The Peyote Road

The Civilization of the American Indian Series

The Peyote Road

RELIGIOUS FREEDOM AND THE
NATIVE AMERICAN CHURCH

THOMAS CONSTANTINE MAROUKIS

UNIVERSITY OF OKLAHOMA PRESS : NORMAN

Also by Thomas Constantine Maroukis

Peyote and the Yankton Sioux: The Life and Times of Sam Necklace (Norman, 2004)

This book is published with the generous assistance of The Kerr Foundation, Inc.

Library of Congress Cataloging-in-Publication Data

Maroukis, Thomas Constantine, 1938–
    The peyote road : religious freedom and the Native American Church / Thomas Constantine Maroukis.
        p. cm. — (Civilization of the American Indian series ; v. 265)
    Includes bibliographical references and index.
    ISBN 978 0 8061 4109 1 (hardcover . alk. paper)
    1. Native American Church of North America—History. 2. Peyotism. 3. Indians of North America—Religion. 4. Indians of North America—Medicine. 5. Indians of North America—Rites and ceremonies. 6. Indians of North America—Government relations. I. Title.
    E98.R3M29   2010
    299.7—dc22

                                                                                    2009041301

The Peyote Road: Religious Freedom and the Native American Church is Volume 265 in The Civilization of the American Indian Series.

The paper in this book meets the guidelines for permanence and durability of the Committee on Production Guidelines for Book Longevity of the Council on Library Resources, Inc. ∞

To my dearest wife, Cassandra, for her love and support during the time-consuming process of research and writing. And also to the many members of the Native American Church who gave their time, help, and suggestions.

Contents

Illustrations

Acknowledgments

This book could not have been written without the help of numerous members of the Native American Church. Their kindness and willingness to offer support and suggestions was overwhelming. My debt to them for what they taught me is beyond what words can convey. I also owe a great debt to a long line of scholars who spanned the twentieth century, from James Mooney to Omer Stewart, who committed much of their lives to doing what they could to protect the constitutional rights of members of the Native American Church. There were many other individuals at the National Archives, National Anthropological Archives, and the University of Colorado Archives who went out of their way to assist me. I am also indebted to attorney James Botsford, director, Indian Law Office, Wisconsin Judicare, for his help on the myriad of legal issues that have plagued the church. In addition, I want to thank Milton Miller, former president of the Native American Church of North America, for meeting with me on two occasions and Sandor Iron Rope, former president of the Native American Church of South Dakota and recently elected vice president of the NAC of North America, for all his help. There are many others, particularly the Yankton Sioux family of the late Asa Primeaux, Sr., specifically his wife, Loretta, sons Gerald and Asa, Jr., and daughter Edith Fool Bull. Many thanks also to Tyrone Smith (Warm Springs Reservation, Oregon) and his family for their help and to Mark and Carol Welsh of the Native American Indian Center of Central Ohio. I also want to thank those individuals who agreed to interviews. Of course, I must mention the voices and the music of the many church people who are recorded in the oral history archives of the Institute of American Indian Studies, University of South Dakota, and I wish to thank the staff members there, especially Margaret Quintal, for their assistance. It would be remiss not to mention the late Leonard Bruguier, former director of the institute and a close friend. His wise counsel will be missed. I also received very kind and valuable assistance from the staff at the University of Oklahoma Press, especially Alessandra Jacobi Tamulevich. I am also thankful to Capital University for granting me a sabbatical in 2006–2007, when much of the research and writing was completed. I want to thank as well the individuals at the U.S. Drug Enforcement Agency and the Texas Department of Public Safety who agreed to speak with me and provide important information. A final thank you is due to my two student assistants, Rebecca Gardlik and Christine Finch, for their invaluable assistance. In spite of all the excellent recommendations from colleagues and readers, I am certain there are errors of omission and commission. For these I take full responsibility.

The Peyote Road

Introduction

Congress shall make no law respecting an establishment of religion, or prohibiting the free exercise thereof; or abridging the freedom of speech, or of
the press; or the right of the people peaceably to assemble, and to petition the
Government for a redress of grievances.

United States Constitution: First Amendment

In August 1918, in the small town of El Reno, Oklahoma, members of the Peyote faith from around the state joined together in an intertribal gathering. The
Cheyennes, Otos, Caddos, Poncas, Comanches, Kiowas, Kiowa-Apaches, and
Arapahos were represented. Their purpose: to discuss the assault on their faith
by the U.S. government. In February and March the United States Congress had
held hearings on the prohibition of Peyote, a cactus plant used as a sacrament
in religious services. Members of the Peyote faith believed that prohibiting their
sacrament would be the equivalent of outlawing bread and wine in Christian
communion. They gathered in El Reno to discuss a plan to defend their right to
practice their religion as guaranteed by the First Amendment, which states that
Congress shall make no law prohibiting the free exercise of religion. They were
defending a faith with ancient roots in Mesoamerica—a faith that led one along
the Peyote Road, a path to a fulfilling spiritual life connecting one to the Great
Spirit, or Creator, thereby restoring harmony and balance in one's life by healing
body, mind, and spirit. The Peyote Road is a metaphor to follow a righteous path
of life, and the sacrament of Peyote is the guide to a long, tranquil life with good
health and well-being for one's children and grandchildren.

In Washington, the House of Representatives would soon vote on restricting the use of Peyote. As members of the faith gathered in El Reno to discuss possible strategies to defend themselves, the world was spinning around them. It was a watershed year as World War I was ending; the winds of prohibition were swirling across the land; influenza epidemics were spreading like wildfire, killing millions, including many American Indians; and the nation was about to begin an antiforeigner campaign, which also affected American Indians. The U.S. government had spent the past half century trying to turn American Indians into Anglo-Americans. Many officials believed this campaign would be successful as the popular image of a "vanishing race" implied. Opposition to Peyote was not new. Since the origin of the faith, missionaries and government officials had opposed it, whether it was the Spanish in Mexico or the Americans in the United States. As the Peyote faith developed from the 1880s through the 1920s, the Department of the Interior's Bureau of Indian Affairs (BIA) saw Peyotism as a threat to its assimilation policies.

(Note: The U.S. government has not been consistent in its terminology for the agency in charge of Indian affairs. It has used Office of Indian Affairs, Indian Service, and Bureau of Indian Affairs. This study follows the practice of the National Archives and Records Administration and uses Bureau of Indian Affairs when referring to the federal government's administrative unit for Indian affairs. Bureau of Indian Affairs became the official name in 1947.)

Those meeting in El Reno were just as determined to protect their right to worship and resist the forces of assimilation. The forthcoming action of Congress was of vital concern to them. Many practices in American Indian ceremonies, such as the Sun Dance, had already been outlawed. Other spiritual traditions such as Sweat Lodge ceremonies and the use of sacred pipes had been discouraged. Many other aspects of Indian culture such as dancing, giveaways, clothing, hairstyle, and language were impeded or suppressed. In addition to the congressional action, various states were enacting similar legislation. In 1917, Colorado, Nevada, and Utah outlawed the use of Peyote.

The events that led to the meeting in El Reno created great tension. Government officials on Oklahoma reservations were opposed to Peyotism as were the many missionaries throughout the state. Church and state were collaborating to stifle an American Indian religious movement. They decided on a legal strategy to defend their faith and drew up articles of incorporation, and like other religious groups, applied for nonprofit corporate status with the state of Oklahoma. On October 10, 1918, the state granted a corporate charter under the name Native American Church (NAC) of Oklahoma. From that time to the present, the story of the NAC is one of persistence by its members to maintain spiritual and cultural autonomy against federal, state, and private interests that would deny them their autonomy. It has been a long continual struggle for religious freedom. Today approximately 300,000 American Indians are members of the Native American Church.

Since its inception the church has been controversial to those outside the faith, primarily because of the use of Peyote, which is ingested as a sacrament during religious services in a manner similar to the sacramental use of wine in Christianity. Peyote is a small, inconspicuous cactus, whose name comes from the Nahuatl (Aztec) word *peyotl*, which refers to a caterpillar's cocoon as the plant has a fuzzy tuft of white silky hair protruding from the center of white-pinkish flower petals, which appear in the spring. Although there are many Spanish descriptions of Peyote, the first botanical illustration appeared in 1847 in *Curtis's Botanical Magazine*. It belongs to a distinct genus, *Lophophora*, with two species: *Lophophora diffusa* and *Lophophora williamsii*. The former is a local cactus in central Mexico; the latter is the Peyote cactus, which American botanist John Coulter classified in 1894. *Lophophora williamsii* is a small, pale bluish green, spineless cactus with a fleshy core that grows either as a solitary stem or as a cluster of stems. The stems are one to two inches in diameter and grow two to three inches aboveground. Each stem has a "button" or top, which is harvested by cutting off the aboveground section. The Peyote cactus has a tuberous root similar to a carrot or turnip that may be five to six inches long, able to absorb moisture in a dry environment (see figure 1).

Peyote grows in limestone soils in semiarid desert scrub usually under dense brush. Its natural habitat is scattered along the Rio Grande in southern Texas and in north-central Mexico, from the Big Bend region of Texas to southeast of Laredo to Brownsville, and down into central Mexico as far south as San Luis Potosi, about three hundred miles north of Mexico City. The Chihuahuan Desert region is the main growth area. The south Texas region, the only place where Peyote grows in the United States, is a crucial growth area for the NAC as transporting Peyote across the border from Mexico is prohibited.

Peyote has been studied by pharmacologists, botanists, and chemists. It has more than fifty-five alkaloids, including anhalamine, anhalonidine, peyotine, lophophorine, and mescaline. The latter is the controversial element because some people claim it produces a mild effect on one's sensory perceptions. It is estimated that 1 to 3 percent of a dried Peyote plant is mescaline. Peyote is not

Figure 1. Earliest illustration of Peyote cactus. From *Curtis's Botanical Magazine*, 1847.

habit forming. There is no evidence that those who use it develop a drug tolerance or have any withdrawal symptoms; it is not harmful when used in the context of a religious service. For many years, those opposed to the Peyote faith have argued that Peyote is a harmful, dangerous drug that should be outlawed; however no scientific evidence has been produced to establish any harmful effects. In fact, in 2005 a medical study from McLean Hospital, affiliated with the Harvard Medical School, indicated that there were no psychological or cognitive problems associated with the use of Peyote. (See chapter 6.)

Part of the misunderstanding concerning the danger of Peyote was its confusion with the mescal bean. In the late nineteenth century, Peyote tops were referred to as mescal buttons or mescal beans, and its users were described as belonging to a "mescal cult." Even Smithsonian ethnologist James Mooney originally called Peyote services a "mescal rite." The origin of the confusion is unclear. The mescal bean plant is the common name of *Sophora secundiflora*, an evergreen bush unrelated to the cacti family. The plant produces pods that contain red beans that are highly hallucinogenic and potentially dangerous. Referring to Peyote as mescal was a mistake. There is an alcoholic beverage called mescal that is made from the plant *Agave angustifolia*. Possibly this is the source of the confusion, since the *agave* belongs to the cactus family. Another possible source of confusion is that some Peyote spiritual leaders wear a decorative necklace made from mescal beans, but these beans are not ingested at any time. In Mexico, this confusion over terminology does not exist. The three different plants are known distinctly as peyote, agave, and frijolillo (the mescal bean plant). In his later writings, Mooney corrected himself and said Peyote is mistakenly known as mescal. Nevertheless the confusion lived on as some scholars continued to misuse the word *mescal* until the issue was fully clarified by ethnobotanist Richard Evans Schultes in the 1930s.

To prepare Peyote for sacramental use, one slices off the upper portion of the plant; from this practice comes the term *Peyote button,* used to describe the cut-off top. When the plant is cut properly, the root will generate another stem. The buttons can be eaten raw, but the most common practice is to dry the buttons in the sun. If dried properly they can be stored indefinitely and are easily transportable, including shipping by mail.

A dried button looks like a dried mushroom except for the white wooly tuft on top. The dried buttons can be chewed and swallowed, or they can be ground into a greenish-gray granular powder for storage. With the addition of water the powder is made into a paste, which is eaten with a spoon. The buttons or powder can also be boiled and made into a "tea," which may be sipped by individuals participating in the Peyote sacrament. The Peyote described here is the central focus of a religious service. It is handled with the utmost reverence. Several times during the all-night service, Peyote is passed around to the congregants and ingested as a sacrament from God. It is a prayerful and sacred moment, a powerful act that is the essential element of the Peyote faith.

This book integrates a narrative history of the Peyote faith with analyses of its religious beliefs and practices as well as its art and music. The historical narrative focuses on the faith's origins, expansion, and development. Since its inception, Peyotism has struggled for survival as it faced a wide array of forces opposed to it. In studying the NAC from its origins to the present, this book focuses on the issue of religious freedom and emphasizes the voices of NAC members. These will come from published autobiographies, published interviews and speeches, including some from the early twentieth century. The oral history collection at the Institute of American Indian Studies at the University of South Dakota provides a valuable resource; it contains recorded interviews with Peyotists from the late 1960s to the present. This is supplemented by the author's discussions and interaction with members of the NAC over the past twenty years. The author's goal in writing this work has been to help bring greater understanding about the Native American Church's struggle for the right to practice its faith. This follows in the words of Reuben Snake

(Winnebago), renowned leader of the struggle for religious freedom, who said his writing was meant "to introduce my Church to the public who knows little about it." In addition to the voices of the Peyote community, this study is built on the work of many scholars, but none as important as anthropologist Omer Stewart (1908–91). His contribution to Peyote studies is unmatched. His list of publications covers five decades. He spent a lifetime of studying, writing, and defending the Peyote faith as an expert witness in many court cases. Whoever writes on the Peyote religion is standing on the shoulders of Omer Stewart.

Throughout this study, Peyote, and all its permutations as Peyote faith, Peyote religion, Peyote art, Peyotist, Peyotism are capitalized. This is out of respect for Native American Church members who regard Peyote as a sacred gift of God. Church members use this capitalization in their writings and documents and in recent years scholars have begun to follow this usage.

A study of the Peyote faith reinforces the viewpoint that American Indians may have been victimized, but they were not victims in the classic sense of being powerless. The existence of the Peyote faith clearly demonstrates the power or agency of Indian communities to shape at least some parts of their lives: in this case their spiritual and cultural lives.

Chapter 1 reviews the origins of Peyote use in Mesoamerica, its development into a Peyote religious complex in the United States, and the incorporation of this faith as a nonprofit religious organization. In Mesoamerica the ritual use of Peyote is thousands of years old. When the Spanish arrived in the early sixteenth century, they found that Peyote was widely used. Peyote usage spread northward into Texas and Oklahoma. It developed into a religious complex on the Kiowa-Comanche Reservation in the 1870s and 1880s and by 1918 had expanded into a legally incorporated church. In 1891, James Mooney, an ethnologist from the Smithsonian Institution, was the first to describe the Peyote religious services that he had attended on the Kiowa-Comanche Reservation. The structure of the ceremony he described has, for the most part, remained virtually the same to the present day. Peyotism spread from the Kiowa-Comanche Reservation to other reservations in Oklahoma, and then north through the central and northern plains and later into the Southwest, the western states, and Canada.

The incorporation of the NAC emerged as one of several responses to the federal government's assault on American Indian cultures. For many American Indians on the reservations, political and economic autonomy proved impossible, but within the NAC they had spiritual and cultural autonomy. As the Peyote religion spread from reservation to reservation, it was perceived by many American Indians as a "traditional" faith even with accretions from Christianity. As Peyotism expanded, government attempts to suppress it increased. As noted above, the BIA feared Peyotism would subvert the bureau's goal of assimilating American Indians. Officials began an intensive campaign to discredit the faith and to label Peyote as a narcotic. Christian groups and prohibitionist organizations joined the anti-Peyote crusade. Anti-Peyote legislation was introduced in Congress in 1916, 1917, and 1918. An anti-Peyote bill passed the House in 1918, but it failed in the Senate as several senators argued that it was contrary to the First Amendment. This did not stop the Department of the Interior from continuing its attempts to eliminate the use of Peyote. In this atmosphere of suppression Peyotists responded in several ways. Some held their services in secret; others added elements of Christianity hoping to gain further protection for their worship. The Peyote communities in Oklahoma, however, took a legal strategy of incorporation, a model that other Peyote communities adopted.

Chapter 2 examines the spiritual beliefs and practices of the Peyote faith. Three main reasons are presented to explain why the Peyote religion spread so rapidly and so widely. First, church members believed in Peyote as a "medicine." The Peyote faith emerged and expanded in an era of great turmoil in the country. The American Indians on the reservations were suffering from illness and disease. In addition to tuberculosis, trachoma, and influenza, there was the scourge of alcohol abuse. Peyote, a "Sacred Herb," is believed to be a gift from God that can heal body and soul. Peyote origin narratives and thousands of testimonials attest to the healing power of Peyote. Church members refer to Peyote as medicine. For example, in Lakota and Dakota, Peyote is called *pejuta*, the word for "medicine." In Navajo, Peyote is *azee'*, also the word for medicine. These indigenous names for Peyote indicate that it is a medicine that acts spiritually, psychologically, and physiologically. A second reason for the rapid expansion of Peyotism is that people saw it as an indigenous American Indian faith, rather than a new phenomenon. Finally, Peyotism offered its adherents an ethical system to follow.

Peyote religious services are usually called meetings. The terms *Peyote meeting*, *prayer meeting*, *prayer service*, and *church service* are used interchangeably. When Peyote people talk about having a meeting or a prayer service, they are referring to religious activities that begin at dusk and end at dawn. Today they are usually held on Saturday nights, weekly or monthly, or whenever requested for a special purpose. Peyote meetings are held for many reasons, but the most common purpose is healing. As indicated above, the followers believe that Peyote cures many ailments, including the disease of alcoholism. Other reasons for religious services are celebratory, such as births, birthdays, graduations, and weddings. Peyote services are also held at all state and national annual conferences. During a meeting, the person who conducts the service and helps guide the congregation along the Peyote Road is called a *Roadman*. The term is used nationwide to designate the spiritual leader who conducts a Peyote service or meeting.

Chapter 3 covers the assault on the Peyote faith by the federal government, state governments, and sectarian and nonsectarian organizations. Since the discovery of Peyote buttons on a reservation in 1886, the government had been determined to suppress it. As the Peyote faith grew, government action increased. The failure in 1918 to get a federal prohibition of Peyote did not stop the BIA. Additional restrictive bills were introduced in Congress up until 1937, all to no avail. Paralleling the legislative strategies were other attempts through various executive branch agencies to weaken the Peyote religion by prohibiting Peyote. The BIA produced and distributed anti-Peyote pamphlets. These included testimonials by people, including missionaries, who claimed they knew the "real" dangers of Peyote. Lobbying state governments was also part of the strategy to suppress Peyotism. From 1917 to 1937 a majority of states west of the Mississippi River outlawed the sale, distribution, and use of Peyote. In response, Peyote groups throughout the West incorporated on the Oklahoma model. For example, in the 1920s and 1930s eleven Peyote groups incorporated in South Dakota.

Chapter 4 analyzes the expansion of the Peyote faith to the north and the southwest. The spread of the Peyote religion to the Diné (Navajo) Nation was the most significant development of the 1940s and 1950s. This alarmed some traditional Navajos, who successfully convinced the tribal council to outlaw the use of Peyote on the reservation. The council rescinded this law in 1967. Nevertheless Peyotism continued to expand as it fulfilled the spiritual needs of many Diné. Today almost half of all Diné are members of the Peyote faith.

Beginning in the late 1920s and into the 1930s and 1940s, the Peyote faith expanded north and westward into the Great Basin, which included Utah, Nevada, southern Oregon and Idaho, and parts of southeastern California. The pattern was similar to previous expansions. People in difficult circumstances or in poor health heard about the healing power of Peyote. When visited by a

Peyote Roadman, they attended meetings, identified with the Peyote faith, and became Peyotists. This expansion included the Gosiutes, Western Shoshones, Bannocks, Utes, Washoes, and Northern and Southern Paiutes. It should be noted, however, with some exceptions, that only a minority of individuals in these groups became Peyotists. In the 1940s and 1950s Peyotists incorporated to gain constitutional protection as the Native American Church of California and the Native American Church of Nevada.

In spite of the federal government's failed attempt to ban Peyote, the Peyote community feared future restrictions. Until the 1940s, there were only state and local NAC chapters. Many followers felt the need for a national organization. In 1944, Oklahoma Peyotists took the lead in chartering the Native American Church of the United States. In 1955, it became the Native American Church of North America. Its most significant function now as then is to coordinate efforts to defend the Peyote faith by developing a unified voice on issues that affect all NAC members. Not all Peyotists are members of the NAC of North America, but they cooperate to maintain First Amendment protection.

Chapter 5 analyzes Peyote music and art as integral parts of the spiritual expression of the Peyote community. Music, prayer, and healing compose essential elements of the Peyote faith. In Peyote meetings, songs, accompanied by a water drum and gourd rattle, are prayers. It is sacred music with social and communal functions. It is a powerful source of bonding among Peyote people. Today Peyote music is very popular and recordings of it are sold nationwide. In 2002 the Grammy Award for Best Native American Music went to well-known Peyote singers Verdell Primeaux (Yankton Sioux) and Johnny Mike (Diné) for their recording *Bless the People: Harmonized Peyote Songs*. In 2007 the Native American Music Awards added a new category: The Best Native American Church Music.

Scholars today consider Peyote art a distinct genre of American Indian art. It is intended to enhance the spirituality of the community and the individual. The art is produced by members of the Peyote community for ceremonial use or, as with jewelry, for personal adornment. It has also been part of the renaissance of American Indian arts. The artwork has a distinct style, using the symbolism and iconography of the faith to express spiritual values. For example, the waterbird is a common motif, as it symbolizes the carrying of prayers upward.

Chapter 6 examines the legal and political issues of the last half century. Religious freedom issues have been in the forefront of NAC concerns. The struggle for religious freedom is part of a larger struggle for American Indian rights, particularly the battle over sovereignty, which includes protecting sacred sites, prisoner's rights, reburial and repatriation issues, and treaty rights, as well as political and economic autonomy. Events of the recent past have clouded the perception of whether the future should be viewed with optimism or pessimism as the Peyote community has had both setbacks and successes.

In the 1960s the American public became aware of Peyote. As drug usage among America's youth increased, including experimenting with Peyote, law enforcement agencies responded with vigorous action. Antidrug campaigns made the Peyote community fearful that its sacrament would be threatened. In 1965, Peyote was added to the government's Schedule I list of controlled substances; however, an exemption was made for American Indians using Peyote as a sacrament in a religious service. Even with this exemption, the NAC still feared that their religious freedom could be curtailed.

In 1978, after many concerns over religious freedom were expressed, the U.S. Congress passed the American Indian Religious Freedom Act. It supposedly guaranteed the free exercise of religion as an inherent American Indian right, but some American Indian leaders argued that the bill was weak and devoid of enforcement mechanisms. Various groups lobbied for a stronger bill. Soon after, in 1984, the NAC was severely jolted when two men who had ingested Peyote as a sacrament in a religious service were fired from their jobs with a drug rehabilitation agency in Oregon for substance abuse. The state of Oregon refused to pay unemployment compensation. The case reached the U.S. Supreme Court (*Oregon v. Smith*, 1990), which ruled against the two men and upheld Oregon's right to refuse to exempt the religious use of Peyote from its drug abuse laws. If this decision held, it would mean that any state could repeal its statues that exempted Peyote for religious use without fear of violating the free exercise clause of the First Amendment.

The ensuing firestorm led to a massive coalition of American Indian and non-Indian groups. The American Indian Religious Freedom Coalition, spearheaded by Reuben Snake, brought together a nationwide coalition to lobby for corrective legislation. In 1993 and 1994 Congress passed two bills that restored the right of free exercise of religion. The first was a broad-based bill designed to protect religious freedom in many areas but did not offer any specific protection for the NAC. The second bill was aimed at specifically protecting Peyote usage by members of the NAC. Although the *Smith* case was overturned by subsequent legislation, it cast a shadow over the NAC's First Amendment protection.

Throughout the late 1990s and into the twenty-first century, the legal right to worship with Peyote as a sacrament has remained protected for American Indians who are enrolled members of a federally recognized tribe. Nevertheless, there are concerns over the possibility of a changing legal and political climate since Peyote is still a Schedule I controlled substance. There are also court cases involving non-Indians who claim the right to use Peyote as a sacrament citing the NAC exemption as a precedent. This is a worrisome development for the NAC community.

The debate over who can use Peyote as a sacrament is complicated by the dwindling supply of Peyote. With an expanding membership and a decreasing supply as the "Peyote Gardens" are being reduced in size by land development, some members see a supply crisis in the future. If non-Indians acquired the legal right to use Peyote the supply could virtually disappear. Nevertheless the NAC today is stronger than ever. The membership, with more allies today, is determined to maintain its rights. Given the problems of the past century, the future seems positive, yet a nagging fear remains that in a changing political climate, a new court, or a new "war on drugs" could be a threat to the NAC's free exercise of religion. The present situation reminds one of the famous statement of Felix Cohen, the great federal Indian law scholar, who wrote, "Like the miner's canary, the Indian marks the shift from fresh air to poison gas in our political atmosphere; and our treatment of Indians, even more than other minorities, marks the rise and fall of our democratic faith."

The Origins and Development of the Peyote Religion and the Native American Church

On any given Saturday night, on many reservations, thousands of American Indians will gather in tepees, hogans, or small church buildings to participate in a nightlong spiritual ceremony that includes the sacramental use of Peyote, a mildly hallucinogenic cactus. They arrive in the late afternoon, rain, shine, or snow. People are well dressed, some wearing Peyote jewelry, carrying the necessary ritual instruments, such as feather fans, gourd rattles, eagle-bone whistle, drumsticks, and personal items in a special "Peyote box." They greet friends, shake hands, hug, and inquire about family and health. Preparations for the service are being finalized. The Roadman, cedar man, chief drummer, and fireman are busy preparing for the service. They set up the altar, clean the area for the all-night fire, and prepare the wood for the fire. Someone may be tying a drumhead to a drum; others may be practicing Peyote songs. Everyone is anticipating a long, powerful night of prayer. They will be engaging in a ritual ingestion of Peyote that is thousands of years old as well as participating in a Peyote service of the Native American Church that is more than a hundred years old.

MESOAMERICAN ROOTS

The use of Peyote in pre-Columbian Mesoamerica is well documented. Desiccated Peyote buttons have been recovered from rock shelters and radiocarbon-dated to 5000 B.C.E. Rock-art panels that depict the ritual use of Peyote have also been discovered in rock shelters in the Lower Pecos River region (south-central Texas, northern Mexico). Archaeologist Carolyn Boyd dates the rock paintings as 2,950–4,200 years old. The rock-art panels depict a Peyote ritual with anthropomorphic figures and antlered deer that are impaled with arrows. The deer have Peyote buttons drawn on their bodies and on the tips of their antlers. This is explained as part of a peyote/deer/rain complex, in which sacred flying deer brought the first Peyote to earth. The same imagery has also been found in a number of other caves and rock shelters. In Oaxaca, Mexico, an effigy pipe depicting a deer holding a peyote cactus in its mouth has been dated to 400–200 B.C.E. In this spiritual complex the rain brings vegetation, including Peyote, the vegetation brings deer, and the deer attract humans. There is also evidence that the Chichimecs and the Toltecs knew of Peyote by 300 B.C.E. More recent sites have been dated to 810–1070 C.E., and others into the Aztec era (thirteenth to fifteenth centuries). The Aztecs, and groups as far north as the Rio Grande, used Peyote for religio-medicinal pur-poses.[1] To support her conclusion that the ceremonial and ritual use of Peyote has ancient roots, Boyd cites three lines of evidence: first, the archaeological presence of Peyote and associated rock paintings; second, ecological and envi-ronmental evidence accounting for the peyote/rain/deer/human interaction; and third, numerous analogies between the animal, plant, and human motifs in the rock paintings and ethnographic analyses of contemporary Indian groups such as the Huicholes of northwest Mexico.[2]

In 1519, Hernán Cortés arrived in Mexico with six hundred Spanish con-quistadores. Within two years, the Spanish had destroyed the Aztec Empire and subjugated the Aztec people. A significant factor accounting for the Spanish victory was the spread of European diseases, such as smallpox, typhus, measles, and influenza. Following the demise of the Aztecs, the Spanish expanded their control over most of present-day Mexico and began the systematic exploita-tion of its human and natural resources. The indigenous people who survived were used as forced labor in mines and farms throughout Spain's New World empire. Along with soldiers and administrators came Catholic missionaries, ready to force the inhabitants to abandon their cultures and indigenous reli-gions and to impose on them what the Spanish believed was a superior culture and faith. This latter mission became one of the justifications for Spanish rule in the New World.

When the Spanish arrived they found the Native population using a wide variety of psychotropic plants for medicinal/spiritual purposes. The Mayas, for example, used water lilies. The Aztecs used morning glories, a variety of mushrooms, jimsonweed, and several types of cacti, including Peyote, which was also in widespread use in northern Mexico. The earliest known written reference to Peyote is from Bernardino de Sahagún, a Spanish priest, in the 1560s. He described its effects among the Chichimec people as seeing visions that are "frightful or laughable." He added, "[I]t sustains them and gives them courage to fight and not feel fear nor hunger nor thirst. And they say that it protects them from all danger."[3] By the end of the sixteenth century, a campaign to completely discredit Peyote and indigenous spiritualities was under way. Juan de Cardenas, writing in 1591, described Peyote as witchcraft. The Jesuits and the Franciscans denounced Peyote as a "diabolic root" whose purpose was to communicate with the devil. Through the efforts of the Catholic Church, the Spanish government outlawed Peyote as the "work of the devil." The church feared its use by Indians who had not converted to Catholicism, and its continued use by those who had converted. The church tried to substitute bread and wine for Peyote in communion, equating the former with goodness and the latter with evil. In 1620 the Spanish brought the full weight of the Inquisition (which served for two centuries as a high court that tried moral transgressions) to bear on the use of Peyote as an act of superstition opposed by the Holy Catholic Faith. The church offered absolution for those who ceased using Peyote immediately.[4]

In confession, priests used a newly prepared catechism that discredited Peyote by associating it with cannibalism and murder. Part of it included:

> Hast thou eaten the flesh of man?
> Hast thou eaten the peyote?
> Do you suck the blood of others?
> Do you adorn with flowers places where idols are kept?[5]

The church held at least ninety documented Inquisition hearings between 1621 and 1779 throughout northern and central Mexico. Spanish commentary on Peyote was usually couched in theological language, but the essential concern was the power of the colonial government to impose their religion, language, and culture on the indigenous people. Yet in spite of the church's attempt at suppression, Peyote usage flourished. In some areas Peyote ingestion existed alongside Catholicism.

The popularity of Peyote in north-central Mexico can be attributed to its diversity of uses among a wide range of people, including the Aztecs, Chichimecs, Coahuiltecs, Coras, Huicholes, Jumanos, Laguneros, Tarahumaras, Toltecs, and Zacatecos. The Coras, Huicholes, and Tarahumaras used Peyote well into the twentieth century. There were other groups close to the Rio Grande that used Peyote, such as the Caddos, Carrizos, Karankawas, Lipan Apaches, Mescalero Apaches, and Tonkawas, all of whom are important as possible transmitters of Peyote into the United States in the mid-nineteenth century.

Peyote was used individually and communally, both internally and externally, for various purposes. Individuals applied it to virtually any type of external infirmity, including wounds, snakebites, and burns. They carried it as a charm or amulet for spiritual protection. People ingested it to induce a vision, diagnose or cure an internal illness, or seek help for personal problems. Some used it to reduce hunger and thirst, or in divination to find lost or stolen objects. On the communal level, Peyote was used in a variety of ceremonies, the most famous being the Huichol Peyote ceremony held before the annual Peyote "hunt." Peyote was part of planting and harvesting ceremonies, which included rain, earth, maize, and fertility. Generally, these ceremonies were carried out under the direction of spiritual leaders, called *curanderos/curanderas* in some areas. Many of these ceremonies were not Peyote ceremonies per se, as with the Huicholes, but they were spiritual ceremonies that included the ritual use of Peyote. Peyote enabled the spiritual leaders to communicate with spirits for the benefit of the community.[6]

Some groups such as the Coras, Tarahumaras, and Huicholes have maintained traditional uses of Peyote up to the present. The Huicholes are the best known, having been investigated by numerous anthropologists (and visited by many young Americans since the late 1960s seeking a "psychedelic" experience). Some scholars claim that the Huicholes have the strongest pre-Columbian spiritual practices of any indigenous group in Mexico. The rituals described by Father Sahagún in the sixteenth century are very similar to the Huicholes' twentieth- and twenty-first-century practices. The Huicholes have a religious complex of peyote/deer/maize, similar to the pre-Columbian peyote/deer/rain complex. As with almost all New World people, spirituality and life are one for the Huicholes, there being no separation between the sacred and the profane. Their spirituality is centered on sacredness, maintaining or restoring harmony, seeking wholeness, and communicating with their deities. Peyote, or *Híkuri* in their language, which they also call the "plant of life," makes this possible.

The Huicholes have a large pantheon of deities that anthropologist Barbara Meyerhoff has put into four categories: Grandfather Fire, Father Sun, Elder

Brother Deer Tail, and a group of earth/rain/growth goddesses called Our Mothers. Peyote is used to communicate with the deities. Grandfather Fire (Tatewari), considered the oldest of the deities, is also known as Hikuri, or Peyote God. He led the gods on the first Peyote pilgrimage in "ancient times" and established the proper ceremonies, offerings, and behaviors. According to the traditions, the deities were suffering from a number of maladies since they had been separated from their homeland. They asked Tatewari for help. He led the male deities on a journey to the sacred homeland of Peyote. On the way they suffered thirst but were saved by the female deities who brought them water. They all proceeded to Wirikuta, the sacred land of Peyote, where they found and shot a deer. The deer is the source of Peyote, which grew in its footsteps and sprouted from its antlers, hooves, and tail. They made a mixture of Peyote and water, drank it, and were restored. Thus they found the "plant of life."[7]

Today, the Huicholes re-create this sacred pilgrimage each year, which is their "hunt" for Peyote. The hunt unites the Huicholes with each other and with their gods and involves the peyote/deer/maize complex. The three are considered one and interchangeable, and refer to a time before humans, plants, and animals were separate. Thus the pilgrimage also reunites human and non-human ancestors. The Huichol pilgrimage of almost three hundred miles takes them from their home in north-central Mexico to the Peyote fields. Before embarking they hold a Peyote purification ceremony with chanted prayers accompanied by a three-legged wooden drum with a deer skin head and gourd rattle. Surrounding a large fire, those going on the pilgrimage make confessions of sexual transgressions. As the names of illicit partners are mentioned, the *mara'akame*, or spiritual leader, ties a knot in a long cord. The knotted cord is thrown in the fire and burned, thus sweeping away the transgressions. One final preparation is the communal smoking of sacred tobacco rolled in maize husks. This ceremony does not involve the use of Peyote, but is called the Peyote ceremony since it is a preparation to harvest Peyote. Once the ritual cleansing and the Peyote ceremony have been performed, the pilgrimage to the Peyote fields can proceed.[8]

The Huicholes make the arduous trek with solemnity, prayer, and contemplation of their sacred undertaking. When nearing the Peyote growth area, they search for the first Peyote as if on a hunt. Once found, the "peyote-deer" is shot with an arrow. To propitiate its spirit, sacred offerings and prayers are made to the "peyote-deer." The arrow, covered with moisture from the fresh Peyote, is used to anoint each person; the Peyote is then cut into pieces by the mara'akame and placed in the mouth of each person as in a sacrament. Next, they harvest Peyote, seeing each plant as the footprint of a deer. Once they find the plants, they cut off the tops, then touch them to forehead, throat, and heart before placing them in a basket. At night there is celebrating, singing, dancing, and eating of Peyote by all. Back home, around the original fire built before the Huicholes left, more Peyote is ingested, and the rest is distributed to the community. Soon after the return home, a deer hunt is undertaken; the blood of the deer is sprinkled on corn seed before planting. The deer, a sacred animal, willingly sacrifices itself for the benefit of its human brothers and sisters. According to Meyerhoff's informant: "The deer, the peyote and maize are one. One is not good without the other." This is the culmination of the peyote/deer/maize cycle without which life for the Huicholes would not be successful.[9]

The Huicholes use Peyote in a variety of ways. Its usage is more ubiquitous than among NAC members in the United States. On the communal level, Peyote is used to ensure the well-being of the community. Without Peyote the annual maize crop would be unsuccessful. The fertility of maize is dependent on deer and Peyote. At the communal level, Peyote is primarily ingested by the spiritual leader during a ceremony so he or she can communicate with the deities, ensure good crops, cure the sick, and protect the community from future illnesses. It is believed that only the mara'akame, through Peyote, can acquire spiritual insights that create more power for communication. On the individual level, Peyote is ingested to reduce pain, allay fatigue, and gain courage and endurance. It is used externally on wounds or is rubbed on the skin to heal infections. It is a panacea for many ailments. Individuals also ingest Peyote to communicate with a particular deity or to have a personal vision, although this is not considered a primary reason for using Peyote.[10]

Perplexing to most outsiders is the peyote/deer/maize complex. According to Ramon Silva, a Huichol spiritual leader, "These things are one. They are a unity. They are our life. They are ourselves." The implication, as mentioned earlier, is one of unity within the spiritual complex, with contemporary Huicholes, the ancestors, and the deities. None can exist without the others; in fact, the success of all ceremonies is dependent on these three items. Their interdependence is described in Huichol narratives. The deer flies to earth bringing Peyote, which is used to communicate with the spirits; the blood of the deer has transformative power that makes rain fall and maize grow. Or according to the Huicholes,

"The animal represents the past—hunting, masculinity, independence, adventure, and freedom; the plant is the labor of the present—food, regularity, domesticity, sharing between the sexes . . . , the cactus which grows far away is plant and animal at once—non-utilitarian, free of time, sex and specifiable meaning, existing for its own unscrutinized, quiet gift of beauty and privacy."[11]

The beauty of Peyote is evident in Huichol art. As with Peyotists in the United States, the Huicholes produce a significant amount of sacred art that reflects and reinforces their belief system. The primary forms are fiber arts, beadwork, and embroidery. The context or symbolism of the art is a representation of their spiritual cosmos and its re-creation in ceremony and ritual. The art is used to preserve tradition and reinforce identity. It is also used as an offering in spiritual activities such as the Peyote pilgrimage. Over the past fifty years, this artwork has also been marketed to outsiders. The most popular art forms, wool yarn paintings, which emerged in the 1960s, are based on older forms of fiber art called *niérika*. Some of these older forms consist of round pieces with a hole in the center, usually made of sticks woven together with yarn; others are wood pieces covered with beeswax into which colored yarn is pressed to create the desired pattern. They are sacred offerings made to a deity; the center hole serves as an opening to see into the spirit world.

The motifs in the fiber arts represent sacred history. For example, they may depict the origin of the world, deities emerging from the underworld, numerous gods and goddesses, the healing power of spiritual leaders, the power of the peyote/deer/main complex or the glorification of Peyote itself. Recently gaining in popularity and renown, the artwork has been shown in museum exhibitions and public galleries, and it can be purchased online through several Huichol websites. Even with the recent commercialization, the Huichol treasure their art as they treasure Peyote and their religion.

It is beyond dispute that the use of psychotropic plants in general, and Peyote in particular, has ancient roots in Mesoamerica. The question posed by scholars is, how was the ceremonial use of Peyote transmitted into the United States and how did it develop into the Native American Church? The Huicholes are a possible source in the export of a Peyote religious complex from Mesoamerica to the north. There are similarities between the Huicholes' practices and those of the NAC, such as the power of Peyote to cure illnesses through ritual ingestion, all-night ceremonies, the use of a drum and gourd rattle, ceremonial smoking of sacred tobacco in maize husks, sacred art, to name several. But the differences between Peyote use in the two groups are even greater. For example, North

American Indians use Peyote only as a sacrament in a spiritual setting, whereas the Huicholes have myriad uses for it. In addition, in the United States, there is no dancing or elaborate ritualized pilgrimage associated with Peyote. There is a commonality of healing through religio-pharmaceutical phenomena, but that is commonality among groups throughout the New World so this cannot be evidence of contact between the Huicholes and the NAC. In fact there is no evidence of direct contact with the Huicholes. Meyerhoff has concluded that "there is no reason to assume any present connection on similarity between Huichol uses of peyote and that of North American Indians."[12] Certainly the use of Peyote north of the Rio Grande has roots in Mesoamerica, but we must look elsewhere to explain the full development of Peyote ceremonialism in the United States.

DEVELOPMENT OF A PEYOTE RELIGIOUS
COMPLEX IN THE UNITED STATES

The absence of evidence of a direct link between Mexican Peyote ceremonies and later Peyote ceremonies in the United States is problematic in attempting to explain the emergence of the latter ceremonies north of the border. Making an explanation more complex is the decline of Peyote ceremonies as well as Peyote usage in nineteenth-century Mexico. After achieving independence from Spain in 1821, Mexico was a nation in turmoil, subject to foreign interference. Mexico lost part of its northeastern territory in the Texas war of the 1830s and lost additional land in the U.S.–Mexican War of 1848. In the 1860s, France sent troops to Mexico in an attempt to usurp the country's sovereignty. The Mexicans resisted successfully only to suffer a pattern of intermittent republics and dictatorships. Catholicism, Hispanic culture, and the Spanish language continued to spread at the expense of indigenous cultures. In this milieu, Omer Stewart concluded, Peyote continued "as a folk medicine but ceased to exist for ceremonial use except among a few tribes that lived in remote areas."[13]

Although Peyote usage declined in Mexico, it did not die out. There is considerable evidence for its continued use, though that use was more on an individual than a communal level. This is also the case north of the Rio Grande in the natural growth area of the Peyote cactus.

In a sense it is inaccurate to ask when Peyote spread into the United States. When this region was annexed in the 1840s, Peyote usage was already several centuries old. The question again is how and when did it spread beyond its natural growth area into Oklahoma and develop into the Native American Church. Three groups, the Mescalero Apaches, the Lipan Apaches, and the Carrizos lived along the Rio Grande in the Peyote habitat region, and outside this area to the northeast were the Tonkawas, the Karankawas, and the Caddos. All six groups were using Peyote in the eighteenth and nineteenth centuries and started to develop a spiritual and ceremonial usage that became the basis for later Peyotism. Thus it is logical to conclude the roots of modern Peyotism can be found in one or more of these six groups. The obvious groups are the three living along the Rio Grande in the Peyote growth region. The two scholars, James Slotkin and Weston Le Barre, who have studied this transition concluded that it was the Carrizos who developed some of the basic features of modern Peyotism and subsequently taught the Lipan Apaches, their western neighbors. Slotkin's and Le Barre's conclusion is conjecture, but they do base it on ethnographic accounts left by outside travelers in the region. For example, a Swiss botanist exploring the region in 1830 reported that the Carrizos and the Lipan Apaches chewed a plant called Peyote.[14]

The Carrizos were the beneficiaries of the long tradition of Peyote usage in Mexico. They lived in the Peyote growth area for centuries, whereas the Lipan Apaches were recent inhabitants; thus the conjecture of a Carrizo origin is supported by ethnographic accounts. In the 1930s, several elderly Lipan Apache Peyotists were interviewed. They said they acquired Peyote from the Carrizos, who they believed also taught it to the Tonkawas. In corresponding interviews, several Tonkawas also credited the Carrizos. The arguments and sources citing the Carrizos as the original purveyors of Peyotism in the southern plains seems solid; however, it was Lipan Apaches who spread Peyotism north to the Kiowas, Kiowa-Apaches, and the Comanches.[15]

The Mescalero Apaches to the west were also in the Peyote-growth region and in contact with Peyote-using groups to the south. Evidence indicates that they did use Peyote in a way similar to that of the Carrizos and the Lipan Apaches. However scholars do not believe the Mescalero Apaches were the original disseminators of the Peyote religion to the north. In the 1890s, when Peyote ceremonies flourished in Oklahoma, they were not widely held by the Mescaleros. In the 1920s, the U.S. government listed the Mescaleros in the category of non-Peyote users.[16]

The Carrizos, who had used Peyote for several centuries, now developed several basic aspects of the Peyote ritual that they then transmitted to their neighbors; those neighbors subsequently spread the practices farther north.

They included ritual use of Peyote in an all-night ceremony, with singing and drumming in a circle around a fire. The Lipan Apaches added additional elements to the Peyote ceremony. They held their ceremonies in tepees, rather than outdoors. They had a special large Peyote button, called Chief Peyote, which they placed on the west side of the fire on a bed of sage. At the beginning and the end of the service, they smoked tobacco rolled in corn husks and prayed, while blowing the smoke toward Chief Peyote. They also had a ceremonial leader, called Chief Peyote Man, who directed the service. Their songs and prayers were accompanied by a drum and gourd rattle. At first, the Lipan Apaches used Peyote for personal visions, but later they began using it for healing during the service. As in Mexico, they used Peyote on an individual basis. A person was free to use Peyote at any time, in any manner. There is no evidence of an altar in the service, and Peyote did not seem to be treated as a sacrament, although it was venerated. Originally the Lipans and the Tonkawas did not allow women in their services, although this changed later. The full ceremony, as we know it today, developed among the Kiowa, Kiowa-Apaches, and Comanches in Oklahoma. The routes of the early diffusion of the Peyote ritual go from the Carrizos to the Lipan Apaches to the tribes now relocated in Oklahoma. The most likely route:

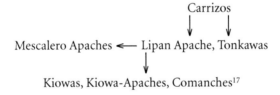

Carrizos

Mescalero Apaches ⟵ Lipan Apache, Tonkawas

Kiowas, Kiowa-Apaches, Comanches[17]

The Lipan Apaches played a key role spreading Peyotism to the Mescalero Apaches and north into Oklahoma. This was happening in an extremely turbulent era exacerbated by the Americans' endless thirst for land. This led to confrontations among settlers, the Indians of the Plains, and the United States military. The federal government was expanding its concentration policy of moving Indian groups onto reservations, using treaties, diplomacy, military pressure, and the destruction of horses and the slaughter of buffalo. As a result, various groups began moving onto governmental designated land, much of it in Oklahoma, then called Indian Territory. In 1867, the Kiowa, Kiowa-Apache, Comanche Agency was established. It included these three groups, plus Caddos, Wichitas, and Delawares. The Peyote religion emerged with the establishment of the reservation system. Within a few short years, many individuals on the reservation were practicing Peyotists. By the 1870s, a wide variety of Native people lived in close proximity in Oklahoma, making diffusion from neighbor to neighbor very possible. In addition, Peyote buttons were legal and widely available.

The primary teachers of Peyotism on the newly established agency were two Lipan Apaches, Chiwat and Pinero. There are many firsthand accounts from Comanche, Kiowa, and Kiowa-Apache sources crediting the Lipan Apaches and Pinero for teaching Peyotism. The Fort Sill Museum in Oklahoma has a 1915 photograph of him with two Comanche Peyote leaders. Chiwat is sitting in a Peyote tepee, holding a gourd rattle and an eagle feather fan. Chiwat and Pinero had gained notoriety from having kidnapped an American boy in 1870 and releasing him in 1879. With this notoriety people wanted to know their story. Years later Pinero described his role in helping bring Peyote to Oklahoma. Pinero was quoted as saying, "I was fleeing for safety and Quanah Parker took me in. I learned Comanche. I married a Comanche. I was the first to teach the Peyote ceremony to Quanah Parker." Parker learned from Chiwat and Pinero to hold religious meetings in large tepees (the Carrizos held Peyote ceremonies outdoors) with the entrance to the east, a fire in a center position, sprinkling cedar, water at midnight, use of feathers, use of sacred tobacco, and most important, doing almost everything in fours as four was a sacred number to many American Indian groups. Other sources also credit Chiwat and Pinero for spreading Peyotism to the Comanches' neighbors, the Kiowas and Kiowa-Apaches. Where and when the Peyote faith spread in its early years is not totally clear, but it is certain that the Lipan Apaches brought it to Oklahoma.[18]

Quanah Parker (c. 1852–1911) (see figure 2) is considered the most significant individual in the early development of Peyotism and its dispersal to other American Indians in Oklahoma. He became the principal chief of the Comanches in a political system that did not have principal chiefs. Parker had an unusual heritage. His mother, Cynthia Ann Parker, a white woman, was captured in a Comanche and Kiowa raid on Fort Parker, Texas, in 1836, when she was nine years old. She remained with the Comanches, married a Comanche, and had Quanah, another son, and a daughter. She seemed to be well integrated into Comanche society. In 1861, the Texas Rangers attacked the Comanche camp and captured Cynthia Parker and her daughter, who were then united with the woman's original family. Parker became grief stricken at having lost her husband and two sons. The daughter, Prairie Flower, died in 1864; Cynthia Parker died in 1870. Her son Quanah was about nine years old when she was taken from him; his father died two years later. Little is known of Quanah Parker's early life, before he surrendered to U.S. authorities at Fort Sill in 1875, except that he had acquired a reputation as a warrior and after learning more about his mother took her last name as his own. He was now relegated to a reservation life. With strong leadership skills he became the undisputed leader of the Comanche nation and soon became a major force within the Peyote faith. The Comanches had known about Peyote from their trade and raids into the south, but in the mid-1870s they developed a Peyote ceremony that became the foundation for today's Peyotism. It is claimed that Parker became an advocate of Peyote when it cured him after a bull had gored him in the stomach.[19] Whatever was the case, he became a major proselytizer for the Peyote faith. The Comanches along with the Kiowas and Kiowa-Apaches developed what was originally called the Quanah Parker Way or the Comanche Way, also known as the Half Moon Way, named after the shape of the mound within the altar.

Given the sense of powerlessness of life on a reservation, the Peyote faith answered both the spiritual and cultural needs of the people forced to live there. Quanah was so determined to ensure the survival and well-being of the Comanches that he made compromises with reservation officials and cooperated with missionaries, while trying to maintain as much of traditional life as possible. He would not give up Peyotism, which was seen as traditional, nor would he give up his several wives. The ceremony that the Comanches developed took place in a tepee with a raised crescent-shaped mound with the open end facing east, toward the morning sun. In the center of the mound on its western-most point a large Chief Peyote button (also called Grandfather Peyote) was placed and kept there all night. It was the central focus of worship. A fire was built within the altar just east of Chief Peyote and tended by a fireman throughout the night. Other items used in the ceremony included a three-legged kettle drum with a deerskin drumhead, a gourd rattle, the leader's staff, an eagle-bone whistle, sage, and Peyote. A Roadman conducted the service and guided the congregation on the right road or the Peyote Road, symbolized by a narrow ridge along the top of the crescent-shaped mound. Almost all the modern ritual elements were present. The drum, rattle, and staff were passed clockwise to singers, who sang a series of four songs. The Peyote was passed around in similar

Figure 2. Quanah Parker, 1890s, holding Peyote feather fan. Courtesy National Anthropological Archives.

fashion. There were special midnight songs and morning songs, followed by sacred foods.[20] (A detailed description of Peyote services appears in chapter 2.)

Parker was a staunch advocate of Peyotism. He is credited with spreading the Peyote faith to the Caddos, Delwares, Otos, Pawnees, Poncas, Southern Cheyennes, and Southern Arapahos. He composed Peyote songs and ran Peyote meetings as a way to teach others. His strength of character and charisma increased his effectiveness and attracted people to Peyotism. Parker's role in the early history of the Peyote religion cannot be overstated. He was an ardent defender of the faith. With his diplomatic and oratorical skills, he was able to protect the use of Peyote from government agents, Oklahoma officials, and Christian missionaries. A strong advocate for Peyote, he was at the same time a critic of the Ghost Dance movement. This may have been a pragmatic response as he was determined to avoid confrontations with American authorities.[21] It is interesting to note that the Kiowas on the same reservation as Parker not only quickly adopted Peyotism but also embraced the Ghost Dance and continued the traditional Sun Dance.

The Kiowas and the Comanches conducted the elaborate Peyote ceremony more or less at the same time so crediting one or the other as the first to adopt the ceremony is impossible. Like the Comanches, the Kiowas were familiar with Peyote before being forced to live on a reservation. Satanta (White Bear), the first reported Peyote leader, was imprisoned from 1871 to 1873 and again from 1874 to 1878, when he committed suicide. Satanta's grandson, Levi White Bear, also a well-known Kiowa Peyotist, claimed his grandfather played a major role in helping to develop the Peyote ceremony. Few sources verify this claim, but Satanta's prison mate, Big Tree, became a prominent Peyotist. In 1950, Levi White Bear gave an extremely detailed description of a Kiowa Peyote ceremony. The ritual he described is virtually the same as the Kiowa ritual described in the mid-1890s by Smithsonian ethnologist James Mooney.[22]

Mooney, who produced the first written description of a Peyote ceremony, was in the West studying the Ghost Dance movement when he heard about the growing Peyote religion. In 1891, he began attending Peyote services with the Kiowas—the first non-Indian, as far as it is known, to attend a Peyote service. He claimed that most Kiowas, except the elderly, were Peyotists. The services he attended were very elaborate, firmly entrenched, and already well defined, meaning they had been in existence for some time by then. In a photograph Mooney took in 1892 (see figure 3), all the important elements of a Peyote

Figure 3. Peyote ceremony, Kiowa-Comanche Reservation, 1892. Photo by James Mooney. Courtesy National Anthropological Archives.

service can be seen. The individuals in the photograph are in a tepee sitting in a circle around an altar, which contains the crescent-shaped mound and the four sacred foods. Visible also are the water drum, the gourd rattle, and the sage on the ground. It is sunrise, and the Roadman is probably getting ready to sing the "quitting song" after a nightlong service.

In terms of theology, ritual, and structure, the Peyote ceremony, while having some regional or local variations, has changed very little in the past century. In the 1890s, Mooney wrote: "[Peyote] is regarded as the vegetable incarnation of a deity and the ceremonial eating of the plant has become the great religious rite of all the tribes of the southern plains."[23] A hundred years later, Reuben Snake (Winnebago), one of the nation's leading Peyotists, would write: "If Jesus was God incarnate in human form, our holy Peyote is God incarnate in plant form."[24]

The basic Kiowa ceremony described by Mooney is the one that spread northward throughout the western United States. The Kiowa-Apaches, Kiowas, and Comanches, along with some of their neighbors, developed the modern Peyote ceremony in the late 1870s and 1880s. They also produced many of the famous Peyotists of the era, including Saddle Blanket, Architah, Daveko, and Apache John (Kiowa-Apache). A 1904 photograph symbolically captured this cofounding of the modern Peyote ceremony, picturing three early Peyote leaders, one from each group—Apache John, Big Looking Glass (Comanche), and Apiatan (Kiowa). The photo was published in the *Handbook of American Indians North of Mexico* (1907–10). Except for the clothing, it could be a photo of a present-day Peyote group. The three-legged drum, the way the drumhead is tied on and tilted as it is played, the eagle-wing fan, the gourd rattle and staff held by the singer, even the semi-squatting/kneeling position while drumming and singing have not changed in the past century.[25]

In addition to developing the Peyote ceremony known today, the three groups actively proselytized throughout Oklahoma and beyond. Their leaders traveled and taught others about the Peyote way and as Roadmen ran Peyote services. Two other early Peyote groups were the Tonkawas and the Caddos. Both had lived in eastern Texas, had knowledge of Peyote, and were familiar with the Carrizo Peyote ceremony. The U.S. government forced both to move to Oklahoma. The Tonkawas were located on a small reservation in the north-central part of the territory near the Poncas and Otos. Although a very small group, the Tonkawas were responsible for spreading Peyotism to the Otos, who were also important in disseminating a Christianized style of the Peyote ceremony to the Winnebagos. The Wichitas, a small but important group, joined the Caddos on the Wichita-Caddo Agency. James Mooney claimed Wichitas had Peyote ceremonies by 1880 and knew about Peyote before that time. They had originally been on the Kiowa and Comanche Reservation, where they had been exposed to Peyotism. The majority of the Wichita Peyote people followed the Big Moon Way of John Wilson (1840–1901).[26]

Wilson is the most important individual after Quanah Parker. He claimed Delaware, Caddo, and French ancestry but spoke Caddo and considered himself a Caddo. Wilson was introduced to Peyote about 1880. His followers claim that he went into seclusion for two weeks, during which he used Peyote and experienced a series of revelations concerning a new style Peyote ceremony that varied from the Kiowa/Comanche-style service. Wilson changed the altar, making the mound much larger and horseshoe shaped rather than crescent shaped. He claimed he had been given new Peyote songs, moral lessons to share with others, and proper ritual techniques to ensure the curing of ailments and illnesses. This ceremony became known as the Wilson Moon or Big Moon, Way or sometimes the Moonhead Way. The name Big Moon emerged in contrast to Little Moon, the smaller altar of the Half Moon Way. The new altar was also more complex. To the east of the fire a small dirt mound representing the sun was built. A straight east-west line ran from the door, through the dirt mound and fire, to Chief Peyote on the altar. This line intersected with a north-south line, thus creating a cross in the center, leading to the name Cross Fire at a later date. The use of this cross illustrates the major difference between the Big Moon Way and the Half Moon Way—the inclusion of Christian symbols and elements in the Peyote service. Wilson not only introduced the use of the crucifix but also made biblical references to Jesus. He claimed that through Peyote he received revelations for these changes and that he was shown the open grave of Christ and the road leading from the grave to the moon that Jesus traveled to join the Creator. Wilson also preached abstinence from alcohol and gambling, condemned sexual license and adultery, and called on his followers to respect their neighbors. He spread the new-style ceremony to the Quapaws, Delawares, and Osages. It was eventually taught to several Winnebagos visiting Oklahoma. They took the ceremony home to Nebraska, where further elements of Christianity were added. After the turn of the century, there were three variants of the Peyote ceremony: the Little Moon (Half Moon), Big Moon or Wilson Moon, and the Cross Fire. Over the succeeding decades, the Big Moon declined in popularity; today only the Osages practice it. The other two variants spread throughout the West. It is important to note that despite ritual variations a unified theology underlay all Peyote services.[27]

Wilson also introduced Peyote to the neighboring Delawares at Anadarko, Oklahoma. The Eastern Delawares were split between the Big Moon and Little Moon services. Elk Hair, the chief of the Eastern Delawares, opposed Wilson and supported the Little Moon Way, even though Wilson had already converted some Eastern Delawares to the Big Moon. The significance of this divisiveness is that the struggle that occurred here was between Peyotists who wanted a Christianized version and Peyotists who wanted a fully "traditional" Peyote service. Elk Hair believed Wilson tainted the Peyote faith with Christianity, claiming Christianity and Peyotism should not be mixed. To him, the Kiowa/Comanche style represented a "pure Indian way." This debate continued throughout the twentieth century. However, all Peyotists stayed within a belief structure in which the primacy of Peyote was unchallenged. The two groups of Delawares, for example, freely attended each others' services.

Another group to disseminate the Peyote faith was the Arapahos. They were located just north of the Kiowa and Comanche Reservation, sharing a reservation with the Southern Cheyennes. Both the Arapahos and the Southern Cheyennes had a tragic history of warfare, smallpox and cholera epidemics, and hunger. A steady stream of miners, homesteaders, and the U.S. Army had forced both groups to move in two directions. From their Colorado homeland part of each group headed north and part headed south trying to escape certain devastation. The Arapahos who headed south were forced to make a home with the Southern Cheyennes in Oklahoma; the Arapahos who headed north ended up in Wyoming with the Shoshones, on the Wind River Reservation. Around 1890, several Southern Arapahos began attending Peyote services with the neighboring Kiowas. Some Southern Arapahos later claimed they had attended meetings run by Quanah Parker.[28] At the end of the century, several Northern Arapahos attended Peyote meetings with their friends and relatives in the south; they then took the ceremony back home. With the Kiowa/Comanche influence, both Northern and Southern Arapahos practiced the Half Moon Way of Quanah Parker. A small group of neighboring Shoshones also became Peyotists. In the tradition of Parker as well, some Arapahos became missionaries and teachers, taking advantage of the contacts and friendships they made in boarding schools. Among them was Jack Bull Bear, a Roadman and active defender of the faith. He was a spokesman for Peyotism at the 1918 U.S. congressional hearings on Peyote.

In the 1880s, government officials on the Kiowa, Comanche, and Wichita Agency became aware of the growing use of Peyote and the rapid expansion of the Peyote ceremony. In 1886, J. Lee Hall, a reservation employee, issued the first written report on the use of Peyote. He claimed that the Comanches and some of the Kiowas ate the tops of a cactus that came from Mexico and produced the same effect as opium. He said Peyote was very injurious and should be declared contraband. Other written reports emerged. E. L. Clark, a reservation farmer, wrote to Hall complaining about the heavy use of Peyote. In response, Special Agent E. E. White issued an order prohibiting Peyote on the Kiowa, Comanche, and Wichita Agency, although he modified the prohibition under a request from Quanah Parker to allow them to use up the Peyote buttons in their possession. White's order said Peyote impaired one's mind and that some Indians had died from using it and henceforth all Indians would be forbidden to partake of Peyote. Anyone convicted of using Peyote would have his or her annuity goods and food cut off. In 1890, Thomas J. Morgan, commissioner of Indian Affairs, sent a similar order to all agencies. He ordered the police to seize and destroy Peyote and directed the Court of Indian Offenses to punish those found guilty of the use, sale, or introduction of Peyote. This court, established in 1883, was charged with eliminating various cultural and religious practices of American Indians, such as "old heathenish dances" like the Sun Dance. Members of the court were also directed to stop plural marriages, the "ritual practices of so-called medicine men," and the use of intoxicants. In 1890 the Bureau of Indian Affairs (BIA) labeled Peyote an intoxicant and a narcotic and initiated a campaign of eradication—but to no avail. In the 1890s, the supply of Peyote remained plentiful and Peyotism continued to flourish.[29]

While the BIA was trying to criminalize Peyote, Oklahoma Territory officials (Oklahoma became a state in 1907) were considering laws to control the use of Peyote. In 1899 the territorial legislature enacted the first law to suppress the use of Peyote. They declared it unlawful to "possess, barter, sell, give, or otherwise dispose of, any Mescal Beans [Peyote Buttons]," with a fine of twenty-five to two hundred dollars and/or up to six months in jail. Reservation officials were told to send in the names of known Peyotists. Fortunately for the Peyote community, implementation of the statute proved difficult, and the statute was not generally enforced. The problem was that while Peyote was now illegal in Oklahoma Territory, it was not illegal under any federal statute and reservations were under federal jurisdiction. There were some arrests and convictions, but they were dismissed on appeal. Peyote leaders began to organize to influence the new legislature that would result from the merging of Indian and Oklahoma Territories into the new state of Oklahoma. They did not want the anti-Peyote law of the Oklahoma Territory to be part of the new state statutes. In 1907, a group of twenty-seven Peyote leaders met with the Medical Committee of the Constitutional Convention. Quanah Parker, whose reputation and his prominence were at a high point, was the main speaker. (He had been invited to attend President Theodore Roosevelt's inauguration in 1905.) Parker used several arguments. The first was the application of the First Amendment's freedom of religion. He said, "I do not think this Legislature should interfere with a man's religion." In addition he argued that Peyote was good for one's health since it was a cure for alcoholism. Parker's arguments for religious freedom and the health benefits of Peyote would become the cornerstone of later arguments against anti-Peyote laws. Led by Parker, the Peyotists won the day. The 1899 statute was repealed, and no action was taken on a new anti-Peyote bill.[30]

The surprising turn of events in Oklahoma frustrated federal officials who had lobbied the Oklahoma legislature for passage of an anti-Peyote bill. The BIA began to plan for federal anti-Peyote legislation. Meanwhile they would do all they could to disrupt the supply of Peyote. Well aware of these efforts, the Peyote community focused their lobbying efforts on officials in Washington to forestall any such prohibition and to keep the supply of Peyote plentiful. In 1908, Parker wrote to the commissioner of Indian Affairs to complain about harassment and the confiscation of Peyote by federal officials. He pointed out that he had a right to acquire Peyote and claimed that it was not harmful. He asked the commissioner to please "send three good men to me and let me make medicine [take Peyote] with them 2 or 3 times, and if there is any harm let them say so."[31] Although these requests fell on deaf ears, Parker's defense of Peyotism and his impact on the growth of the Peyote religion remains unparalleled to this day, a century after his death (in 1911).

The intrinsic nature of the Peyote faith with its focus on community, healing, renewal, and spiritual uplift partially explains the spread of Peyotism, but there were other factors that contributed to its expansion. In the last decades of the nineteenth century, there was a tremendous movement and interaction among American Indians. The reservation system brought disparate people together in Oklahoma and elsewhere. This increased contact and communication made it possible for the rapid spread of Peyotism and the Ghost Dance. An expanding railroad system facilitated this movement of people. The Texas Mexican Railway from Corpus Christi to Laredo, which opened in 1881, passed directly through the Peyote fields. Other rail lines crisscrossed the Southwest, including a line from Laredo into Oklahoma. By the mid-1880s, travel between reservations was easier, facilitating proselytization in new areas. In southern Texas, Mexican Americans made a living harvesting, drying, and selling Peyote. It was shipped in boxes and barrels by rail and through the postal service. The low cost of shipping lightweight Peyote made supplies plentiful in Oklahoma, and if the Peyote was dried properly, there was no risk of spoilage. Other factors accounting for the diffusion of the Peyote faith included the increasing use of English and, as mentioned above, the emergence of boarding schools.

In 1879 the Carlisle Indian Industrial School opened in Carlisle, Pennsylvania, the first of many such boarding schools. The schools brought American Indian youth from western states together. The goal of the BIA, which ran the schools, was to "civilize" the students by removing them from their families. The bureau was following the maxim of Captain Richard Pratt, the founder of Carlisle: "Kill the Indian, Save the Man." Many of the early Peyote adherents were young men who had gone to boarding school, been exposed to Christianity, and learned to speak English. The contacts and friendships they made in these schools helped spread the Peyote faith. With English as a *lingua franca*, the different groups of American Indians could use it as an "enabling factor" in the spread of Peyotism. There were individual contacts, but when people joined a Peyote community, they usually did so as an entire family. Peyotists were a group that had considerable contact with each other. For example, Jim Blue Bird (Oglala) went to Carlisle and performed in Wild West shows, as did Sam Lone Bear (Oglala). William Black Bear (Oglala) and Sam Blowsnake (Winnebago) performed in Wild West shows. Albert Hensley went to Carlisle and Jonathan Koshiway (Sac and Fox) attended Chilocco Industrial School. Southern Cheyenne Peyotists William Cohoe, Roman Nose, and Little Chief attended Carlisle or Hampton Institute in Virginia or both. In fact these three men had been together in the Fort Marion POW camp in St. Augustine, Florida, where additional contacts were made. Cleaver Warden (Southern Arapaho) and Henry Murdock (Kickapoo) attended Carlisle. Paul Boynton (Cheyenne/Arapaho), an interpreter for James Mooney, also attended Carlisle. Yankton Peyotists such as Sam Necklace and Joe Rockboy went to boarding schools as well. Omer Stewart has listed by name, tribe, and dates of attendance 109 Peyotists who attended Carlisle. This list does not include the 50 Oto Peyotists who went to Carlisle but whose names have been lost.[32] These contacts obviously facilitated the diffusion of the Peyote religion, a pattern that continued throughout the twentieth century. Today it would be virtually impossible to find a Roadman who has not conducted Peyote meetings on many reservations. The same is true for Native American Church members who freely attend meetings wherever they happen to be. As a result of this historical experience, the contemporary members of the NAC perceive themselves as a nationwide Peyote community. These contacts, the ease of travel as well as the spiritual needs of many people, all account for the rapid dissemination of the Peyote religion. Peyote congregations emerged in all states west of the Mississippi River.

Another major event that assisted the dissemination of Peyotism was the Ghost Dance movement, which began in early 1889 in Nevada and spread to California and the northern, central, and southern plains. It started with Wovoka (Jack Wilson), a Northern Piaute from Nevada. At a time when the reservations resembled outdoor prisons, the Ghost Dance promised the restoration of American Indian cultures. Wovoka preached peace and said the changes would come from supernatural intervention. He promised the disappearance of the American settlers, the resurrection of the ancestors, the end of disease, and the return of the buffalo. As the Ghost Dance spread from reservation to reservation, the American government came to see it a threat to its authority and declared the dance illegal. This resulted in the murder of Sitting Bull and the tragic massacre at Wounded Knee on the Pine Ridge Reservation in December 1890. The troops of the U.S. Seventh Cavalry massacred several hundred men, women, and children.[33]

The Ghost Dance was not related to the Peyote religion, but it indirectly facilitated the spread of Peyote. Peyotism clearly predates the Ghost Dance; in 1889, when the movement began, many American Indians in Oklahoma, New Mexico, and Texas were already Peyotists. In fact, well-known Ghost Dance leaders such as John Wilson and Frank White (Pawnee) were active Peyotists before joining the Ghost Dance movement. However, Peyotists did not join the movement because there was a theological linkage between the Peyote faith and the Ghost Dance. The link between the two was related to the widespread movement of people and the many intertribal contacts that occurred with the Ghost Dance.

Not all Peyotists participated in the Ghost Dance. (Nor did all participants in the Ghost Dance become Peyotists.) There were active Peyote groups that the Ghost Dance did not penetrate, such as the Comanches, Lipan Apaches, Mescalero Apaches, Menominees, Omahas, and Winnebagos.

The Ghost Dance certainly heightened the sense of spirituality and hope and that may have benefited the Peyote religion, but the real significance of the Ghost Dance was its intertribal nature—the same connection found in the Peyote religion. As discussed above, the contacts made in government boarding schools and Wild West shows and rodeos as well as the expanding linkage of roads and railroads made it possible to develop a network of Peyote people, facilitating the growth of the Peyote religion throughout the western states. By 1900 the following groups were conducting Peyote ceremonies on their reservations: Arapahos, Caddos, Cheyennes, Comanches, Delawares, Kansas, Kiowa-Apaches, Kiowas, Lipan Apaches, Mescalero Apaches, Missouris, Osages, Otos, Pawnees, Poncas (Southern), Quapaws, Tonkawas, and Wichitas.[34]

In the central plains, the Winnebagos of Nebraska were one of the first people of the region to accept the Peyote faith. They were to the central plains what the Comanches and Kiowas were to the southern plains. The Winnebagos had originally been located in Wisconsin. Because of the steady encroachment of American settlers in the mid-nineteenth century, their landholdings and their population declined, victims of a deadly combination of warfare, food shortages, and disease. In 1863, the United States government moved them to a reservation in northeast Nebraska. Some refused to stay in Nebraska and went back to their home in Wisconsin. The result was two groups of Winnebagos, one in Wisconsin (who now call themselves Ho-Chunks), the other in Nebraska. They maintained close contact, and both groups adopted the Peyote faith. Like the Comanches, the Winnebagos became renowned teachers, innovators, and proselytizers. They may have learned about Peyote in 1889, but soon after they developed the full Peyote ceremony. This was certainly the case by 1905, when the superintendent of Winnebago Reservation in Wisconsin reported to Washington the presence of Peyote on the reservation. The Winnebagos credit John Rave (c. 1855–1917) with the introduction of Peyote. Rave said he first ate Peyote in 1889 when he was in Oklahoma with "peyote eaters."[35] He returned home convinced of its value for his people as he had experienced something very holy that had turned his life around and changed him from being a heavy drinker, living an irresolute life, to a spiritual person with a definite direction. He dedicated the rest of his life to proselytizing, first among his own people, then among people in surrounding states.[36] Paul Radin, the well-known ethnologist who did considerable fieldwork among the Winnebagos from 1908 to 1913, described Rave as:

a very remarkable man, the leader and directing power of the peyote religion. He became a convert to it in Oklahoma and introduced his version of the cult among the Winnebago. . . . [H]e molded the cult he had borrowed into something quite new. He possessed the proselytizing zeal to an unusual degree. Through his activity the Winnebago form of the peyote cult has been spread among the Fox, Menominee, Ojibwa, and Dakota.[37]

Albert Hensley, also a Winnebago, played a similar role. He attended Carlisle Indian School and became the Winnebago spokesman for Peyote. Hensley defended Peyotism against the increasing attacks from government officials and missionaries. His approach to legitimizing Peyotism was to make it part of Christianity. He and others began corresponding with the BIA, trying to convince them that Peyotism was a Christian faith. Hensley wrote that they called it "medicine," not Peyote or mescal: "Our favorite term is medicine, and to us it is a portion of the body of Christ even as the communion bread is believed to be a portion of Christ's body." He explained how it cures "temporal spiritual ills" and "takes away the "desire for strong drink."[38] In their attempts to legitimize the use of Peyote, both Rave and Hensley became informants to Paul Radin. They supplied some of the most significant accounts of the Peyote church in its early days. Today both men are credited with helping to establish the Peyote church on a firm foundation.

With the influence of Rave, the Omahas of Nebraska adopted Peyotism about the same time as did their Winnebago neighbors. By 1906, the Peyote Cross Fire ceremony had been introduced onto their reservation. The Omahas were one of the first groups to organize against and protest federal restrictions. At first they referred to themselves as the Mescal Society. In 1912, a delegation went to Washington to testify for the right to use Peyote. Nebraska attorney Harry Keefe wrote an introductory letter to the BIA on their behalf, commenting on the positive influence of the Peyote faith. Keefe had attended Peyote services and wrote that "the effect of Peyote is very slight. I have never been able to observe any effects one way or the other." In 1915, under the name Omaha Indian Peyote Society, the Omahas petitioned for the right to use Peyote. Eventually more than half of the Omahas became Peyotists.[39] Milton Miller, elected president of the NAC of North America in 2006, comes from this long line of Omaha Peyotists. In 1921, Hensley helped the Peyotists in Nebraska to incorporate as the "Peyote Church of Christ." Their charter had thirty-eight signatories, including

Hensley and Jesse Clay, and most significantly members of the Half Moon and Cross Fire Way were represented. According to the charter:

> We recognize all people who worship God and follow Christ as members of the one true church. . . . We believe in the sacrament and sacramental bread and wine, but in so much as the use of the same is forbidden to Indians, we of the people who cannot obtain or use the same have adopted the use of bread as Peyote and water as wine.[40]

In 1922, they changed the name to the Native American Church of Winnebago, Nebraska, deleting the word *Peyote* from their name.

While establishing the Peyote religion among the Winnebagos, Rave and Hensley developed the Cross Fire ceremony. Rave, who introduced it, apparently coined the term Cross Fire. Hensley added some significant innovations. What became known as the John Rave Cross Fire, however, was partially an adaptation of Jonathan Koshiway's First Born Church of Christ in Oklahoma, and Wilson's Big Moon ceremony. Rave, who spent several years in Oklahoma, said that he visited the Otos and credited them with teaching him about Peyote. He also probably attended Peyote meetings with the Big Moon ceremony. Rave returned to Nebraska and modified what he had learned in Oklahoma. He eliminated the use of tobacco in the ceremony and added additional Christian elements. Rave first came in contact with the use of Christian elements and interpretations to explain Peyotism when he attended Koshiway's First Born Church of Christ.[41] Rave and Hensley, however, are credited with increasing Christian references in Peyote songs and the use of the Bible in Peyote services. Rave attended Oto services where the Bible was used, probably lying open on the altar. As Rave and Hensley were proselytizers, the Peyote way they taught included considerably more use of the Bible, such as midnight sermons based on biblical passages or biblical references to sanction the eating of Peyote. One such example is from Exodus 12:8—"and they shall eat the flesh in the night, roast with fire, and unleavened bread; and with bitter herbs they shall eat it." In addition certain aspects of the Peyote religion were given Christian interpretations.[42] Hensley gave the following interpretation of the Peyote religion by drawing parallels with early Christianity:

> It is true religion. The peyote is fulfilling the work of God and the Son of God. When the Son of God came to the earth he was poor, yet people spoke of him; he was abused. It is the same now with the peyote. The

plant itself is not much of a growth, yet the people are talking about it a good deal; they are abusing it, they are trying to stop its use. When the Son of God came to earth the preachers of that time were called Pharisees and Scribes. They doubted what the Son of God said and claimed he was an ordinary man. So it is today with the Christian Church; they are the Pharisees and Scribes, they are the doubters. They say that this is merely a plant, that it is the work of the devil. They are trying to stop its use and they are calling it an intoxicant, but this is a lie.[43]

Hensley also told his followers that the Bible was intelligible only to those who partook of Peyote. This allowed for the continued primacy of Peyote as well as significant use of the Bible. Both Hensley and Rave had considerable influence on the development of the Peyote religion. However, their proselytizing among the Winnebagos was not without opposition. In the early years many traditionalists opposed the introduction of the Peyote religion.[44]

A more serious threat to the Winnebagos and the growing Peyote religion was the Bureau of Indian Affairs, which initiated an active campaign to abolish Peyotism. This was particularly threatening to the Winnebagos as BIA investigator William "Pussyfoot" Johnson regarded them as major proselytizers. In 1908, he wrote: "The Winnebagos have sent out missionaries to other Indian tribes, teaching this doctrine, administering the rites and arranging for the supply of peyote." Johnson had been appointed by President Roosevelt in 1906 to enforce the prohibition of alcohol on Indian reservations. An activist in the national prohibition movement, Johnson took to his new job with a vengeance. With approximately a hundred deputies, he became the BIA's chief enforcer. The legislation outlawing intoxicants on reservations did not mention Peyote, but Johnson took it upon himself to interpret the law to include Peyote.

The Winnebago Peyote leaders took a dim view of Johnson, but they had few options open to them in opposing him. At this point, the only possibility would be to mount a lobbying campaign to convince Washington of the value of their religion and get federal officials to ease on its suppression and leave the Peyotists alone. Only at a later date would Peyote groups incorporate and seek constitutional protection. Hensley, Rave, and Oliver La Mere, the three most prominent Peyotists, began corresponding with officials in Washington. In a 1908 letter, Hensley tried to convince Francis Leupp, the commissioner of Indian Affairs, that the Peyotists were a Christian denomination and that Peyote was a gift of God that cured temporal and spiritual ills, including addiction to alcohol.[45] The BIA relented slightly by allowing Peyotists to possess a small number of Peyote buttons for personal use, but it continued the effort to stop the sale and shipment of Peyote as the bureau believed that it was dangerous and habit forming. By stopping the sale of Peyote, BIA officials hoped that a dwindling supply would cause the Peyote faith to fade away. Dissatisfied with this situation, Peyote leaders continued to protest and lobby. "Pussyfoot" Johnson's strategy to stop the supply of Peyote was to buy and destroy it. In 1908, he reported that he had bought and destroyed 176,400 Peyote buttons. He did the same thing in 1909. In Laredo, Texas, he went to wholesale companies and warned them against shipping Peyote; he also went to Pacific Express and Wells Fargo Express and convinced them not to ship it. Johnson had an infamous reputation within the Peyote community. His campaign against Peyote was on shaky legal grounds as Peyote had not been criminalized; therefore authority to enforce a Peyote prohibition was unclear. Johnson, however, had no misgivings about his activities. He wrote: "I believe that we have got things in such shape now that we will be able to snuff out this peyote nuisance." It was not to be. Peyotism continued to grow, as the law enforcement community in general did not follow Johnson's interpretation of the ban on intoxicants to include Peyote. Becoming very frustrated, he told the superintendent of the Yankton Sioux Reservation that he had been ordered to limit his work to liquor suppression and had to "suspend all operations concerning peyotes." In 1911, Johnson left government service and joined the Anti-Saloon League of America.[46]

In spite of the efforts of the BIA and Johnson's belief that destroying the supply of Peyote would weaken Winnebago Peyotism, the religion continued to grow. Johnson had claimed that the Winnebagos were renouncing Peyotism; in reality it was expanding. In 1912, Jesse Clay, a Winnebago Peyotist, introduced the Half Moon ceremony to the Winnebagos. In an interview with Paul Radin, Clay said he had attended an Arapaho Half Moon ceremony in Oklahoma. A year later, a man Clay called Arapaho Bull (Jock Bull Bear) visited Clay in Nebraska and led a Peyote meeting in the Arapaho manner.[47] This became the Jesse Clay Half Moon ceremony of the Winnebagos. They claimed that the Half Moon Way was more traditional than the Cross Fire, particularly with its ceremonial use of tobacco during prayer. The ceremony differs from the Cross Fire primarily in the degree of Christian influence. Some Half Moon services do not contain any Christian elements, but some do so to a limited extent, such as using Christian references in Peyote songs and using Christian references to explain Peyote symbolism. For example, in Clay's account to Radin, he said, "The reason for drinking water at midnight is because Christ was born at midnight and because of the good tiding that he brought to the earth, for water is one of the best things in life and Christ is the savior of mankind." Clay added that "the purpose of going to the four directions and blowing the flute is to announce the birth of Christ to all the world." For the Winnebagos, as for other American Indians who follow the Peyote faith, the introduction of Peyotism with a lesser or greater degree of Christianity does not represent a break with the religious traditions of the past but is considered an expansion of and integration with the spiritual beliefs of their ancestors.[48]

The Jesse Clay Half Moon ceremony became popular with many Winnebagos. Clay became the first president of the Native American Church of Winnebago, Nebraska, and like his counterparts Rave and Hensley, he was an active proselytizer. By 1918, the Wisconsin and Nebraska Winnebagos were practicing both the Cross Fire and Half Moon ceremonies. Most people attended either service. Both groups opened their doors to non-Winnebagos, and both traveled to spread the Peyote way. A 1911 report from the reservation superintendent claimed that 37 percent, or five hundred to six hundred, of the Winnebagos were Peyotists. Another source claimed 50 percent in 1914. This large membership with its strong proselytizing ethic made the Winnebagos very influential in the spread of the Peyote religion. Local opposition to Peyote eventually dissipated, and by the 1950s, a wide cross section of Winnebagos were Peyotists, including some important political leaders. By 1960 one scholar estimated that the majority of the Winnebagos had become members of the Native American Church. Most of what Rave and Hensley taught is still practiced among the Cross Fire Winnebagos.[49] It should be noted that despite the scholarly interest in the patterns of diffusion of the Peyote religion and the degree of Christian influence on various Peyote ceremonies, the Winnebagos and all other American Indians who are members of the Native American Church believe that Peyote is a "medicine" and is a direct gift from God. A Winnebago man told Paul Radin:

> The Winnebago were decreasing in number, so the Creator gave them a medicine [Peyote] which would enable them to get accustomed to the white man's food; that, also, they might know the Creator and that he is the true bread and food. This they found out by using this medicine. They are going into it deeper and deeper all the time, they who had been lost, and this has all been accomplished by the medicine.[50]

In the first two decades of the twentieth century, the Peyote faith continued to expand across the west. The BIA reported that the number of Peyotists in various Indian groups in Oklahoma ranged from 15 to 50 percent. The major exception in Oklahoma was the so-called Five Civilized Tribes (Creeks, Cherokees, Chickasaws, Choctaws, and Seminoles), who had been removed from the southeastern United States to Oklahoma in the 1830s and 1840s and were highly Christianized. In the central plains, the Winnebagos were the primary missionaries of the Cross Fire Way. Many groups gave them credit for introducing Peyote. John Bearskin (Winnebago) told an interviewer that Rave went to South Dakota, Minnesota, and Wisconsin in 1903–1904 to teach Peyotism to those willing to listen. The various Sioux groups in South Dakota also credit the Winnebagos for introducing them to the Peyote religion. After the turn of the century, important Peyote communities emerged on the Pine Ridge, Rosebud, and Yankton Sioux reservations. Although Sioux Peyotists were a small minority on their respective reservations, they played a significant role in the history of the Peyote faith. The earliest known Peyote ceremony on a Sioux reservation was in 1904 on Pine Ridge. Albert Hensley and John Rave were the teachers.

Two years earlier, however, Jim Blue Bird (Oglala Lakota, 1887–1976), one of the founders of the Native American Church of South Dakota, had visited Oklahoma and attended a Peyote meeting run by Quanah Parker. Blue Bird said he immediately considered himself part of the Peyote religion. In spite of his Half Moon experience, it was the visits of Hensley and Rave that convinced Blue Bird and others on Pine Ridge to follow the Cross Fire Way. By 1911, a Peyote community had emerged. Three men—Harry Black Bear, Willie Red Nest, and Charles Red Bear—wrote to their local superintendent asking for permission to acquire Peyote. The BIA denied them permission, claiming it was an unresolved issue. In the teens and 1920s, a Half Moon following emerged. Lakotas living in Oklahoma returned home after becoming Half Moon Peyotists, and some Winnebago and Omaha Half Moon people visited Pine Ridge. Both influences led to the emergence of a Half Moon group. The Cross Fire, however, remained the much larger group.[51]

Blue Bird and other Lakotas such as Sam Lone Bear and William Black Bear traveled widely throughout the plains, teaching the Cross Fire Way. Blue Bird proved very influential in integrating Christianity with Peyotism. He wrote to Omer Stewart that "we use the Bible [and] adopted the teaching of the Gospel of Jesus Christ."[52] In many ways Blue Bird and Lone Bear are archetypes of

Peyote proselytizers. Both went to the Carlisle Indian School, both worked in Wild West shows, and both had a wide range of contacts with people who also spoke English. They became Roadmen and teachers of the Peyote faith. Blue Bird was also the chief organizer, along with William Black Bear, in chartering the Native American Church of Allen, South Dakota, which eventually became the Native American Church of South Dakota.

Even with the Christian focus, the Peyotists on Pine Ridge were not immune from harassment by federal officials. Upon occasion the police would confiscate the drum and the Peyote buttons. In 1916, Harry Black Bear was arrested for distributing Peyote. Based on the Indian Prohibition Act of 1897, the prosecutor argued that Peyote was an intoxicant. Black Bear was found guilty in a jury trial, but the judge dismissed the case on a request from the defense attorney and ruled that the 1897 law applied only to alcohol and not to Peyote. Federal officials were not happy. There still was no consistent federal policy as there was no federal statute criminalizing Peyote. However, the same year that Black Bear was arrested, one would be introduced into Congress.

The Peyotists on the Rosebud and Yankton reservations also credit the Winnebagos with introducing them to the Peyote faith. In both places there is no exact date for the introduction of Peyote, but it was certainly in the first decade of the twentieth century. In his autobiography, Leonard Crow Dog (born 1942), a Roadman and lifetime member of the NAC, as well as a traditional spiritual leader, claims Peyote came to Rosebud "around 1903." His elders told him that it was the Winnebagos who taught them about Peyote. The Crow Dogs are the most famous family to come from Rosebud. Leonard's great-grandfather, Crow Dog, shot and killed Chief Spotted Tail in 1881. In a famous Supreme Court case, charges against Crow Dog were dismissed. The court argued that the federal government had no jurisdiction over Indian-on-Indian crimes. As a result, Congress passed the Major Crimes Act (1885), which gave the federal government jurisdiction over certain crimes committed on reservations. Decades later, the Crow Dog family, starting with Leonard's father, Henry Crow Dog (1899–1985), who joined the NAC in the 1920s, became devout Peyotists and defenders of the faith. Leonard, who claims "Grandfather Peyote had chosen me to be a road chief in the Native American Church," continues to be a leading spokesman today.[53]

Among the Yankton Sioux, the Peyote religion became established amid the turmoil caused by the loss of land and the rapid change in everyday life as well as their continuing political divisiveness. The first recorded government acknowledgement of the presence of Peyote on the Yankton Sioux Reservation came from Walter Runke, superintendent of the Yankton Agency. In 1911, he sent the following to "Pussyfoot" Johnson:

> A number of Indians of this reservation have recently taken it upon themselves to introduce the use of Mescal [Peyote] among the people of this agency. . . . I am putting forth all possible effort to prevent the use thereof by the Indians under the jurisdiction of this Agency. It will be much easier at this time to prevent the introduction and general use of Mescal on this reservation than it will be later to stamp out its use. I have taken drastic measures with the ringleaders of our new so-called Mescal [Peyote] Society and have them now lodged in the Agency jails.[54]

In Runke's Annual Report for 1911, he gave more details on how he was jailing the "bean eaters" and would soon see the suppression of the use of "mescal or peyotes."[55] Runke's optimism about suppressing the Peyote religion proved premature.

The above report indicates that in 1911 Peyote had only recently been introduced onto the reservation or at least that it had recently come to the attention of Runke. The exact date for the introduction of Peyote to the Yanktons is difficult to determine but was probably between 1904 and 1910. There are several versions of how Peyote was first introduced, but all versions agree that it was Charlie Jones, a Yankton, who introduced Peyote to the reservation. In 1912, the year after the Runke report, Jones gave Adelbert Leech, the new superintendent, information on the Peyote religion. Leech heard that Charlie Jones and other Yanktons were holding Peyote meetings. He reported that "they were locked up again, until such time as they are willing to come into this office here and sign a statement to the effect that they will quit the use of Peyote and its attendant practices." Leech also confiscated the Peyote, a drum, feathers, and a rod or staff with carved symbols on it.[56] Jones agreed and signed the statement. He also gave Leech additional information. He said that four years earlier (1908) Albert Hensley, a Winnebago, had introduced him to Peyote. Jones claimed he spent two years with the Winnebagos in Nebraska, where he attended a Peyote meeting every Saturday night. After he returned home, other Yanktons joined him in Peyote meetings. He described a typical meeting:

> They met on Saturday night at Charlie Medicinhorns [sic] place, sing Indian songs, and prayed to the Great Spirit. They have a drum and

several rattles, a bunch of feathers, and some other paraphernalia. . . . They eat the peyote and beat the drum and shake the rattles, and keep this up all night and sometimes the next day.[57]

It is obvious from the above that by this time the issue for federal officials was not the Peyote buttons, but the full Peyote religious ceremony. All the essential elements of the Peyote religion were in place.

Leech's incarceration of the Peyotists was a bit precipitous. In March 1912, the BIA told him: "The mere fact of holding such meetings or the use of peyote or mescal cannot be considered an offense . . . and if Jones is at present imprisoned he shall be released at once." The fact that the Peyote was not illegal did not deter reservation officials from attempting to suppress it. In his 1913 Annual Report, Leech admits Peyote usage had been revived and said he would continue a policy of harassment and confiscation of Peyote buttons until the religion was stamped out.[58] This pattern of suppression continued throughout the decade but with little effect. In 1914, S. A. M. Young, the superintendent of Indian Schools on the Yankton Sioux Reservation, wrote to the BIA that the use of "mescal or Peyote" was increasing. He encouraged the BIA to find a legal means to punish the men using Peyote, because not punishing them will have a bad effect on reservation discipline and make the Peyotists more brazen. Again, the reply from the bureau was that the Yanktons could not be locked up but that anti-Peyote legislation was under consideration. Since threats and arbitrary arrests did not restrain the Peyote community on the Yankton Sioux Reservation, Superintendent Leech asked the BIA to give him the power to eliminate Peyote by labeling it a narcotic, like morphine and opium. Another strategy was to have medical authorities attack Peyote. Dr. David A. Richardson, the BIA physician on the Yankton Reservation, reported many "horrors" associated with Peyote. He wrote that it "undermines health" and had caused "several sudden deaths," including those of children. He denied that Peyote cured alcoholism by saying that "every peyote fiend uses alcohol," and he added that Peyote meeting were nothing but orgies.[59] These horror stories were always told by people who had never attended a Peyote service. What is ironic about Dr. Richardson's report is that drug companies such as Parke, Davis and Company sold Peyote until the 1920s because of its alleged therapeutic uses.

As Peyotism continued to expand throughout the West, opposition to it grew. The opposition came from both the executive and legislative branches of the federal government as well as from state governments, from many Christian denominations and various humanitarian groups. Opposition also came from a significant number of American Indians who supported assimilation and saw the Peyote religion as retarding progress toward "civilization." Many of these groups formed an alliance to eradicate Peyotism. The response to this repression took several forms. First, some people went underground by holding Peyote meetings in secret and publicly downplaying the expansion of Peyotism. However, this was neither a practical nor an effective approach. Another option was to focus on the Christian elements in the Cross Fire ceremony; or, if Christian elements were absent, to add several to the service. Peyotists hoped that having Christian elements in the service, such as the use of the Bible, would mute the opposition. They also developed theological interpretations to parallel Christian theology. For example, Peyotists compared Peyote as a sacrament that was ingested as the body of God to the Christian belief in bread and wine as the flesh and blood of Jesus Christ; they said the fire in the center of a Peyote service represented God in the Old Testament saying, "Let there be light." Blowing the eagle bone whistle to the four directions was symbolic of announcing the birth of Jesus. The fire chief shaped the ashes into a heart or cross to symbolize Jesus, or one claimed the Peyote Road represented Jesus' road. Whether some of these were contrivances or sincerely held beliefs, it made no difference; they had no impact on muting the opposition to Peyote. There was another option to counter the opposition to Peyotism: Seek constitutional protection.

INCORPORATION OF THE NATIVE AMERICAN CHURCH

The drive to seek First Amendment protection for the Peyote religion emerged in response to a widespread campaign to prohibit the possession, sale, and use of Peyote. The Bureau of Indian Affairs, several state legislatures, and a wide range of religious and humanitarian groups joined forces in an assault on Peyotism. With such an array of enemies many Peyotists believed that only through incorporation could they gain legal protection for the free exercise of their religion.

The first fully incorporated group with a clear articulation of Peyote as a sacrament was established in Oklahoma in 1918. This was a watershed event in the history of the Peyote religion. This was neither the first Peyote organization nor the first to incorporate, but it was the first to publicly proclaim Peyote as a sacrament. Prior to an actual incorporation by Peyotists in Oklahoma, there

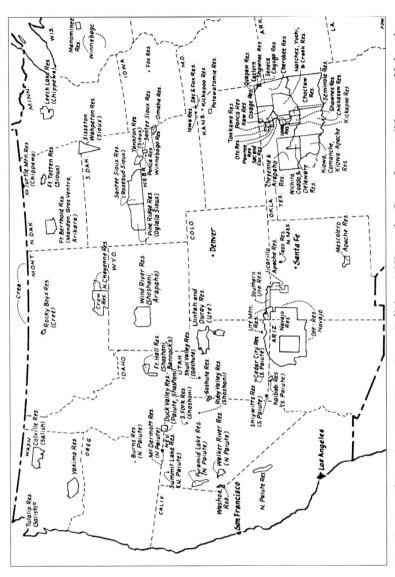

Distribution of Peyotists, 1985. From *Peyote Religion: A History*, by Omer Stewart (Norman: University of Oklahoma Press: 1987), 149.

was a middle stage between Peyote ceremonies by individuals on a reservation to a fully state chartered corporation. After the turn of the century, Peyotists were organizing into wider groups. Reservation superintendents were sending in reports about these activities to Washington. For example, Superintendent H. M. Noble of the Ponca Reservation in Oklahoma reported in 1906 that "one or two quasi-religious societies of mescal bean eaters were organized." He noted that the societies were having a beneficial effect on younger men by reducing the use of alcohol. He added that he did not detect any physical harm among the users of Peyote. The BIA ignored remarks such as this about Peyote not being harmful as it did not fit their assimilationist agenda, especially given the fact that other superintendents reported that it was dangerous. A 1906 report from the Winnebago Reservation in Nebraska says the "mescal bean" was introduced two years ago and the Indians have established an organization known as the "Mescal Society."[60] A local medical doctor referred to a sect he called "Mescal Bean Eaters." Another 1906 report mentions that a loose intertribal association of Peyote groups known as "Mescal Bean Eaters" has expanded from Oklahoma to Nebraska. The same source claimed that in 1909 the name "Mescal Bean Eaters" was changed to "Union Church."[61] Albert Hensley made a similar comment in a 1909 interview. He said, "[W]e now call our church the Union Church instead of Mescal Eaters."[62] In 1914, there is also testimony in a U.S. District Court case in Wisconsin concerning an association called the Peyote Society.[63] It is difficult to assess the degree of organization that was occurring; it seems to have been informal. Yet one point is certain: as the anti-Peyote forces increased in influence, the Peyote communities were taking defensive measures, including the development of semiformal organizations and the use of Christianity as a foil to the opposition.

In 1914, Jonathan Koshiway incorporated a group of Oto Peyotists (his wife was Oto), forming the First Born Church of Christ in Red Rock, Oklahoma; however, Peyote was not mentioned in the articles of incorporation. Koshiway told anthropologist James Slotkin that he incorporated to acquire legal protection, that he had to find a way to defend his religion. He said that he chose a biblical passage for the name of his church from Hebrews 12:23— "One Church of the First-born"—so that they could spread the word of God and the Holy Bible. They purposely focused on the Christian elements in their ceremonies and charter to lessen opposition to their religion.[64]

As knowledge of the expansion of Peyotism filtered into Washington from reservation employees, BIA officials became quite alarmed. The BIA's Annual

Report for 1909 stated that Peyote people were organizing and expanding the use of a "powerful narcotic," and that the development of a "religious cult" was just an excuse for using a narcotic substance. Because it lacked legislative tools to stem the tide of Peyotism, the BIA turned to administrative measurers. For example, in 1910, the bureau requested that the Treasury Department, through its Customs Office, prohibit the importation of Peyote from Mexico. The department refused, claiming it had no legal basis to do so. In 1914, when Congress passed the Harrison Narcotic Act, the BIA tried, unsuccessfully, to get Peyote added to the list of narcotics. The bureau did have one success in 1915. The Department of Agriculture issued an order prohibiting the importation of Peyote as it was considered a danger to the American public (order rescinded in 1937). Two years later, based on the Department of Agriculture's decision, the U.S. Postal Service banned the shipment of Peyote through the mail system (order rescinded in 1940). The BIA also began a systematic effort to collect more information on Peyote from its employees in the field. The bureau hoped to use the information to mount a public campaign against Peyote.[65]

The BIA also hoped to get support from the courts; that support was not forthcoming. In the cases in which arrests for Peyote usage were made, charges were eventually dropped or guilty verdicts were dismissed. Even when reservation officials arrested Peyote people, the BIA had to order them released as the bureau did not have the authority for such arrests because no laws had been broken. Nevertheless pressure continued to build to do something about the "mescal craze." The ongoing use of Peyote alarmed various Christian churches and humanitarian organizations. These groups exerted pressure on Congress to pass a law prohibiting Peyote. Groups such as the National Indian Association, Indian Rights Association, Society of American Indians, Native American Student Conference, and the Lake Mohonk Conference also supported such a law. They believed that the Peyote faith threatened their attempts to "save the Indian," to civilize and Christianize them. These and other groups published a steady stream of anti-Peyote literature. Herbert Welsh, president of the Indian Rights Association, issued a pamphlet with an alarming title, *Peyote— An Insidious Evil*. He claimed that connecting Peyote to religion was just a pretense for drug use. One group that may best epitomize the "save the Indian" mentality, however, was the Lake Mohonk Conference.

The Lake Mohonk group of clergy and humanitarians was founded in 1883 and met annually at Lake Mohonk, New York. Their mission was to save American Indians by supporting the government's assimilation programs.

They issued position papers, developed resolutions, lobbied Congress, and informed the public. They believed that American Indians should give up their cultures, religions, and languages and become Christianized Anglo-Americans. For example, they supported sending American Indian youth to boarding schools; they supported the Dawes Act or allotment system designed to eliminate communal aspects of Indian life and replace it with American-style individualism. They and other groups hoped to close the reservations. In 1914, the Lake Mohonk Conference added the Peyote faith to their list of Indian practices that should be eliminated. In their 1914, 1915, and 1916 conference reports, the group used language such as "peyote menace" and "mescal fiends." The reports added that "thousands of our Indians are now Peyote drug fiends." The Lake Mohonk group called on the U.S. Congress to outlaw Peyote. Yet the group realized the dilemma of this position when one member said we "are up against the fact it is a religious institution and comes under the Constitution of the United States." In a 1916 speech, retired general Richard Pratt, former head of the Carlisle Indian School, asked the members to support the new legislation in Congress that would outlaw the use of Peyote.[66]

The BIA, thwarted in its many nonlegislative attempts to stop the use of Peyote, was behind the new legislation. In 1914, the BIA began a campaign to get a legislative prohibition against Peyote. Two years later, Representative Harvey L. Gandy of South Dakota introduced the first such bill in the House of Representatives. The same bill was introduced in the Senate. Support for the Gandy bill came from the Department of the Interior, Christian denominations, reform groups, and some American Indian converts to Christianity. These groups issued more anti-Peyote literature, some of which made its way into the media. In 1916, journalist Gertrude Seymour published an article titled "Peyote Worship: An Indian Cult and a Powerful Drug." She quoted various "authorities" on the pernicious nature of Peyote and expressed concern about the "rapid spread of peyote worship in the past decade." She called for legislation outlawing Peyote. In spite of the nationwide campaign, the Gandy bill failed in 1916 and again in 1917, but in 1918, as the nation focused on World War I, the anti-Peyote forces coordinated their activities in a final push to convince Congress to criminalize the use or possession of Peyote.[67]

The BIA asked the highly respected representative from Arizona, Carl Hayden, to reintroduce the anti-Peyote bill in the House of Representatives. The Hayden bill differed slightly from the previous Gandy bill. It did not directly outlaw Peyote but sought to revise the liquor traffic laws to include Peyote as an intoxicant.

This time congressional supporters of the bill called for extensive hearings to build a case against Peyote through the testimony of expert witnesses. A subcommittee of the Committee on Indian Affairs conducted the hearings in February and March 1918. Equally troubling to Peyotists, Nevada, Colorado, and Utah had passed anti-Peyote laws in 1917. As noted above, the intensity of the assault on Peyote was stimulated by the growing fear that the Peyote faith would thwart the BIA's ongoing "civilizing" mission. It was in this atmosphere of prohibition and suppression that Oklahoma Peyotists considered incorporation as a strategy they hoped would give them First Amendment protection.

During the subcommittee hearings, a wide array of spokespersons on each side of the Hayden bill testified. The BIA, several government scientists, missionary and church groups, humanitarian organizations, and medical doctors supported the bill. Opposing the Hayden bill were several government ethnologists, scientists, and doctors as well as American Indians who were Peyotists and several who were not but supported the Peyote faith.[68]

Many groups and individuals submitted supporting documentation at the hearings. They included the Anti-Saloon League of America, the National Women's Christian Temperance Union, the YMCA, the National Congress of Mothers and Parent Teachers Associations, the Bureau of Catholic Indian Mission, and the Home Missions Council. This was by far the most determined attempt to pass a federal law prohibiting the use of Peyote. A leading spokesman for the Hayden bill was General Pratt. Interestingly, he began his testimony by admitting that he had no direct knowledge of the harmful effects of Peyote, that his belief in these effects was based only on hearsay evidence, yet he wanted to challenge the previous testimony of James Mooney, the leading defender of the Peyote faith. He accused Mooney of promoting, if not originating, the Ghost Dance and the Peyote religion. He added that Mooney's testimony and that of other ethnologists from the Bureau of American Ethnology could not be trusted as they were guilty of leading Indians back to the past.[69]

The key witness for the anti-Peyote group, however, was Gertrude Simmons Bonnin (1876–1938), a Yankton Sioux who later took the Dakota name Zitkala-Ša (Red Bird). She was a very prominent person at the time, and supporters of the legislation hoped that as an American Indian she would carry extra weight in testifying in favor of the prohibition. Bonnin was a noted author and an officer of the Society of American Indians, founded in 1911 in Columbus, Ohio. Its members were American Indians who for the most part had considerable accomplishments in American society. They valued their heritage but saw little future for their past. They saw their future paralleling the future of America as equal citizens. The strategy to achieve this goal was continually debated. At their inaugural conference in 1911, the society's members debated the issue of Peyote but took no official position. Four prominent Peyotists, Thomas Sloan and Hiram Chase (Omahas) and Oliver La Mere and Albert Hensley (Winnebagos), were in attendance at the conference. Several of the members, including Bonnin, Dr. Charles A. Eastman (Santee), and Arthur C. Parker (Seneca), opposed Peyote and pushed the organization in that direction. In 1914, the society began to cover Peyote issues in their quarterly publication. The first article to appear was titled "Peyote: A Drug-Induced Religion." Two years later, as the anti-Peyote movement increased, the society reprinted Gertrude Seymour's harsh article "Peyote Worship" (mentioned above). At their 1916 annual conference, members voted to support the anti-Peyote legislature before Congress. Bonnin and her husband, Raymond, also a Yankton Sioux, worked for the BIA among the Utes on the Uintah and Ouray Reservation. She claimed extensive knowledge of Peyote. She said she watched it spread among the Utes and considered Peyote the same as alcohol and that a belief in its powers was mere superstition. In 1915, she and her husband joined with Episcopal and Mormon missionaries to try to stem the tide of Peyotism by lobbying the Utah legislature to outlaw Peyote. In January 1917, after the failure of the Gandy bill, Bonnin traveled to Denver. She brought a collection of documents on Peyote with her and was able to convince the Women's Christian Temperance Union and the Anti-Saloon League to help her lobby the Colorado legislature for a state law prohibiting Peyote. They were successful.[70]

Four days before the congressional hearings began, Bonnin, aware of the impact of public opinion on the hearings, agreed to an interview with the *Washington Times* (February 17, 1918, Sunday edition). She appeared in a photograph wearing traditional American Indian clothing. The headline read "Indian Woman in Capital to Fight Growing Use of Peyote Drug—Mrs. Gertrude Bonnin, Carlisle Graduate, Relative of Sitting Bull, Describes Effects of Mind Poison." At the hearing, Bonnin vigorously attacked the use of Peyote while claiming that she was the granddaughter of Sitting Bull and a graduate of the Carlisle Indian School. Continuing in the self-publicist mode, she appeared before the House subcommittee wearing the same American Indian clothing as in the newspaper photo and proceeded to testify to the supposed horrors of Peyote. She denied that Peyotism was an Indian religion and claimed that the use of Peyote led to wild intoxication and orgies that involved men, women, and children and had caused the deaths of several people. In her testimony, she tried to link Peyote to increased alcohol abuse and warned that if it was not stopped immediately Peyote would spread like "wildfire," including its introduction into the Anglo-American community. She became angered by the idea that Peyote should be given constitutional protection. Bonnin even played the race card, pointing out that James Mooney was white and she was Indian; therefore, she was in a better position to know the truth about Peyote. She proved to be an intriguing and dynamic witness for the Hayden bill. Testifying for the Hayden bill as well was Samuel M. Brosius, of the Indian Rights Association. He is noteworthy because of his statement that he had not had any experience with Peyote, but he knew it was evil. There were also representatives from the YMCA and the Bureau of Catholic Missions, scholars from Yale University and the University of Utah, and Dr. Eastman and Arthur Parker.[71]

Both Eastman and Parker were highly educated, prominent men and well-known authors. Each became president of the Society of American Indians. They also opposed the Peyote faith. Eastman grew up in Minnesota speaking Dakota. He attended Santee Indian School and went on to Dartmouth College and Boston University Medical School. He was the physician at Pine Ridge in 1890 during the massacre at Wounded Knee. After this traumatic experience and conflict with reservation authorities, Eastman moved to Minneapolis, began a private practice, and became involved with organizations committed to supporting American Indians. His agenda was to pressure the government to allow American Indians to move away from dependency to full citizenship. He believed the Peyote faith was a step backward and that defending Peyotism on religious grounds was a falsehood. At the hearing, he testified that it was not an Indian faith and that Peyote was a dangerous substance that should be prohibited by law.[72]

Parker was equally prestigious. He grew up on an Iroquois reservation in New York State. He claimed descent from the prophet Handsome Lake. He spent much of his life studying and writing about Iroquois history. His family moved to New York City, where he became fascinated with anthropology after visits to the Museum of Natural History. This led him to Columbia University, where he studied under the famous anthropologist Franz Boas. Parker wrote hundreds of articles and fourteen books. He believed the future of the American Indian lay in working together across tribal boundaries. This led him to Eastman, Bonnin, Carlos Montezuma (Apache), and the founding of the Society of American Indians and to his conceptualization of a pan-Indian identity. He became editor of the society's quarterly and eventually its president. He believed the Peyote faith was not in the best interests of American Indians. During his time as editor of the society's quarterly, he published the first articles that were hostile to the Peyote faith. He believed the government had not done enough to stop Peyotism. All this led him to the hearings where he testified in favor of the Hayden bill. Parker and Eastman were powerful voices against Peyotism. It was difficult to ignore their testimony.[73]

As the anti-Peyote forces amassed their arsenal of evidence and testimonials, the Peyote community began the defense of its faith. As noted above, James Mooney led the defense. He angered the anti-Peyote forces, who saw him not only as a threat but as a traitor to the government that employed him. By 1916, Mooney was well known for his study of the Ghost Dance movement and had been studying and participating in Peyote meetings for the past twenty-five years and thus had many years of field experience. Mooney had argued for almost three decades that Peyote was not harmful and that Peyotism was a genuine American Indian religion that deserved First Amendment protection. His experience and knowledge was such that some of his colleagues nicknamed him "Indian Man." In his testimony, Mooney presented a history of the Peyote faith, a description of the Peyote cactus (he showed the congressmen a small box of Peyote buttons), explained how it was harvested and sold, and gave a detailed account of a Peyote ceremony. Mooney also tried to weaken the credibility of Gertrude Bonnin. His testimony against her proved to be high drama. He pointed out that although she claimed to be Sioux, her regalia were not Sioux, her dress was from a southern tribe, her belt was a Navajo man's belt, and ironically she was holding a Peyote feather fan. He said that she had never attended a Peyote meeting nor had ever tried Peyote. Mooney's comments about her clothing during the hearings and her admission that she had never attended a Peyote service were embarrassing, but not as embarrassing as the misleading *Washington Times* article. He pointed out that she had never been a student at Carlisle and Sitting Bull was certainly not a relative of hers. Mooney denied the accusations of orgies, or any other type of immoral activity, and defended Peyote as a curative for alcohol addiction and for its medicinal uses. For example, he thought it could have medicinal value like quinine and reminded the committee that quinine, originally used by Indians, had been condemned by the Spanish.[74] In the end, Mooney's dynamic testimony, peppered with sarcasm, did not impress the committee. They questioned his assumptions and ultimately did not accept his arguments.

Several other government employees testified against the Hayden bill. William E. Safford, an economic botanist from the Department of Agriculture who had previously written about the "Peyote Gardens" and the harvesting, drying, and sale of Peyote, had claimed that there was no problem with eating Peyote, except in excessive amounts. He added that even excessive amounts of coffee were bad for a person. He reaffirmed what Mooney had said, that Peyote was not habit forming and that nothing immoral occurred in Peyote services. He said he saw much harm to American Indians if Peyote was taken away. Dr. Truman Michelson, an anthropologist from the Bureau of American Ethnology, confirmed that Peyotists did not use alcohol. Many Peyotists also traveled to Washington for the hearings and gave additional testimony.

Almost all of the Peyotists who spoke confirmed the lengthy testimony of Mooney. Most of them were Peyote Roadmen in their communities and prominent in their own right. Thomas L. Sloan (Omaha) was an attorney as well as a former president of the Society of American Indians. He had become a lonely voice within that organization in defending Peyote. Other speakers included Paul Boynton (Arapaho, Cheyenne), Cleaver Warden (Arapaho), Wilbur Piawo (Comanche), Otto Wells (Comanche), Chief Little Hand (Cheyenne), and Arthur Bonnicastle (Osage). Two of the most impressive Native speakers were Fred Lookout (Osage) and Francis La Flesche (Omaha), an ethnologist in the Bureau of American Ethnology and coauthor of *The Omaha Tribe* (1911). Lookout was a prominent religious and political leader of the Osage nation and a lifelong defender of the Peyote faith. He had been principal chief of the Osage for twenty-six years and a Peyote Roadman. He argued that Peyote was not harmful and was only used in church services to pray to God. He referred to Peyote as "medicine," a term all Peyotists used. When asked how many Osage were members of the Peyote faith, he said, "Most all full-blood members." La Flesche made a lengthy and moving statement. He was a significant witness. In addition to being a noted author and a government employee, he was the only Native speaker who was not a Peyotist and had never tried Peyote, but he had attended Peyote services. He said he watched as Peyote spread among his people after 1906. He gave very dramatic testimony on how Peyote reduced alcoholism on his reservation. He also explained how Peyote benefited his Osage and Ponca neighbors.[75]

After all the testimony was heard, supporting documents submitted, and questions asked by the subcommittee, the members recessed and voted in favor of the Hayden bill. Their last action was to print a twenty-four-page report, *Prohibition of the Use of Peyote*. In supporting the Hayden bill, the report reaffirmed Bonnin's assertion that Peyote was dangerous and that the Peyote faith was a cover for narcotic use. The report included her paper "Peyote Causes Race Suicide." The chair of the subcommittee, John H. Tillman of Arkansas, concluded that Peyotism should not be defended on religious grounds.[76]

In early July 1918, after the hearings, but before a full congressional vote on the Hayden bill, Mooney returned to Oklahoma fearing the worst. He visited many of his old friends among the Comanches, Kiowas, Wichitas, and Caddos. Knowing of his testimony, they gave Mooney a warm welcome. He attended a number of Peyote services and collected information from Peyote people as he continued working on his history of the Peyote religion. The welcome by the Indian communities was countered by the hostile treatment by reservation officials and missionaries. They saw him as a threat and wanted him removed from Oklahoma. Fearing an outright prohibition of Peyote, Mooney came to the conclusion that the incorporation of the Peyote religion as a duly constituted church was the only way to ensure constitutional protection. Peyotists from all over Oklahoma met in August 1918, in El Reno, to draw up a charter. Many of those gathered had just returned from the congressional hearings in Washington and realized the gravity of the situation. For them, the hearings became a springboard to action. They decided on a new organization. Mooney was at the meeting, and according to Jim Whitewolf (Kiowa-Apache) who was also there, Mooney recommended that the Peyotists there organize, choose officers, and pick a new name. Whitewolf said in a 1949 interview that it was Mooney who recommended the name Native American Church.[77] There had been other incorporations, but this was different as it included Peyotists from many reservations. There already existed Koshiway's First Born Church of Christ among the Otos, but some of the delegates did not want to be associated with it. Koshiway had forbidden the use of tobacco in his church's services, whereas many Peyotists believed tobacco was an essential element of prayer. Others argued that Koshiway's service was too Christian. In addition, his charter did not mention Peyote. Everyone knew that Peyote was the primary issue and that it had to be front and center in the charter. All this prompted the decision to form an entirely new organization. The articles of incorporation included a new name, an organizational structure, a governing body, and a clear articulation of Peyote as a sacrament. The delegates were very careful in choosing the name Native American Church. The name is pan-Indian in character, and *Native American* implied it was an indigenous faith. The term *Church* was chosen specifically with the hope that this would give the members the protection of the free exercise of religion clause in the First Amendment of the U.S. Constitution. This was especially significant since the full Congress had yet to vote on the Hayden bill. The document was signed by ten prominent Peyotists from six different tribal groups and submitted to the state of Oklahoma for incorporation, which was granted on October 10, 1918. The process of incorporating as a church to seek First Amendment protection became the model for Peyotists throughout the country.[78]

Mooney's role in the incorporation was not well received in Washington. The superintendent at Anadarko, Oklahoma, wired the commissioner of Indian Affairs requesting that Mooney be removed from Oklahoma. He claimed that Mooney advised and assisted in writing the Native American Church charter. The commissioner then ordered the Smithsonian to remove Mooney from Oklahoma. He was ordered off the Kiowa and Comanche Reservation and charged with obstructing administrative policies and being detrimental to the peace and welfare of the Indians. On November 12, 1918, Mooney left Oklahoma, never to return. The anger against Mooney was intense. Gertrude Bonnin wrote a letter to General Pratt asking him to use his influence to have Mooney removed from government service. In 1919 and 1920, Mooney asked to be allowed to return to Oklahoma reservations, but his request was denied. In 1921, at the age of sixty, he died of a heart attack before he was able to complete his history of the Peyote religion.[79]

The issues discussed during the congressional hearings were clear and framed the debate for decades to come. One basic question concerned the safety of Peyote. The anti-Peyotists argued that it was physically and psychologically damaging and led to immoral behavior. Mooney and the Peyotists argued that it was not only harmless and not habit forming but also a positive good, especially as a remedy for alcohol addiction. Another question was whether the Peyote faith deserved constitutional protection. Some people argued that the Peyote faith was a smoke screen for narcotic use; others argued it was a bona fide religion with pre-Columbian roots. The testimony in the congressional hearings was often fiery and acrimonious, especially the Mooney/Bonnin exchanges as they tried to discredit each other. It was also interesting in other ways. American Indians spoke on both sides of the issue, and non-Indians spoke on both sides of the issue. Government employees and expert witnesses were also divided. The only groups that consistently supported the Hayden bill were the non-Indian humanitarians and missionaries who believed they were acting in the best interests of American Indians. In the end the subcommittee accepted the arguments of the anti-Peyotists and reported the bill to the House of Representatives.

The full House passed the Hayden bill; however, the bill ran into difficulties in the Senate. The two senators from Oklahoma, under pressure from their own constituents, persuaded their colleagues not to support the prohibition of Peyote. They argued it was a First Amendment, religious freedom issue and were able to convince a majority of senators not to vote for the bill. The bill failed, and a federal prohibition of Peyote was not enacted into law. Many individuals and groups inside and outside the government were unhappy with this turn of events. The BIA did not accept this defeat. Throughout the 1920s, they continued to promote additional legislation and also sought other means to suppress the use of Peyote. The Peyote community breathed a sigh of relief, though it knew this was only temporary reprieve as a wide array of groups still opposed the Peyote faith. The pressure from anti-Peyote forces, plus the experience of the congressional hearings, made one point clear to the Peyote community: they had to unite and seek the full protection of the Constitution. This was an unintended consequence of the attempt to prohibit Peyote. It mobilized the Peyote community to organize and defend itself against its many enemies. This strategy would be employed throughout the twentieth century.

CHAPTER TWO

Religious Beliefs, Ceremony, and Ritual

The use of Peyote, as well as other plants, in religious ceremonies has ancient roots in Mesoamerica; however, Peyote's use as a sacrament within a specific religious complex developed in the United States in the early reservation era. It evolved into an institutionalized church under the name Native American Church. As described in chapter 1, Peyotism diffused throughout the West despite considerable opposition. This chapter describes not only how the Peyote faith expanded but also why it expanded and what made it attractive to diverse groups of American Indians. As Peyotism evolved, it developed a theological base, a ceremonial and ritual structure, and an ethical system for its members to follow.

Three major beliefs or factors are examined to show how a small cactus plant became the basis of a major faith that expanded from reservations in Oklahoma to other parts of the United States and Canada. Any of these three factors could be involved in an individual's decision to become a Peyotist. The first and most significant belief is that Peyote can heal or cure a variety of illnesses. It is considered a medicine and is called "medicine." Members of the Native American Church claim Peyote is a gift of God, or even a part of God, that was sent to help needful human beings just as the Christian sacrament of bread and wine is believed to be the body and blood of Jesus, who also was sent for the benefit of humankind. The second factor in the spread of the Peyote faith is the perception of it as an indigenous American Indian religion. There are elements in Peyotism that parallel many American Indian traditional spiritual beliefs and practices and fit into traditional cosmological frameworks. For example, the traditional mode of healing and Peyote healing are both holistic in that they heal the spirit, mind, and body. The third factor contributing to the diffusion of the Peyote religion is the belief that Peyote is a teacher. It teaches a way of life to be lived twenty-four hours a day. It provides an ethical system for its members as well as a sense of belonging to a community of believers. Peyote teaches one to follow the Peyote Road, a metaphor for the path to a righteous and spiritual life.

When the Peyote religion emerged among the Caddos, Kiowas, Comanches, and others in Oklahoma, it had developed a formalized ceremonial and ritual structure. It included an all-night meeting, preferably in a tepee, led by a Roadman, who was accompanied by a chief drummer, a cedarman, and a fireman. A crescent-shaped mound and a fire were built in the center of the tepee. Attendees sat in a circle around the fire. There was singing, accompanied by a water drum and a gourd rattle. There were opening prayers and a special midnight ceremony. At various times during the night, Peyote was passed around the tepee and ingested as a holy sacrament. At dawn, special songs marked the entrance of the Morning Water Woman, who brought a pail of water, which was blessed and passed around for all to sip. A series of four closing or quitting songs ended the service.

The Peyote religion has maintained this basic ceremonial structure for more than a century although some variations have been introduced. By the early twentieth century, there were two major variants of the Peyote ceremony and several minor ones. Today the major divisions are the Half Moon Way and the Cross Fire Way.

PEYOTE AS "MEDICINE"

There are many theological, ceremonial, and ritual elements involved in explaining the diffusion of Peyotism, but there was one belief that was universal in its initial acceptance: Peyote is a medicine. This conclusion is not new, but it needs to be emphasized to understand the spread of Peyote. More than a century ago, James Mooney wrote that the Kiowas described Peyote as having medicinal properties. In 1914, anthropologist Paul Radin explained how John Rave promoted the curative power of Peyote as the way to attract Winnebago converts. In the 1930s, ethnobotanist Richard E. Schultes and anthropologists Weston La Barre, Omer Stewart, and Vincenzo Petrullo reinforced this viewpoint. These men were part of a new generation of young scholars who participated in Peyote meetings and interviewed Peyote people as part of their research. They saw healing as the essential element in the diffusion of Peyote. Schultes differed from the other three, arguing that Peyote was accepted as a curative in a pharmacological sense, while La Barre, Stewart, and Petrullo argued that Peyote was accepted as a curative in a spiritual, holistic sense. Stewart wrote that "first and foremost, the initial appeal to converts was for a cure." More recently, Ake Hultkrantz, a comparative religion scholar, wrote that healing was essential, especially with the prominence of health problems on reservations.[1]

Prominent Peyotists who are authors or spokespersons, such as Leonard Crow Dog, Reuben Snake, Douglas Long, Emerson Spider, and Vincent Catches, also focus on the healing power of Peyote.[2] The expression of this power is reflected in two sources: the Peyote origin narratives and more than one hundred years of testimonials by Peyote people. There is no "official" narrative of the origin of the discovery of Peyote; although each group has its own variant, there are several common themes. Origin narratives tell of a person, usually a woman, who is lost, as a result of war, searching for a loved one who did not return, or seeking help for her people, who are in distress. The lost person, suffering from hunger and thirst, is facing death. In some versions, the Peyote plant reveals itself and gives instructions for ingestion. In other versions, the lost person is helped by strangers and given Peyote. Other narratives describe Peyote being found in a miraculous way. Once the plant is discovered, the individual ingests it, becomes cured of illness or hunger, and is saved. In some of these narratives, the Peyote reproduces itself to offer an endless supply. With newfound strength, endurance, and a keen sense of direction, the lost person returns home and shares Peyote with the members of the community, who are also healed or saved. The people then begin practicing the Peyote faith. The underlying themes of the origin narratives are salvation in a crisis, redemption of the individual, healing of the ill or injured, followed by a reunion with the community and the sharing of Peyote.[3] A very significant underlying theme is the role of a woman in the discovery of Peyote.

The Kiowas have several variants on the theme of a lost woman finding Peyote. In the 1890s, James Mooney was told the story of two young brothers who went on a raiding party but did not return. Assuming they were dead, their sister went into the mountains to mourn for them. That night, exhausted, she fell asleep. She heard a voice in a dream that said her brothers were alive and that when she awakened she would find something that would help her. She awoke, found a Peyote plant, and took it home with her. She told the elders what had happened, and following the directions she was given in the dream, they set up a tepee with a crescent-shaped mound. The people prayed, sang, and ate the Peyote, which had multiplied. During the ceremony, they envisioned the young men still alive. A rescue party was sent out, and two were saved. The people continued to eat Peyote and honor the "Peyote woman."[4]

A variant, collected in the early 1970s by the Kiowa Historical and Research Society, begins: "Long ago a woman and her people had left their village, searching for food." The woman, "heavy with child," became separated from the group. She gave birth alone, terrified and fearing death. She then heard a voice say, "Eat this plant growing next to you. This is life and a blessing for you and your people." She ate the top of the plant and quickly regained strength to feed her newborn baby. She gathered more Peyote and was guided home. She told her story to her mother's brother, who followed her directions and established a ceremony through which the blessings of Peyote could be bestowed on all the people. The woman in the story is portrayed in a painting, *Peyote Meeting*, by Cecil Murdock (Kiowa).[5] As Peyotism developed, the woman came to be represented by the Morning Water Woman, who at dawn brings in sacred water and food for the participants in Peyote meetings.

Another variation, told by the Kiowa-Apaches, concerns the Lipan Apaches, whom many consider to be among the earliest disseminators of Peyotism. According to a version of the narrative collected in 1949, a Lipan Apache group was attacked and scattered. "There was just one woman and boy left. . . . It was hot and dry. All the water had dried up. They had no food or water." The woman told her son to go in search of food or people. As he was walking, he heard a voice: "I know you are hungry. Look down ahead of you. You will see something green. Eat it." He saw a green plant, ate some, and the hunger disappeared. He looked around and saw many more plants. He dug them up and took them to his mother. She ate some of the plants, satisfying her hunger. That night, the mother dreamed that she was to take the plants back to her people. She was told that she and her son would teach her people how to have a Peyote ceremony in a tepee, how to sing, and how to drum. This version includes the previously mentioned themes of salvation in a difficult situation, the role of a woman in finding Peyote, and the introduction of Peyote to the community.[6]

The power of Peyote to heal is a universal concept among Peyotists. Healing testimonials reinforce the origin narratives. As noted, Peyotists refer to Peyote as medicine, and the process of healing in a Peyote meeting is usually called doctoring. There are hundreds of published and unpublished testimonials by people who claim they were healed by Peyote or who describe how a family member was healed by it. These testimonials are willingly shared and can be heard whenever Peyote people gather. The testimonials also are used when Peyotists are proselytizing as a way to attract new members. There are many explanations for the expansion of the Peyote faith, but the essential element is the belief in the plant's power to heal. Many early leaders of the Peyote community claimed they had an injury, illness, or disease or were living an irresolute lifestyle that usually included alcohol abuse. These leaders claimed that after hearing about Peyote and participating in Peyote ceremonies, they were cured or healed. One typical example of a conversion narrative is the story of Quanah Parker. Once Parker settled on a reservation, he decided to find out more about his deceased mother. While visiting her brother in Mexico, Parker was gored by a bull and suffered an abdominal wound, infection, and fever. A local Indian gave him a drink of boiled green cactus juice. It was Peyote tea. After his health improved, Parker returned home and became a staunch advocate of Peyote, helping to expand the Peyote faith throughout Oklahoma. Another example is from Roger Stops (Crow), who was interviewed in 1970. He said Peyote came to the Crows in Montana about 1909, when a person very ill with pneumonia met a Cherokee man who brewed Peyote tea and "made him drink it and this guy came out of it, so from right then it had religious significance."[7] Subsequently, the Crows adopted both the Half Moon and Cross Fire forms of worship.

There are many similar healing/conversion narratives throughout the western states. Alice Bulltail (Crow) told a dramatic story of recovering from blindness. In a 1970 interview, she claimed she had fallen, severely injured her head, and lost consciousness. Upon regaining consciousness, she could not see. Her family took her to a hospital in Billings, Montana, where she stayed for three weeks with no improvement in her vision. Upon returning home, Alice, her husband, and her two sons decided to go to a Peyote meeting. During the service she ate several Peyote buttons while everyone prayed for her. At

3:00 A.M. the Roadman conducted a "doctoring." When he finished, he asked her to look around. She saw her sons, cousins, nephews, nieces, and best friend, many of whom were crying. She claimed that a blood clot had disappeared and that now she could see as well as anyone. Other Peyotists have similar accounts of healing. The late Douglas Long, former president of the Native American Church of North America, described how Peyote saved his life as a child and how the sacramental use of Peyote cured his mother, who had heart problems, and his niece, who had cancer.[8]

Anthropologist Charles S. Brant collected similar testimonials from the Kiowa-Apaches. After a Peyote meeting, a person told Brant that "peyote saved me when I had ulcers." Another said that during the influenza epidemic of World War I, he was saved by drinking Peyote tea. Brant was told by a Cheyenne Peyotist that thirty white doctors diagnosed him with incurable tuberculosis, but after he reluctantly went to Peyote services, he was cured. He became a dedicated believer in the Peyote faith.[9]

These narratives are significant in that whenever Peyote people proselytized they focused primarily on the healing power of this "Sacred Herb." This is the essential explanation for the rapid expansion of Peyotism. Healing remains one of the most common reasons for having a Peyote prayer service. In addition to attending the regular weekly or monthly meetings, an individual can request a special healing meeting, or more typically, one's family can sponsor a special meeting for the sick or injured person.

The appeal of Peyote as a curative came at a time when there was physical and spiritual disequilibrium among many American Indians. There was a decline of traditional spiritual leadership and pressure to discontinue traditional ceremonies. Sickness and disease, such as tuberculosis, trachoma, influenza, pneumonia, cancer, and the general ill health that goes with poor nutrition and poverty, had also increased. The most serious health problem, however, was the abuse of alcohol. Few reservations escaped its scourge. It affected the individual, the family, and the community. Poor living conditions, unemployment, powerlessness, idleness, and the assault on traditional culture all led to alcohol use, then to alcohol abuse and addiction. Aside from legally prohibiting alcohol on the reservations, there were no answers to this crisis until Peyotism began to diffuse throughout the western states. Peyote was perceived as a generic curative, and because alcoholism was considered a sickness, Peyote could be used to cure it.

There are more testimonials about curing alcoholism than about curing any other illness. One well-known example of a conversion narrative is from the autobiography of Sam Blowsnake (Winnebago, aka Crashing Thunder). He described an irresolute life of brawling, alcoholism, promiscuity, crime, and prison. He was introduced to Peyote by acquaintances who told him it would stop his craving for alcohol. He claimed that after attending Peyote meetings his life was transformed, and that all he now knew, he had learned from Peyote. He said, "Before my conversion I went about in a pitiable condition, but now I am living happily." John Rave and Albert Hensley, the two founders of Winnebago Peyotism, also had reputations as heavy drinkers in their early lives, but with Peyote they stopped drinking alcohol. In fact, Rave said that he first saw Peyote as a "curative herb."[10]

There are similar examples from other places. From the 1930s to the 1950s, a growing number of Diné (Navajos) became attracted to the Peyote faith because of its reputation as a curative. Anthropologist David Aberle, who interviewed many Diné, estimated that about 80 percent initially joined the Peyote faith for health reasons. In another example, a Washoe Peyotist claimed that when Sam Lone Bear (Lakota) came to his reservation in the late 1920s, he told them he had a "new medicine" and a new way of curing people.[11]

The belief in the healing power of Peyote helps explain how Peyotism expanded. It was spread from reservation to reservation by traveling Roadmen such as Albert Hensley, John Rave, John Wilson, and Jim Blue Bird, who visited kin, friends, and acquaintances on various reservations. These connections came from attending boarding schools, working in rodeos or Wild West shows, or even being in POW camps together. Many people had heard rumors about the healing power of Peyote and wanted to learn more. Sometimes they invited Peyote leaders to teach them about the faith, or the Roadmen traveled to other reservations, made contact with people they knew, and offered to teach them about Peyote. Wherever the Roadmen traveled, their message focused on the healing power of Peyote. John Rave, for example, preached about Peyote's curative powers and recited testimonials about its positive effects. By focusing on healing, the Roadmen attracted people to their services. Sometimes individuals who were not Peyotists traveled to reservations that had a Peyote community. They attended the services, learned about the faith, heard the stories of healing, experienced the sense of community, felt the power of an all-night religious service, and went home determined to introduce Peyotism to their own communities.

Since Peyote was introduced and accepted as a medicine, Peyotists call it *medicine* when speaking English; when not speaking English, they use the generic word for *medicine* in their own languages. In Lakota/Dakota/Nakota (Sioux), Peyote is called *pejuta*, which means medicine and is the generic word for any substance that induces physical and/or spiritual healing. In Diné the word is *azee'*, which also means medicine. Reuben Snake said, "[W]e call it Peyote, but more often, because of what it does for us, we call it our Medicine." He added that it heals both mind and body.[12] This implies much more than does the English word *medicine*. In Diné healing, for example, the term explicitly refers to the whole spiritual complex, that the power of Peyote, prayers by the patient, the Roadman, and the participants, and the singing and drumming all make it possible for the spirit world to intervene for the benefit of those who are injured or ill. It means that physical healing and spiritual healing are insepa-rable, that they occur together and are considered one and the same.[13]

Another essential belief of Native American Church members is that the power to heal is a gift of God or the Great Spirit. Healing is not pharmaco-logical, it is spiritual. Peyote is a gift called medicine; it is also called sacred herb, sacred medicine, holy medicine, and holy sacrament. Healing is holistic—spirit, mind, and body are one; in fact, only through a holistic interpretation can one understand the power of Peyote to heal.[14] Healing comes not only from the Peyote cactus itself but also from participation in one's own healing through prayer and ritual. The beliefs about Peyote as a curative, in the American Indian sense of the word *medicine*, meant that it was accepted within a familiar cosmo-logical structure or worldview. Peyote may have been new, but the structure and process of healing were not. The tradition of healing in American Indian cultures and the curative power of Peyote in the Native American Church are on the same cosmological plane. This helps explain the acceptance of the Peyote religion among many of the Native people in the western part of the United States. This is where the tradition of healing in the pre-reservation era by spiritual leaders paralleled the process of healing in Peyotism: in both cases healing could only occur by supernatural means. Hultkrantz argues that curing is facilitated by Peyote being integrated into the traditional curative patterns. This viewpoint is reinforced by recent studies of Peyotism as a health care delivery system among the Delawares of Oklahoma and the Diné. On the basis of ethnographic and historical analysis, the authors conclude that the integra-tion of religion and health care is an essential element of both Peyotism and Delaware and Diné spiritual beliefs, and that the significance of Peyote as a medicine is an essential factor in its acceptance. The Gosiutes offer another example of the belief that curing is the chief function of Peyote. One person said that "the room is not only our church, it is our hospital." Dick Fool Bull (Lakota), a longtime Peyotist from the Rosebud Reservation, interviewed in 1971, at age eighty-one, said he had been eating Peyote since he was a boy because when one got sick "we take this medicine and heal ourselves. That's what it's for. God gave it, God's gift for us, so people can learn about Him." This view of healing reinforces the viewpoint that Peyotism and many aspects of traditional American Indian spiritualities have a common theological and cosmological basis.[15]

Many non-Peyotists have questioned how Peyote could cure alcoholism. No studies have demonstrated that Peyote has the pharmacological properties that would lead to a physical cure. Some non-Native scholars offer a psychosomatic analysis or a sociological view that it is being part of a close-knit community that eschews alcohol that gives a person the strength to move toward abstinence. NAC members have a spiritual answer. Peyote cures alcoholism through the power of God. For Peyotists, there could be no other answer. However one may view various interpretations, the fact is that alcohol abuse has been greatly reduced among members of the Peyote community.

PEYOTISM AS "INDIAN" RELIGION: SACRED COMMONALITIES

Another major factor in the diffusion of Peyotism was the belief that it was an American Indian spirituality with ancient indigenous roots. Healing is the major power implicit in Peyote, but equally important is that the belief that the healing processes and methods of Peyotism parallel the pre-reservation beliefs in regard to the philosophy of healing. In other words, Peyotism was accepted for its essential qualities as a body of spiritual beliefs that resonated with the pre-reservation belief structures. Peyotism seemed to be part of a traditional spiritual complex and not something new. The Peyote cactus was new north of Mexico, but its role and purpose in a sacred universe was not new. The spiritual basis for healing did not change. This does not mean that traditional spirituality and Peyotism were the same; they were not. In many places, traditional spiritual leaders opposed the introduction of Peyote, particularly among the Diné and the Winnebagos. What it means is that the Peyote faith functioned within the same sacred universe as traditional beliefs. One example is the Lakota/Dakota/Nakota people. They believe the Sacred Pipe, which is the center of their traditional belief system, was brought to them by the White Buffalo Calf Woman. She was delivering a gift sent by Wakan

Tanka (Great Spirit/Creator) to help people during difficult times. Now during a similar difficult era, Wakan Tanka sent Peyote. The Peyote was new, as was the Sacred Pipe at one time, but seeking and receiving help from the Great Spirit, who takes pity on suffering humans, was not new. On this basis, Peyote could be accepted and perceived as being a traditional form of spirituality.

Other examples include the Ute Peyotists, who believe that Peyote is part of Ute curing ceremonies, though practiced separately from traditional curing rituals. The Washoes in their narratives about the power of Peyote describe the Peyote way as "living in the old Indian way." It seems that each cultural group makes Peyote its own. The people know Peyote was brought to them by others, but they integrate some of their traditional beliefs into Peyotism to make it their own, such as developing Peyote origin narratives.

The Diné (Navajos) are an example of this. At first glance, the Peyote faith may appear quite different from Diné traditional spiritual beliefs, yet today many Diné are Peyotists. Upon closer examination, it appears that the main appeal is that Peyotism was a curing ceremony with structural and cosmological elements similar to traditional Diné healing rituals. As mentioned above, a majority of Diné converts were first attracted to Peyote by its reputation as a healer. This was particularly true with its claim to cure alcoholism and two previously unrecognized illnesses, cancer and tuberculosis. The concept of healing through ceremony, ritual, and prayer paralleled traditional Diné healing ceremonies on a spiritual level. Traditional Diné healing is holistic. Its goal is to reestablish balance and harmony, leading to a return to wellness. In the Diné cosmology, balance, harmony, and good health are reestablished when proper ritual and prayer encourage Diné Holy People (Diné deities) to intervene. Healing in the Peyote faith is also holistic. Prayer, communication with God through the power of Peyote, can bring about healing; thus Peyotism, with its similar conceptualizations of healing, did not seem foreign.[16]

Given the above, the Diné perceive Peyotism as an American Indian spirituality. Some go further and claim it is a Diné faith and is so defended by some of today's leadership. James Tomchee, former president of the Native American Church of Navajoland, said in the 1980s:

> [T]he way the peyote ceremony is practiced, I would say about 99 percent of whatever is taking place in there is basically Navajo. Prayers are in Navajo; many Navajo traditional prayers have been integrated and incorporated into the ceremonies.[17]

Reinforcing the above, Paul Radin wrote almost a hundred years ago that only Peyote and a few Christian elements were new, and that everything else was "typically Winnebago and in consonance with shamanistic practices." Anthropologist Weston La Barre also concluded many years ago that "despite the apparent and superficial syncretism with Christianity, peyotism is an essential aboriginal American Indian religion, operating in terms of fundamental Indian concepts about power, visions and native modes of doctoring." More recently, the late American Indian scholar Vine Deloria wrote that the "attraction of peyote lay in its origins in traditional practices and that it was designed for Indians by the Creator." The Native American Church is not indigenized Christianity. It is an indigenous faith, and so perceived by its members, in spite of Christian accretions to its ceremonies.[18]

In addition to parallel beliefs about "medicine" and healing, there are many other aspects of Peyotism that paralleled traditional American Indian ceremonial elements as well as fitting within traditional cosmologies. In addition to healing, Peyotism also parallels other areas within the traditional way of defining one's spiritual existence. Upon close comparison, one finds many commonalities in ritual and symbolism, again helping us to understand why or how Peyotism was perceived as an "Indian religion." This was essential if the Peyote faith were to be able to meet people's spiritual, social, and aesthetic needs.

The use of language in ceremonies is such a commonality. Prayers and songs are sacred; the words are sacred. This is true for traditional American Indian religions and Peyotism, even though the use of English became more common throughout the twentieth century. A Peyote meeting may have people from a variety of groups, thus necessitating the use of English, but nevertheless the Roadman may pray or sing in his own language. For example, both the Lakotas and the Diné value prayer in their own languages whether it is prayer in Peyotism or traditional ceremonies. The commonality is the belief that prayers are more efficacious if spoken, recited, or sung in one's own language. In Peyote meetings with only one group in attendance such as Lakota, Diné, or Kiowa, the prayers and commentary may be in the local language.

Another commonality which contributed to the perception of Peyotism as an "Indian religion" is the similar use and function of sacred foods. Such foods are used in traditional religious ceremonies by almost all American Indian cultures and are also used in Peyote services. In both instances, they are ritually prepared by women and usually brought into the ceremonies by women. The sacred foods, including water, are offerings to the spirit world as well as being a source of protection and spiritual sustenance to the participants. In Plains cultures, sacred foods are part of vision quests and naming ceremonies; they are also part of Diné healing ceremonies. In Peyote services, water is brought in at midnight. At dawn, water and sacred foods are brought into the service. In the 1890s, James Mooney noted and photographed sacred foods in a Kiowa ceremony. They are still used in a similar manner today. The sacred foods are blessed and prayers are offered, then the foods are placed on the ground in front of the fire. They include water, corn (maize), meat, and fruit (or something sweet). They are passed clockwise to the participants. To an individual who is familiar with the traditional use of sacred foods, the use of them in a Peyote service seems quite familiar and very "Indian."

As the Peyote faith expanded it came to have much in common with traditional American Indian spiritualities, though at the time there were many who did not see Peyotism that way. Another commonality, for example, is the sense of the sacred or the belief in the sacredness of the universe in both traditional religions and Peyotism. American Indian spiritualities believe all things are sacred, but some things are more sacred than others and have special powers. The traditional belief in sacred sites—such as mountains, forests, or particular local spots—in sacred objects of plant, animal, or mineral origin (such as claws, feathers, rocks, tobacco, and manmade items, such as pipes, masks, rattles), and medicine bundles, was pervasive. Even words as in prayers or incantations could be sacred. This spiritual sense of sacredness also pervades the Peyote faith. The ultimate sacred item is Peyote. The Peyote Gardens, the natural growth area of Peyote, is considered sacred land. The paraphernalia used in the services are sacred, such as the water drum when tied and blessed, gourd rattles, the Roadman's staff, feather fans, the central fire, and even the ashes. The water drum is a significant example. After the meeting is over in the morning, and the drum is untied, the water inside is considered sacred and used for blessings and prayers. It may be sipped or used to purify oneself. The Kiowa-Apache put a drumstick in the water drum. It is then passed around, with individuals placing the wet end of the drumstick in their mouths four times. Some participants rub the water on their heads and hands. The use of what is now sacred water is for protection and good health. The remaining water is poured alongside the altar. Other material used in the service, such as tobacco, sage, and cedar, are also used in prayer, purification, and protection.[19]

There are obvious ceremonial and ritual differences between traditional American Indian religions and Peyotism, but both are practiced within a dynamic sense of sacredness. Both have a common function, which is the use of the sacred to connect oneself, one's family, or community to more powerful forces in the universe. In other words the use of the sacred is a way of seeking power to protect, to purify, to repent, to heal, to learn. In this manner, Peyotism was perceived as an American Indian spirituality. It was accepted by many because it fit the old way or traditional way of interpreting one's spiritual existence; thus the spread of Peyotism was facilitated by the large number of parallel ritual and structural elements as well as fitting within the traditional cosmological framework.

There are also several parallels in the ceremonial functions of Peyote Roadmen and traditional spiritual leaders. Both guide you, lead you along the "right" path, pray for you and with you, and most important assist you in opening a communication channel to the supernatural to receive the requested assistance for yourself or others. These spiritual leaders reinforce, in a material and abstract way, the belief that all things in the universe are related. This does not mean that there are no differences between the two. Traditional spiritual practitioners are thought to have access to spiritual power, which can be used to call spirits into a ceremony, or to diagnose and cure an injury or illness. These leaders are believed to be repositories of special or secret knowledge, which they may have acquired though visions or dreams, or been invested by a spirit. Their power may be used to influence the temporal world for the betterment of individuals or communities. It is believed they have the power to call for aid from supernatural powers to restore balance and harmony. Whether venerated or feared, they are central to spiritual life. Peyote Roadmen are important people, but they do not have special powers, nor are they repositories of secret knowledge. As the name implies, Roadmen are guides. They conduct Peyote services and guide the participants along the Peyote Road. Roadmen do not have spiritual power that can be used for others. Peyote, as the repository of power, has that function. Roadmen have the power of prayer, but so do all NAC members. There is healing in Peyote meetings, and Roadmen play a role, but it is the Peyote that heals. One becomes a Roadman by reputation as there is no formal training. One grows up in a Peyote family, learning to drum and sing, learning the functions of those who assist in a Peyote service. After becoming knowledgeable in Peyotism, having a sincere depth of belief in Peyote, and having a reputation as an ethical human being, one may be asked to serve as a Roadman. A Washoe Peyotist once said, "He [Roadman] ain't no better than anyone else. He just got a job to do—keep everything going the right way for the meeting. . . . He takes care of the medicine [Peyote]."[20]

In spite of the many parallels there are significant differences between Peyotism and traditional Indian spiritualities. The Cross Fire Way, for example, has incorporated elements of Christianity and eliminated the use of tobacco. There is no dancing in Peyotism, and the Roadmen play a less significant role in healing than do the traditional medicine men and women.

Another aspect of the development of the Peyote ceremony was the pattern of gender roles. Initially, Peyote ceremonies followed the pattern of most traditional American Indian societies. These roles have often been described as complementary, or as Bea Medicine (Sioux) has defined them with the term "complimentality," where each gender had its own social, cultural, and economic roles that created balance and harmony.[21] Women as the givers of life were honored and respected. As discussed above, most Peyote origin narratives credit a woman for being chosen by the Creator to receive the gift of Peyote. The woman, as the bearer of life, commemorates this by bringing the sacred water into the tepee at dawn, when the morning star is rising. The Morning Water Woman, the star, and the water represent renewal, a new beginning, a new day. This is an essential role. The rest of the service was left to the men. The only exceptions were women and girls brought into the tepee for doctoring or for special occasions such as baptisms, weddings, and funerals. In the early twentieth century, this began to change in some areas. Whether women could attend services was a local issue—there were no "official" policies concerning their attendance—so the inclusion of women did not occur in a uniform manner and not without dissent. But more and more women began participating in Peyote services as the century progressed, although at first they were not necessarily allowed to sing. In time, this too would change. As the decades passed, women and children began attending Peyote services, usually with their husbands, sitting as families. One indication of this changing trend was the inclusion of women in the paintings of Peyote artists, who from the 1930s on have women among the participants in their depictions of Peyote meetings. Eventually, women's inclusion became universal.

THE SACRED CIRCLE

A further reinforcement of the commonality thesis is the symbolism of the sacred circle. It is ubiquitous in American Indian cultures and in Peyotism. The circle in its literal usage and symbolic meaning pervades many spiritual beliefs and practices and is a metaphor for life. The circle represents the continuity of the universe or the cosmos, which has no beginning and no ending, or as Vine Deloria, Jr., has written: "The circle was the emblem of eternity for the Sioux."[22] It represents a circular universe in which there is harmony, balance, and interrelatedness. The structure of the cosmos is re-created symbolically in ceremony and ritual. Within the cosmos there is the circular motion of the sun, moon, and stars, which people perceive as moving clockwise; thus, most spiritual activities must replicate this pattern. The Sun Dance arbor is a large sacred circle; the dancers move around the arbor in a clockwise direction. Virtually all the ritual activities in the Sun Dance arbor are conducted in a circular fashion. The creation of the circle begins on the opening morning of the Sun Dance. The head dancer leads the other dancers around the outside of the arbor, from the west side, clockwise to the east side, in a semicircle entering the arbor at the east gate. At the end of the fourth day, the head dancer leads the other dancers out of the arbor, through the east gate, around the outside of the arbor to the west gate, thus completing the circle begun on the first day and officially ending the Sun Dance.

There is similar symbolism of the circle associated with the sweat lodge or sweat bath used widely throughout the United States. The lodge is a dome-shaped structure with a round base. The "sweat" is a purification ceremony. Water is poured over hot stones, creating steam, which along with prayer and song, purify, cleanse, protect, or heal the participants. Inside the lodge, everyone sits in a circle, and everything takes place in a clockwise direction. The person on the left of the entrance prays first, followed by the person to his or her left, and on around the circle. At the conclusion, everyone leaves in a clockwise direction. In the plains, where many pray with the sacred pipe, the ceremonial smoking of the pipe is conducted in a circle. The pipe is passed around the circle for each person to smoke and share in the prayers. Because of its inherent power, the circle is used in a wide variety of ways. It is the shape of dream catchers and medicine wheels; it is the shape of drums. A circular motif is used in the logos of many American Indian nations, organizations, schools, and universities. The symbolism of the circle is widely recognized as is its role in creating a spiritual environment for communication with the supernatural and a social environment for communication between people (e.g., talking circles). Leonard Crow Dog said that by "[s]moking in a circle we renew the sacred hoop of the nation."[23] The traditional ritual patterns of the Diné are also based on a circular view of the cosmos. Inside the hogan, ritual items are passed clockwise in a circular pattern. This replication of the universe increases the potential power of the service.

The circle has virtually the same function in the Peyote faith. Reuben Snake claims the circle in Peyote services conforms to the patterns in nature. He says, "[T]he stars circle, days become nights then days again, summer turns into winter then returns to summer—gyres and turnings are everywhere."[24] Wherever possible, the circle is replicated. A tepee with its round base is the choice structure for a Peyote meeting. Participants circle the tepee before entering. Inside the tepee, hogan, home, or church building, everyone sits in a circle around the fire. During the all-night service, everything is passed clockwise around the circle. This includes the holy sacrament, which is passed around the circle to the participants. If it is a Half Moon service, tobacco is passed the same way. Other religious paraphernalia, such as the water drum, the Road-man's staff, and a small bundle of sage are also passed around the circle for each individual to use while singing. The Roadman's wooden staff, three to four feet long, is a very significant ceremonial object and a symbol of unity. The staff is also passed around the circle, so everyone has the opportunity to sing and pray while holding it. When the staff gets back to the Roadman, it has been held or touched by everyone, completing the circle. The same pattern continues all night. The Peyote, the ritual paraphernalia, and the songs and drumming continue around the circle until morning, when the sacred food is brought in and is passed around the circle. Like traditional religious ceremonies, the symbolism of the circle permeates Peyotism. The NAC of North America recognizes the importance of the circle. Its official logo depicts Peyotists praying in a tepee encased in double concentric circles.

SACRED NUMBERS

There are also significant parallels in the role of sacred numbers in traditional American Indian cultures and in the Peyote religion. They share the idea that particular numbers can be sacred and imbued with power as well as the widespread belief in the sacral nature of the numbers four and seven. Four is a particularly sacred number in many American Indian societies. This parallel facilitated the acceptance of Peyotism. Four represents the sacred directions: north, east, south, and west. Seven represents the same four directions and three additional directions: up for the sky, down for mother earth, and the center for the universe or Creator Spirit. Specific examples include the numbers four and seven in the symbolic and ritual structures of the Lakota/Dakota/Nakota people. They are divided into the Seven Council Fires, some of which are divided into seven bands and practice the seven sacred rites, which include the use four sacred foods.

Throughout the plains, the numbers four and seven have ritual significance in the sweat lodge ceremony. The person preparing the wood for the fire offers a prayer to each of the seven directions, with the first seven rocks placed on the fire. After the rocks are heated, the first seven are brought into the lodge and placed in a particular pattern, one that again recognizes the various directions. Throughout the ceremony, the sacred numbers of four and seven are integrated into the ritual; songs, for example, are sung in sets of four. There are regional and local variations of the sweat lodge ceremony, the sacred pipe ceremony, and the Sun Dance; however, in all cases sacred numbers are essential.

Just as the spiritual power of the circle permeates the Sun Dance, it is the same with the use of sacred numbers. Many of the Sun Dance rituals are patterned in sequences of four. When a Sun Dance is sponsored, it must be held for four consecutive years. The Sun Dance chief and the dancers make a commitment to participate all four years. The Sun Dance itself lasts four days. The inside of the Sun Dance arbor reflects the significance of the four directions. There are four openings to the Sun Dance circle, facing each of the four directions. A tree is placed in the center of the arbor, and when "fed" four of the sacred foods it becomes sacred. During the Sun Dance, patterns of four guide the dancers. They are positioned by the Sun Dance chief sequentially at each of the four directions; they face the sacred tree, dance, and pray. Subsequent rounds of dancing follow the same sequential pattern based on the number four. Four represents power and enhances the possibility of communicating with the Creator and increases the efficacy of the ceremony.

Because the use of sacred numbers may enhance the power of a ceremony almost all American Indian cultures employ these numbers in various ways. As discussed above, the number four in particular is believed to hold special power. For example, in the Diné creation narrative, the people traveled through three underworld levels to earth, the fourth level. They live within the four sacred mountains, with four seasons, and pay homage to the four cardinal directions. They replicate the four directions in their sand paintings, some of which have multiples of four. A Cheyenne ceremony, the Sacred Arrow Renewal, is a four-day event involving four arrows given to the Cheyennes by the Creator to protect them from harm. The Apaches pray to the four directions. In the Great Basin, the Gosiutes use the numbers four and twelve in their ceremonies. The Washoes believe four is the Creator's number as there are four races of humans and four sacred directions. One informant said "You have to have four to make things come out right. Just like in [Peyote] Meetings, you have four of everything."[25] The Poncas use four, seven, and twelve as sacred numbers. The first is the four directions; the seven is the same as described above with one exception: the seventh is the individual, recognizing one's place in the cosmos. There are two interpretations of the importance of twelve. Some say it represents the twelve feathers in the tail of the eagle. Christian Poncas claim it represents the twelve apostles.[26] The Lakotas/Dakotas/Nakotas use the number four to help protect individuals undertaking a vision quest. As a person seeks a spiritual vision through fasting, others offer a prayer for him or her as they sing the "Four Directions" song and blow an eagle-bone whistle four times to each cardinal direction with four different length notes.

This use of sacred numbers in traditional ceremonies has its counterpart in Peyotism, especially the number four, which is an essential part of Peyote ritual. According to Omer Stewart's "Peyote Element Distribution List," all Peyote groups in North America place ritual significance on the number four.[27] The structure of the entire Peyote meeting reflects this significance. The all-night Peyote service is conducted in patterns of four. The service is divided into four parts: the opening, the midnight ceremony, the morning water ceremony, and the closing ceremony. Each segment begins with four songs. There are four sacred foods, and four "officials" conduct the service. The underlying cosmology is similar to traditional beliefs in that the four directions encompass a uniform and interdependent cosmos. Using four in a ritual pattern re-creates unity and balance and creates a path or a way, the Peyote way, for communication with the supernatural. The essential core of Peyotism is the sacramental ingestion of Peyote. It is a gift: it teaches, it heals, it purifies, it blesses, it protects. It is the center of the service. During the course of a Peyote meeting, Peyote is usually passed around four times, with each person ingesting the Peyote each time. This is a sacred act, and one prays during it. The entire night reflects the pattern of fours.

At the beginning of the meeting, the Roadman and the chief drummer sing four songs, then the drum and staff are passed to their left and the next person sings four songs. The pattern continues around the circle until the drum and staff return to the Roadman. At midnight there is a break; the Roadman goes outside and blows the eagle-bone whistle toward the four directions.

The number seven is used less often in Peyote services, but it is also significant. The water drum used in Peyote music has four or seven pieces of charcoal placed inside the drum. The drum is covered with a drumskin, which is fastened around the top of the drum by seven small stones placed in the drumskin and, when tied together around the drum, anchor the drumskin to the drum. Some Cross Fire people claim that the seven stones represent the seven Christian sacraments. Lakota/Dakota Half Moon people claim the stones represent the Seven Council Fires. Others claim they represent the seven days of the week. Patterns of four are also used to purify the religious paraphernalia used in a meeting. Cedar is sprinkled on the fire to produce smoke. The rattle, drum, staff, and Peyote are purified by being passed through the smoke four times. This is referred to as "smudging" or "cedaring off."[28] This use of sacred numbers, especially the number four, in indigenous traditions and in the Peyote faith is one additional factor helping to explain the acceptance of Peyote as an indigenous Indian spirituality.

SACRED PLANTS

Another significant commonality between traditional religions and Peyotism is the spiritual/medicinal use of plants in ceremonies and healing. This is universal among American Indians, who believe that the Creator/Great Spirit has imbued certain plants, just like certain animals, with the spiritual power that can protect, purify, enlighten, or heal human beings when used in a prescribed manner. It is part of the interrelationship of all living things. Two plants in particular are used extensively by American Indians and considered sacred— red cedar (*Juniperus virginiana*) and prairie sage (*Artemisia gnaphalodes*). They are used in two ways: as plants in themselves, and as smoke or incense from burning them. Sage is considered a powerful protector. It may be rubbed on a person for spiritual purification and protection. The smoke from a smoldering bundle of sage provides protection and purification. In some areas, the smoke is employed as a blessing for a marriage, a birth, a new home, a funeral, or other significant life event. Small bundles of sage are found today in people's homes, offices, and cars. These bundles serve as spiritual protection. During the Cheyennes' Sacred Arrow Renewal ceremony, the spiritual leader sits on a bed of sage. Cedar is primarily used as incense when sprinkled on hot rocks or coals or thrown into a fire. Cedar and sage are used in Sun Dances, vision quests, and sweat lodges in virtually the same manner as they are used in Peyote meetings. During the Sun Dance, sage and cedar are used throughout the four days of dancing. Both are essential to purify and protect the dancers. For protection, the dancers wear crowns of sage and sage wristlets and anklets while dancing. During the piercing ritual, the dancers lie on a bed of sage.

Cedar is also used throughout the Sun Dance, and like sage it purifies and protects, blesses and strengthens. During the Sun Dance, all the spiritual paraphernalia and all the people are "cedared off" or "smudged." The smoke from smoldering cedar is fanned over objects and people to purify and protect them. Along with a Sun Dance chief and a head dancer, there is a cedarman who assists with the Sun Dance and is responsible for cedaring off everything and everyone with smoke from the smoldering cedar. During a typical round of dancing, smoke from the cedar purifies each dancer. In addition the four entrances, the sacred pipes, the altar, the singers, and the drum are purified by cedar smoke. During the piercing rounds, cedar is used profusely to protect and strengthen the dancers who are undertaking the sacrifice of piercing. During sweat lodge ceremonies, cedar is used to give spiritual strength and protection. As the first heated rocks are brought into the sweat lodge, each one is blessed with a sprinkling of cedar. During the ceremony, more cedar is placed on the rocks to help people with their prayers.

In addition to sage and cedar, tobacco is a widely used sacred plant. The belief that tobacco is sacred is almost universal among Native North Americans, who consider tobacco a gift from God. It is used as a medicine, as a purifier, as a protector, and as a means of communication with the spirit world. Often it is smoked in pipes in a communal setting where individual and collective prayers are carried skyward, the smoke becoming a medium of communication between humans and the spirit world. Tobacco or tobacco smoke is used in healing. Tobacco juice or smoke may be applied to an injury. Sometimes tobacco is used to bless crops. It is also used as a prayer offering when tied in small pieces of cloth (called tobacco ties) and hung in special places, such as sweat lodges. Tobacco is offered to spiritual leaders when one is requesting their help. Throughout Native America, tobacco has multiple spiritual applications.

The Peyote faith adopted the use of tobacco in prayer. In 1891, Mooney reported that in Peyote meetings "everyone smokes handmade cigarettes, the smoke being regarded as sacred incense." The importance of this continuity cannot be overstated. In the early days of Peyotism, virtually everyone used tobacco to assist in prayer during religious services. By the turn of the century, however, the use of tobacco with prayer was discontinued among some Peyotists, such as John Rave's Cross Fire group in Nebraska; nevertheless, the majority of Peyotists continued to pray with tobacco as the Half Moon groups do today.

In the Half Moon ceremony, once the paraphernalia has been purified the Roadman passes tobacco and corn husks to the participants. Each person rolls his or her own cigarette and prays while smoking. Tobacco may also be used at midnight and dawn when a bucket of water is brought in. At midnight the fireman smokes tobacco while praying over the water. At dawn a woman does the same thing. In both cases, the tobacco smoke blesses the water and the participants while carrying the prayers upward.[29] In place of tobacco, the Winnebago Cross Fire group used the Bible in Peyote services to assist in prayer. The Winnebago claim that Albert Hensley was the person who introduced the Bible into Peyote services and initiated the addition of Christian elements into the Cross Fire Way. The truth is unclear as Hensley may have learned of the use of the Bible from his visits to Oklahoma. Some time earlier, John Wilson, who died in 1901, had added Christian elements to the Big Moon Peyote service, but it not clear if he actually took the Bible into the service. His nephew George Anderson told anthropologist George Speck in the 1930s that Wilson did not actually use the Bible for his teachings but used Peyote as the basis for his revelations about Jesus and His empty tomb, and the modifications of the Peyote ceremony. Nevertheless, while in Oklahoma, Hensley came in contact with those running the Cross Fire services.[30]

In Peyote meetings, both sage and cedar play a central role. Again, as in traditional ceremonies, they purify, protect, bless, and strengthen. Four people conduct a Peyote meeting: the Roadman, the chief drummer, the cedarman, and the fireman. The cedarman sits to the left of the Roadman and has a bag of cedar that is used throughout the night. At the beginning of the meeting, just like the beginning of the Sun Dance, the cedarman cedars off all the paraphernalia that will be used throughout the night, including the Peyote, the drum, the drumstick, the gourd rattle, the staff, the eagle-bone whistle, and the feather fans. Cedar is sprinkled on the fire, and each item is passed through the smoke. All the participants use the cedar smoke to purify themselves in preparation for ingesting Peyote. During healing, the Roadman, using his eagle-wing fan, fans cedar smoke on the ill person. Being in charge of the cedar is an important responsibility. The smoke purifies and protects everything and everyone. The late chief priest of the Native American Church of South Dakota, Emerson Spider, Sr., described the role of the cedarman:

> The cedarman who takes care of the cedar throughout the night has to be a man who knows how to pray to the great creator. . . . Everytime a person prays, he burns cedar. We use the cedar smoke as incense, just like the Catholic Church. . . . During our church services in the tipi we burn that cedar whenever somebody prays, so that the smoke goes up. Our understanding is that we are making smoke signals to the Great Spirit so that He will hear our prayers.[31]

Sage is used in the Peyote meetings as a purifier in the same way it is used as a purifier in traditional religions. At the beginning of a Peyote meeting, a bundle of sage is passed around the circle of participants. Each person holds the sage in his or her hands, lightly brushing the sage across his or her body as an act of purification. If someone arrives late, the sage is passed to the latecomer for the same purpose. Since Peyote is considered a holy sacrament, purification is an essential precursor to ingesting it. During the rounds of singing, sage is passed around the circle with the drum and staff. Because the songs are prayers, they are considered to be more effective if sung while the singer is in a purified state. Emerson Spider makes the important point that sage is used in a "traditional way of praying."[32]

Sage, cedar, and tobacco are widely used in traditional spiritual ceremonies throughout the western states. All three are also essential elements of Peyotism. Their functions and their symbolism closely parallel each other, adding one more commonality, helping us to understand the expansion of the Peyote faith.

THE VISION EXPERIENCE

The relationship of the vision experience in traditional American Indian religions and Peyotism has long been debated. Some scholars have seen this as a commonality and a major factor in the spread of the Peyote. Others have denied the relationship. Scholars have debated whether the rapid diffusion of Peyotism was facilitated by the existence of spiritual beliefs that included vision-seeking ceremonies such as the Sun Dance and the vision quest. Some scholars (Ruth Shonle, Weston La Barre, Ake Hultkrantz, Gloria Young, George Anderson) have argued that Peyotism was primarily accepted because Peyote induced visions. Anderson stated recently that "[o]ne of the major reasons for eating peyote is to induce visions." Hultkrantz has written that visions "primarily" facilitated the diffusion of Peyote. Gloria Young, an anthropologist, argues that the rapid expansion was because Peyote facilitated visions and that curing illness, though important, was not essential.[33] Other scholars (Vincenzo Petrullo, J. S. Slotkin, Omer Stewart, Richard Schultes, Paul Steinmetz, Hazel Hertzberg) have argued that that diffusion was influenced by many factors, with visions being just one factor. Schultes, who attended Peyote meetings in Oklahoma in the 1930s, said healing and curing were primary and visions secondary. Petrullo wrote in 1940 that "white investigators" have overemphasized the chemical-physiological effects of Peyote. He added he did not think the drug effects of Peyote had much value in explaining the religious aspects of Peyotism and that its primary purpose was to heal and that Peyote was not a giver of visions, but "the healer supreme." More recently, Omer Stewart wrote that it was reiterated in Half Moon and Cross Fire ceremonies that Peyote was taken not to induce visions but to help concentrate and learn. In addition, he claims that the expansion of Peyote did not follow the path of vision-seeking societies. The Poncas of Oklahoma specifically reject the idea that Peyote is hallucinogenic.[34]

It is a complex issue because some groups of American Indians without a vision-seeking tradition have accepted Peyotism, while others with a vision-seeking tradition have not. In the case of the Lakotas/Dakotas/Nakotas, there was and is a vision-seeking tradition in their spiritual heritage and yet the majority have not become Peyotists even through Peyotism was known to them and probably practiced by some of their neighbors. Among the Lakotas in particular, the Sun Dance and the vision quest are essential ceremonies on the Pine Ridge and Rosebud Reservations, but only a small minority became Peyotists. If visions were the central element in the expansion of Peyote then one would expect many more Lakotas to be Peyotists. There is also the case of the Diné. They do not have a vision-seeking tradition as in the Sun Dance, yet almost half the population are Peyotists today. This certainly weakens the argument that visions are a primary cause of the expansion of Peyotism.

The issue of visions is complex for another reason. In the early years of Peyotism, when many forces were allied against it, the main accusation was that it was a drug-using cult, so there was an excessive emphasis on Peyote as a destructive substance. An example, from 1925, is Shonle's "Peyote, the Giver of Visions," an influential article with missionaries and government officials.

Shonle, an anthropologist, claimed the visions or hallucinations explained the diffusion of Peyote. In addition, there were many so-called scientific tests in which the alkaloids in Peyote were isolated and tested in a laboratory. Some testers claimed Peyote was a powerful drug that could produce hallucinations. As a result, many scientists came to believe that American Indians were attracted to Peyote because it was a strong narcotic. To other scientists and anthropologists, and to all Peyotists, this was pseudoscience since those doing the testing and the writing had never been to a Peyote meeting (see chapter 3).

The diffusion of the Peyote religion did not follow a consistent pattern; it was quite differential and sporadic even within a particular group. To explain the diffusion of Peyotism a wide range of spiritual, social, political, and economic factors must be considered. The parallel of vision experiences between certain traditional religions and Peyotism is clearly not a major factor leading to the acceptance of Peyotism. If the vision experience was the critical element in diffusion, then Peyotism would be more widespread among the plains cultures. There are only a few groups in the northern and southern plains in which a majority of people are Peyotists. More analyses of diffusion on the micro level is needed before a satisfactory macro analysis can be considered tenable. Another point to consider when assessing the role of the vision experience in diffusion is that many of the early Peyotists were younger people, with day school or boarding school experience. They had grown up in the 1880s and the 1890s when the Sun Dance was outlawed and other spiritual practices were repressed. Traditional spiritual practices never totally disappeared; they were held in secret, but with fewer participants. The older generation, who grew up in the pre-reservation era or early in the reservation period when traditional spiritual practices were still common, did not, in any great numbers, become Peyotists even though they may have had intimate knowledge of the significance of visions. In fact, one could almost make the case (especially from the plains) that those most involved with vision-seeking experiences were least likely to become Peyotists. Among the Yankton Sioux, for example, many of the first generation of Peyotists were young people with boarding school or day school experience. It is doubtful any had experienced a Sun Dance or a vision quest.[35]

In those places where one could make a connection, the cosmological place of visions in the Peyote religion is similar to visions in traditional religions. Visions serve a similar function in that they are vehicles of communication between humans and the spirit world. Peyote, as the sacrament, opens a channel, like the sacred pipe, making it possible to receive a revelation. It could help an individual follow the Peyote Road to a fulfilling life. The fact that Peyote contains mild hallucinogenic substances should not be overstated. The true spiritual power is beyond the particular chemical properties of the Peyote cactus. Visions, however, are not common today; they are not part of Peyote meetings. For example, the following testimonial by Patricia Russell (Southern Cheyenne) is not unusual. "I have never seen colors or delusions of any sort while taking Peyote. What it feels like is that I am sitting by God the Creator."[36] It seems that visions were either overstated in the early twentieth century or the significance of the visions declined throughout the century to the point that today's Peyotists rarely mention them except when discussing their ancestors or famous Peyote people from the past. Some of the older narratives may be metaphorical, such as, "My great uncle had a vision after he ate 100 buttons." Virtually no one today says he or she became a Peyotist because Peyote could produce visions; in fact the vast majority of Peyotists would say the physiological effects of Peyote are overstated. This viewpoint is best summed up by Jay Fikes, who worked with Reuben Snake in the struggle for legal protection for Peyote. He wrote that "Peyote is regarded as a gift of God. It counters the craving for alcohol and is not eaten to induce visions." Daniel Swan says that in his many conversations with NAC members he has not encountered anyone who said he or she had a hallucinatory experience. He sees visions as insights that come from religious experiences, not a psychic effect.[37] The vision thesis of earlier scholars has been overstated.

OTHER COMMONALITIES

There are other parallels between traditional spiritualities and the Peyote faith. These include the use of feathers, the eagle-bone whistle, the fire and fireplace as the center of the spiritual activities, and the central role of drumming and singing. Throughout Native cultures, feathers, particularly eagle feathers, have a powerful significance. The eagle is recognized as having spiritual power. Eagles represent protection and strength; they carry special blessings, as well as being messengers to and from the spirit world. In the pre-reservation era, the Sioux believed that the spirit of the eagle presided over the tribal councils, hunters, war parties, and battles. Eagle feathers are sacred and highly prized.

They must never touch the ground or be defiled in any way. They must be cared for and protected when not in use. They were used to make the war bonnets of the Plains tribes; they were used to adorn shields and lances; and they were used in ritual and ceremony. Sun Dancers wore eagle feathers; the Sun Dance chief carried an eagle-wing fan. An eagle feather is used to protect someone on a vision quest; it is given as an honor in naming ceremonies. Eagle feathers are a sign of honor and an affirmation of identity and status.

The sacred nature of eagle feathers is also part of the Peyote religion, although the feathers of other birds (e.g., hawks, scissortails, flickers, pheasants, macaws, and parrots) are also used. Birds symbolize the carrying of messages or prayers upward toward the sky. The waterbird is also highly venerated. It represents a generic water fowl that most closely resembles the water turkey (*Anhinga anhinga*). Leonard Crow Dog says, "The greatest symbol of the Native American Church is the water bird."[38] The stylized bird, which is represented in virtually all Peyote art, has a long, slender neck, sleek wings, and elongated tail feathers. The bird symbolizes swift skyward flight. The waterbird design is made into jewelry; it is sewn as an appliqué on women's shawls, men's vests, and pillows; it is painted on water buckets and appears in many paintings and prints as a symbol of the Peyote religion. The waterbird appears in the logo of the Native American Church of North America. The Roadmen use eagle wing fans to fan cedar smoke on the ritual items and the participants. The fan is especially significant in healing. The Roadman will wave the fan vigorously across the body of the ill person. With the ingestion of Peyote and the utterance of intense prayer, and in conjunction with the fan, the supernatural power of healing is transmitted to the individual.[39]

The sacral power of the eagle is also represented by the eagle-bone whistle, which is made from a hollow wing bone. The wing bone (five to six inches long) has a precisely cut single stop about an inch from the end. It emits a high-pitch sound when one blows into the end. The whistle is used during many traditional ceremonies in the Southwest and the plains. Roadmen in the Peyote religion have an eagle-bone whistle as part of their ceremonial paraphernalia. The whistle plays a special role at midnight when there is a break in the singing and drumming. The drum and staff are returned to the Roadman, who sings the midnight song. The midnight pause may also be a time for special prayers or individuals may share their thoughts with everyone, or in a Cross Fire service a sermon may be delivered. The Roadman then leaves the tepee and blows the eagle-bone whistle four times while facing each of the four cardinal directions. Sometimes the same procedure is followed at dawn.

Fire and fireplaces are central to traditional American Indian religions and Peyotism. Ceremonially they are the literal center; cosmologically they are the symbolic center. The fireplace is sacred and is essential in almost all ceremonies. The person who is responsible for the fire has an important duty to perform whether it is for a sweat lodge ceremony, a Sun Dance, a vision quest, or a healing ceremony. The fire and the fireplace are the focus of the Peyote meeting. The fire is located in the exact center of the tepee between the door (east) and the Roadman (west). If a meeting is held in a home or another building, a fire can be built on a platform or earthen bed; if that is not feasible, the fire is built outside and hot coals are carried inside. The fireman is one of the four people who conduct a Peyote meeting. The role of the fireman is special and very difficult. Wood for an all-night fire must be gathered. This is not a casual undertaking, as only the right kind of wood can be used, and it must be cut and split in a very specific manner. The fireplace itself is very special to Peyote families. Many people speak of a family's particular fireplace since it may include ritual elements handed down from previous generations. In addition, the term *fireplace* is a metaphor for the type of Peyote service conducted. One can refer to a Roadman who runs a Cross Fire fireplace or a Half Moon fireplace. In this context the term *fireplace*, sometimes referred to as the altar, has a broad meaning. It includes the fire, wood, coals and ashes, and the crescent mound, as well as specific ritual practices associated with the "sacred fire." The fire itself represents the eternal power of the Creator. The fireman prepares the inside of the tepee or hogan before the meeting begins, then prepares the wood for the fire, which he cares for the rest of the night.

Singing and drumming are an integral part of traditional American Indian spiritual life as they are of Peyotism. The drum in particular is an essential element in both. When blessed, the traditional drum is considered sacred. Its construction, from choosing the wood for the frame to tanning the skin for the head, is very elaborate. Before the instrument is used, it is blessed. The drum must be cared for and protected, usually with tobacco ties or with a sprinkling of tobacco on the drum before drumming. The sound of the drum represents the human heartbeat. In the 1930s, Black Elk said, "The round form of the drum represents the universe, and its steady strong beat is the pulse, the heart throbbing at the center of the universe."[40] The Peyote water drum is quite different from the large drum used at Sun Dances and powwows and the small handheld drum used in some healing ceremonies. The water drum is made from a three-legged iron or brass kettle, filled with water, and covered with a deer skin. Although the Peyote drum may differ in design, the function is similar to that of traditional drums in their ritual and ceremonial roles as well as in their symbolism as stated by Black Elk. Gerald Primeaux, Sr., Yankton Sioux Roadman and well-known singer, sees the drum as a representation of the "whole world." "The drum is four elements, the kettle is mother earth, stretched hide is blue sky, seven marbles [stones] are the continents; the water in the drum is oceans, rivers and lakes; the rope ties all together; the star [on the bottom of the drum] is the universe. When you drum the whole world is in your hands: animal, plant, human." He added that the charcoal in the drum represents the "spirits of the deceased." According to Leonard Crow Dog, the drum reflects the spirit of Peyote and the sound represents the "Indian heart beat." Vincent Catches puts it another way: Through the night the Peyote drum is the heartbeat of the meeting.[41]

Another similar function of the drum is the sense of community it creates in both traditional ceremonies and Peyotism. Although the Peyote drum is played by one person at a time and the large traditional drum is played by four to eight people together, both types of drumming reflect the communal nature of spiritual experiences. The Peyote drum is passed around the circle to give each person the opportunity to drum. The traditional drum is played collectively by a group of people sitting in a circle. In both cases the method of drumming re-creates the unity and continuity of the sacred circle.

In this same manner, the sense of community provided in the past by the extended family, the band, the clan, or the village is now provided by the Peyote community. By the 1920s, traditional social, economic and political entities were rarely functioning as corporate groups, but Peyotism re-created community when community was in decline. For example, respect for the elderly and the kin network remained intact as the use of vernacular kinship terms for grandparents, uncles, aunts, and cousins continued. This helped to reinforce the extended family within the Peyote community, especially as families attended Peyote meetings together.

In reviewing the literature on the history of Peyotism, one finds many theories and models that attempt to explain the religion's origins and diffusion. These include acculturation theory, relative deprivation theory, nativistic movements, reformative movements, revitalization movements, and crisis cult theory, recently renamed crisis religion.[42] There are relevant elements in each of the paradigms. One could amass the necessary data from the historical experience of almost any Native group to support several of these perspectives. Yet on closer examination, these perspectives do not offer an interpretation that fully explains the Peyote experience in a holistic sense. Some groups were relatively deprived, they were in crisis, and acculturation was a reality. These can be measured and compared with the models. What is missing is the nature of the Peyote faith itself. These theories analyze external phenomena, but by focusing on Peyotism itself and the pre-reservation traditional spiritualities, one can gain an internal perspective that corresponds with the viewpoints of Peyotists that they accepted the Peyote religion for its intrinsic worth, relevance, and truth as a spiritual complex that articulated well with their spiritual roots. The conclusion to be reached is that Peyotism had so many commonalities with pre-reservation spiritual beliefs that it could provide a meaningful spiritual life. Peyote communities acquired a degree of autonomy. Peyotism provided spiritual and cultural autonomy over one's life, when political and economic autonomy was not possible. This is not a proposal for a general hypothesis on the diffusion of the Peyote faith; it is simply a conclusion about Peyotism drawn from the voices of NAC members, from ethnohistoric analysis, and ethnographic descriptions based on field experiences.

PEYOTE AS TEACHER: AN ETHICAL SYSTEM

In addition to Peyote as medicine, the Peyote faith offers its followers and potential followers a moral code and an ethical way of living. All Peyotists believe that Peyote is a teacher and that it is the basis for one's ethical standards. Peyote teaches a way of life; it gives one a path to follow, the so-called Peyote Road. Members of the NAC credit Peyote with teaching them how to live, how to behave, how to treat their family and community, and how to be one with all humanity. The altars in Peyote services serve as the literal and symbolic basis of an ethical system. Along the top of the crescent-shaped or horseshoe-shaped mound, there is an indentation or groove that is incised from one end to the other. This represents the Peyote Road, the path of life on earth that all Peyotists should follow. Some people see this as the path of life from youth to old age. Some simply view it as the route one follows for a meaningful spiritual life. Others claim it is the path that prayers follow to the Creator. The significance of the Peyote Road is emphasized by the large Grandfather Peyote button placed exactly in the center of the mound.

The power of Peyote as a teacher has been recognized since the origins of the Peyote faith. Early leaders such as John Wilson, Quanah Parker, Jonathan Koshiway, Albert Hensley, and John Rave extolled the virtues of Peyote as a teacher. There were no official instructions or written guidelines to learn about the Peyote faith or how to become a Roadman. Only Peyote, the source of knowledge, could teach one about the faith. Even today if one asks a Peyotist about his or her faith, the likely answer is that only Peyote can teach. Anthropologist Vincenzo Petrullo commented on this in the 1930s after attending Peyote meetings in Oklahoma. When he asked questions about the Peyote religion's beliefs and rituals, he was offered a handful of Peyote buttons and told to eat them if he wanted answers. Dick Fool Bull said, "I told white people you'll never understand unless you eat it." John Wilson, the founder of the Big Moon ceremony, gave detailed moral instructions, but he made it clear that he was not the teacher; it was the Peyote that encouraged him to tell his followers to lead a moral life through marital fidelity and avoidance of gambling and alcohol. He warned against lying, repeating falsehoods, losing one's temper, fighting, and revenge. Through Peyote, he preached a humanistic message to respect one's neighbors, to maintain a peaceful disposition, and to forgive others.[43]

As with Peyote and healing, there are multitudes of testimonials about the power of Peyote to teach. When NAC members are interviewed, they focus on this power. For example, Bernard Ice (Lakota) said Peyote is not a narcotic. "When you eat it, your mind turns to the Great Spirit. In one song I can learn what takes twenty-years in school." Joe American Horse (Lakota) states, "[Y]ou take Peyote, you have an inner eye that clears up and tells you what is right and wrong." These same types of teachings have become the basis of Peyotism's ethical values as expressed by Ted Strong (Yakima): "Our Holy Medicine has within it four powers: love, hope charity and faith."[44]

The ethical values implicit in the testimonials have also been included in various state charters. The original NAC charter of 1918 describes its moral values as deriving from the "Christian religion with the practice of Peyote sacrament." The charter states that the foundation of the value system is respect for self and others. It includes sobriety, morality, industry, charity to others, and a "brotherly union among the members of the Native Race of Indians." Other charters followed suit. For example, the 1922 charter of the Yankton Sioux Peyote church states that their purpose is to teach morality, kindly charity, right living, self-respect, brotherly love, and union among all American Indians.[45]

These testimonials and statements reinforce the belief in Peyote's power to teach. Among the Diné, the moral and ethical dimensions of Peyotism are intertwined with the spiritual. Their ethical prescriptions are similar to those of other Peyote communities: work hard, plan for the future, be responsible for your family, and avoid gambling and alcohol. One is expected to be a "man of peace," even to those who criticize you. One should follow the "prayer circle" and pray for oneself, one's family, one's church, one's tribe, all Indians, all Americans, and all humankind.[46] In essence, Peyote is transformational. The drinkers become the abstainers, the lazy become the hard working, the angry become peaceful, the boastful become humble, the selfish become the generous, the irresponsible become responsible, and the immoral become moral, as the sacred herb teaches members of the Peyote faith.

In the Cross Fire Way, Christian values have been incorporated although they are not different in any appreciable way from the values described above. After the use of the Bible was introduced into some Peyote services, biblical references became more commonplace as expressions of values such as "Let brotherly love continue" (Hebrews 13:1). There is also a biblical sanction for eating Peyote. "For one believeth that he may eat all things: another, who is weak, eateth herbs" (Romans, 14:2). The "herb" that will make the weak strong is believed to be Peyote. In Cross Fire services the Lord's Prayer is recited; there are references to the teachings and sacrifice of Jesus, the use of the cross as a symbol; and Christian terms such as *baptism* and *ordination* are used along with titles such as priest and reverend. However, despite the intertwining of Peyotism with Christianity, there is one essential reality for all Peyotists—Peyote remains primary. It is believed that the Bible can only be understood through eating Peyote. This began in the late nineteenth in Oklahoma and in the early twentieth century among the Winnebagos. Peyotist Albert Hensley said the Bible was intelligible only to those who took Peyote. Another Winnebago said, "After eating peyote, I grasped the meaning of the Bible, which before had been meaningless to me." According to a Kiowa-Apache: "God put peyote on earth for the illiterate Indian so he could get the religion of the Bible."[47]

PEYOTE AS PROTECTOR

In addition to serving as a healer and a teacher, Peyote is believed to be a protector. With virtually all traditional American Indian societies, protection from harm, including injury, disease, witchcraft, and warfare, was part of one's spiritual life. Individuals and communities sought assistance from medicine men and women to protect them from danger. They could be protected by ritual and ceremony, by avoiding taboos, and by possessing sacred objects or talismans. With the spread of Peyotism, Peyote buttons became a source of protection, especially in warfare. There are many testimonials from American Indian veterans who served in the United States military from World War I to the present and who carried Peyote buttons into war. Families sponsored Peyote services for their sons or daughters before they left for military duty. They were given special Peyote buttons and prayers. The Peyote might be carried in a small medicine bundle or placed in a leather pouch and worn around the neck. Many veterans have claimed that Peyote protected them and brought them home safely. One Washoe veteran said:

> When I went in the war my friends gave me a fine big chief Peyote button to keep on me all the time. . . . Well I was all over that war [World War II] in France and Germany and Africa. I saw people dead all around me, but I came through and never got hurt.[48]

Another veteran, Johnny White Cloud, said, "They prayed for me when Vietnam was going on. I took the Medicine [Peyote] with me. The Medicine took me over there and brought me back." George Palmer (Kiowa), a World War II Air Force veteran, carried a special Peyote button sewed in a beaded pouch made by his mother. He wore it attached to his dog tags. He claimed the power of Peyote protected not only him, but all the members of his airplane crew as well. Upon return from war, the soldiers' families sponsored Peyote meetings. The individuals received special blessings and prayers and a ritual purification by the Roadman. The soldiers also offered thanks to those who prayed for their safe return.[49]

MULTIPLE AFFILIATIONS

There is another significant factor to help explain the acceptance of the Peyote faith. When a person becomes a Peyotist, he or she is not expected to give up previous spiritual beliefs or religious affiliations. Sometimes there is a double or triple affiliation. Exclusive membership in the NAC is not a requirement. One may be a Peyotist, a member of a Christian denomination, and a traditionalist, that is, a believer in the spiritual traditions of one's ethnic group. Although this is not universal, the majority of Peyotists do not see contradictions with multiple religious affiliations or practicing multiple faiths. Being a member of the NAC and participating in a variety of traditional ceremonies such as sweat lodges, chantways, sacred pipe ceremonies, medicine societies, vision quests, and Sun Dances is not unusual. In fact since the 1960s it has become more common. Among the Lakotas/Dakotas there are Peyote Roadmen who are also traditional spiritual leaders. For example, on the Rosebud Reservation Leonard Crow Dog, and his father before him, are traditional spiritual leaders and Peyote Roadmen. Each summer Crow Dog sponsors a four-day Sun Dance and also has Peyote meetings through the night. On the nearby Yankton Sioux Reservation, the late Asa Primeaux and his family sponsored a series of four Sun Dances (sixteen years). Each year on the last day of the Sun Dance, the family sponsored a Peyote meeting which some of the Sun Dancers attended.

A common viewpoint is that all these religious groups worship the same God, but take different paths. Individuals are quite open about this. For example, a majority of Southern Poncas are Peyotists, but many are also practicing Christians. They also participate in traditional ceremonies such as the Sun Dance. They believe people use different means to reach the same end. One Ponca questioned about religious attitudes said, "The Poncas give thanks to God in their different ceremonies and religious worships. In the Sun Dance, the Peyote church, or in the Christian church, it is all the same God." Many individuals define themselves by more than one faith. Prior to an interview, while giving personal information, Charles Kills Enemy (Lakota/Yankton) listed his occupation as "Medicine Man" and his religion as Catholic. In his interview he described himself as a Pipe Carrier (traditional faith), an NAC member, and a Catholic. There are many similar examples. Albert Hensley, an important proselytizer of the Peyote faith was also active in the Episcopal Church. Among the Taos Pueblo there are Peyote members who participate in traditional ceremonies in kivas and at the same time are active in the Catholic Church. Stewart tells the story of Joe Green, an active Paiute medicine man, who also is "devotee of Peyotism" and a "devout Episcopalian." He believed in and practiced all three religions simultaneously. Sometimes this double or triple affiliation is expressed in other ways. For example, a recent text depicts a photo of a Navajo Peyote Roadman with a print of Leonardo da Vinci's *Last Supper* on the wall.[50] In NAC cemeteries a single tombstone may display symbols of several different faiths. There may be a sacred pipe or eagle feathers (traditional), a Peyote drum or tepee (NAC), and a cross (Christian), all on the same headstone.

Many Diné, for example, are active in more than one faith. If an individual is ill, he or she may seek help through the Peyote faith, a traditional Diné healer, and go to a western hospital. Traditional Diné spirituality and Peyotism have remained distinct, but today there is mutual respect with some individuals attending the ceremonies of both, and others also attend Christian services. The Diné believe that the God worshipped by Peyotists is the same God worshipped by Christians and Jews and that Peyote is a special gift of God to Indians.[51] This is exemplified by the fascinating life story of a Diné Catholic nun. "Sister Grace" (pseudonym) participated in a recent study on Diné healing. She said when she was confronted with a serious illness she turned to three different spiritualities for healing. She sought help in Peyote services, traditional Diné healing ceremonies, and a Catholic charismatic prayer ritual of the laying on of hands. She also went to a western hospital. She has combined some of these beliefs and is now a spiritual healer. In an interview she said that "healing is being in oneness with God." Another example comes from a recent *Navajo Times* article on centenarians. The family of Tom Lee (Diné, age 101) attributes his longevity to his faith. When asked what his faith was, family members said he attended traditional Navajo ceremonies, the Native American Church, and Christian services. One relative added, "I think to our elders, it was all kind of the same thing."[52]

HALF MOON AND CROSS FIRE CEREMONIES

The modern ceremonial and ritual structure of the Peyote faith's religious services developed in Oklahoma in the 1870s and 1880s. By the 1890s a distinct ceremonial structure was well established. There are two major styles of worship within Peyotism today: the Half Moon Way and the Cross Fire Way. The earliest ritual was today's Half Moon, also known as the Little Moon, Tipi Way, or Kiowa Way. By the turn of the last century a variant developed which is today's Cross Fire, also known as Big Moon, or Wilson's Moon (after John Wilson). There are also minor variants, such as the Osages' West Moon Altar and the Diné V-Way Altar. The various names come from the shape and size of the altar. The majority of Peyotists today follow the Half Moon Way. The most common-shaped mound within the altar is the crescent or half moon. According to Reuben Snake, the half moon represents one's life on earth. The half moon is part of a universal circle. He said we existed in the spirit world before we were born and will return to the spirit world when deceased. The

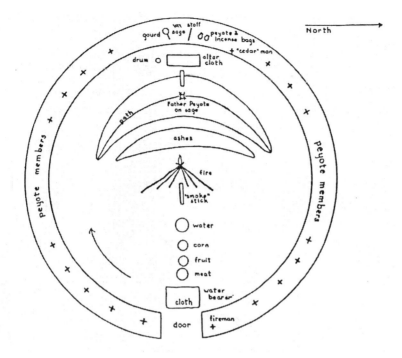

Figure 4. Half Moon altar. From La Barre, *Peyote Cult*, 154.

half moon represents the road of life on earth or the "earthly portion of the unending cycle of life."[53]

Altars are prepared with great care and reverence: they must be just right. The term *altar* refers to the central part of the tepee or hogan, which contains the fire, the ashes, the crescent or horseshoe-shaped mound, and an area where the Roadman lays out the ritual items. There are two major types of altars, but they have basic similarities in form and function. The Half Moon (see figure 4) is an ephemeral altar built for each Peyote service. It includes a crescent-shaped mound four to five inches high with an arc approximately eight or nine feet in length and a groove, or Peyote Road, along the top with Grandfather Peyote placed in the center.

The Cross Fire altar, as in the earlier Big Moon altar (see figure 5) is more complex. The Big Moon has a large horseshoe-shaped altar eight to ten feet long on each side and four to five feet wide. Some people claim the horseshoe shape seen from above is the heel print of Jesus. The fire is in the center in a slightly sunken area. As the Big Moon developed into the Cross Fire, the use of tobacco for prayer was eliminated and replaced by the Bible, but other elements remained the same including two intersecting lines through the altar. One line extends from the door (east) to the west side of the tepee, and another line going north/south, intersect in the center of the fire forming a cross, thus the name Cross Fire. The cross represents the four directions and is an obvious Christian symbol. Emerson Spider, an NAC church leader, claimed that the cross at the center of the altar represents the place where Jesus gave his life for humanity. In addition, in the Cross Fire service, a cross may be incised on the top, in the exact center of the raised mound. A sprig of sage is placed on the cross, and Grandfather Peyote is placed on top.[54]

Peyote religious services or meetings are held on a regularly scheduled day or on an ad hoc basis related to a special need or event. Most Peyote communities have all night services on each Saturday, or alternate Saturdays, or once a month, such as the Yankton Sioux Peyote church that has a regularly scheduled service the first Saturday of the month. Saturday became the day of choice for a service to conform to the American work week and school schedule. Other services are held in conjunction with holidays such as Memorial Day, Independence Day, Veteran's Day, Easter, New Year's, and Christmas. Meetings are also held for a variety of specific purposes. The most common purpose is healing, but they are also held for life events such as graduation, marriage, birth of a child, and funeral and memorial services. If a special service is needed, an individual or family will sponsor it. They contact a Roadman and offer tobacco to run the service. The family is responsible for all the arrangements. Whether the service is Half Moon or Cross Fire depends on the Roadman in consultation with the sponsor.

Peyote meetings are also held during annual state and national conferences. When the Native American Church of South Dakota has its four-day annual conference, Peyote services are held at night. At the annual convention of the Native American Church of North America, multiple Peyote services are held. Given the large attendance at the 2006 convention held on the Omaha Reservation (Macy, Nebraska), six tepees were set up to conduct Half Moon and Cross Fire services.

As described earlier, once a Peyote meeting is planned, the sponsor begins preparations. It may be held in a tepee, a hogan, or a permanent structure such

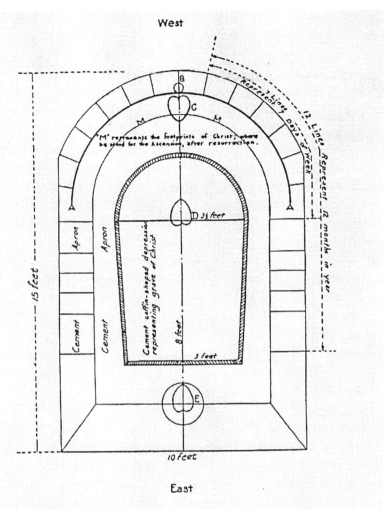

West

"M" represents the footprints of Christ; where he stood for the Ascension, after resurrection.

Representing Days of week

Line Represent 12 month in year

B

C

M   M

A   A

D 3½ feet

15 feet

Apron   Apron

Cement   Cement

Cement coffin-shaped depression representing grave of Christ

8 feet

3 feet

E

10 feet

East

Figure 5. John Wilson Big Moon–style altar, La Barre, *Peyote Cult*, 44.

as the octagon-shaped church houses of the Osages and Quapaws, or in a private home. The latter occurred mostly in the past when a tepee was not available or when secrecy was necessary, or if there is inclement weather. As noted earlier, if the service is held in a home or permanent structure, the fire is built outside and hot coals are brought in and used for the service as if it were a fire. Some groups also have church buildings. The Yankton Sioux had a small church from the late 1930s to the 1990s. As the building aged and fell into disrepair, Peyote meetings were held in a tepee on the church grounds. After several years of fund-raising, Peyotists built a new church and began conducting their Peyote services in 2010.

Throughout the twentieth century and into the twenty-first century, with several exceptions, there has been a standardization of the Peyote ceremony, the ritual instruments, and the structure of the altar. From the 1930s to the 1980s, Omer Stewart, as a participant-observer, compared ritual elements among dozens of Peyote communities. Noting the variations between Cross Fire and Half Moon, he concluded that the ritual of each is virtually the same through time and space throughout the United States and Canada. Where there are differences within each, they come from Roadmen who are able to make minor modifications within a standardized ritual structure.[55] The major difference between the Half Moon and Cross Fire is the degree to which Christian elements have influenced the ceremony. The Half Moon uses tobacco to pray. As discussed in an earlier section, the Cross Fire eliminated the use of tobacco and substituted the Bible to use in prayer. Some people argue the Half Moon is more "traditional" and that the Cross Fire is more syncretistic with Christian influences. The latter has more references to Jesus in its songs, sometimes a Bible is on display, a midnight sermon based on a biblical passage is delivered, and the Lord's Prayer is recited. Christian elements are not entirely absent from the Half Moon, particularly Christian references in Peyote songs.

These two variants of Peyotism should not be seen as separate denominations as are found in Christianity. They are not equivalent to, for example, Methodists and Lutherans. These are two approaches to worship within one denomination. The fundamental beliefs are the same, based on the primacy of Peyote and its power to heal and to teach. The similarities greatly outnumber the differences. Members of both groups openly attend each other's services and most Peyote communities are under the umbrella of the Native American Church of North America. Both groups are also members of almost all state and local NAC organizations.

Whether it is a Half Moon or Cross Fire service, there is a similar ritual order to the ceremony. What follows is a composite description of the all-night service with brief commentary on the differences between the several styles of worship.

Once a Roadman has accepted an invitation from a sponsor to conduct a Peyote meeting, three individuals are invited to serve as chief drummer, cedar-man, and fireman. The sponsors begin planning for the acquisition of a tepee, inviting individuals, purchasing food for the congregation, obtaining a sufficient supply of Peyote, and preparing wood for the all-night fire. All this is at considerable expense to the sponsor. During the day before the beginning of the Peyote meeting the tepee is set up with the doorway facing east. The firewood is stacked outside the door. The grounds are cleared, the grass is cut, and all is put in order. Inside the tepee, the altar is prepared with meticulous care. All those who help with the preparations have a late afternoon meal as people begin arriving for the service. An hour or two before dusk, the Roadman and his assistants will carry their ritual instruments into the tepee. The instruments are carried in a creatively designed container, called a Peyote box or gourd box. Almost all NAC members have such a box for personal items and religious accoutrements that are used through the service (see chapter 5).

Sometime during the late afternoon or early evening (the time varies), the fireman starts the ritual fire, which burns until dawn. The fireman (some Cross Fire services may have more than one fireman) sits next to the door, controlling access in and out of the tepee, carrying in the wood, and tending the fire. The wood, cut in three- to four-foot-long pieces, is placed in a precise way to form a V-shape with the apex toward the west. The wood is lit at the apex and during the night produces a significant amount of ashes.

The ashes and hot coals from the fire are an essential part of the altar arrangement. As the fire burns, the fireman adds wood in a very precise manner while moving the ashes into a pile. After a sufficient amount of ashes have accumulated, the fireman arranges them in a variety of patterns throughout the night. Using one or two pieces of firewood, the fireman arranges the ashes into symbols of the Peyote faith, such as an eagle, a waterbird, or a star, or in the Cross Fire, a heart or a cross. The Half Moon symbol of a cross represents the four directions; in the Cross Fire service it represents a Christian cross. Each of the symbols has its own iconic significance but all have the same function of harnessing prayers and carrying them skyward.

Attire worn for Peyote services has changed during the past century. Peyotists originally wore local-style Native clothing. Some groups, mostly in Oklahoma, used face paint, through this soon died out. Roadmen in various areas wore otter skin caps or turbans. By the 1910s and 1920s, traditional clothing styles had for the most part disappeared and been replaced by Anglo-American-style clothing. Today men wear slacks and a long-sleeve shirt, sometimes with a vest and a bolo tie. The women dress modestly with a long skirt and blouse, or a dress, and a traditional fringed shawl over their shoulders. The attire may be embroidered with NAC symbols such as a tepee or waterbird. Everyone believes it is important to dress well and look your best.[56]

As dusk approaches, the Roadman gathers everyone to begin the service. He leads the congregation clockwise around the outside of the tepee before entering. Once inside the participants continue clockwise finding a place to sit. Everyone brings a blanket or pillow to sit on. The Roadman sits on the west side, the cedarman to his left, the chief drummer to his right, the fireman seated north of the door. As all are seated, the Roadman lays out an altar cloth and proceeds to take out the ritual items that were in the Peyote box. The cedarman sprinkles cedar on the fire for the Roadman to purify the objects by passing them through the cedar incense four times and returning them to the altar cloth. The Roadman's carved and beaded staff is placed upright in the ground or sometimes laid flat on the altar cloth. Special care is taken to place the "Grandfather Peyote" or "Chief Peyote" on the crescent moon. The Grandfather Peyote button is the focus of prayer throughout the night. In the Half Moon, the Roadman distributes tobacco, usually Bull Durham, and three-inch-long corn husk wrappers to everyone so they can roll their own cigarettes. In the Big Moon, only the Roadman prays with tobacco; tobacco is not used in the Cross Fire.

The Roadman, and usually the sponsor, takes the opportunity to explain the purpose of the meeting and beseech all to focus their prayers on that purpose. Meanwhile the fireman has a special fire stick that is removed from the fire with one end glowing red. The Roadman's cigarette is lit first. The stick is then passed clockwise for all to light up. Once the cigarettes are lit, all pray. It is a ceremonial smoke. The Roadman recites a prayer, either in English or a Native language, the congregants pray themselves. Each person pulls the smoke toward his or her body. The smoke is considered sacred as it carries everyone's prayers. When the prayers are finished, the fireman collects the cigarette butts and places them along the ends of the crescent moon. The Roadman now prepares for the opening song by readying the Peyote to be passed around the circle. As more cedar is added to the fire, the Roadman passes the Peyote through the cedar smoke four times. Meanwhile a bundle of sage is passed clockwise around the tepee. Each person rubs the sage on his or her hands, head, and body, as an act of purification, before ingesting the sacred herb. The Roadman takes the first Peyote and then passes it clockwise for each person to ingest. It is now time for the opening song.

The Roadman, with the help of the chief drummer, cedars-off his staff, bundle of sage, feather fan, and gourd rattle. The drummer does the same with the drum. Everything has been purified. The Roadman holds his staff, sage, and feather fan in his left hand, and with the rattle in his right hand, and accompanied by the chief drummer, he sings a fixed opening song, followed by three more songs. As the Roadman sings, the power of the Peyote service is felt by all. The rapid intensity of the drum, with the higher pitch of the rattle, intensifies the spirituality of the service. Everyone is praying intently, with eyes closed, or focusing on the bright flames of the fire and Grandfather Peyote. After the opening songs are completed, the staff, rattle, sage, and fan are passed to the chief drummer. The drum is given to the Roadman, who drums for the chief drummer, who is singing. He sings four songs. The cedarman is next and so on, going clockwise around the circle, until each participant has the opportunity to sing four songs accompanied by a drummer. As the ritual items and instruments are touched by all while being passed around the circle, a communal feeling envelops the service. This continues until midnight, when the first part of the service is over.

At 12:00, the ritual items are returned to the Roadman in preparation for the Midnight Water Ceremony. Cedar is added to the fire so all can use the smoke for purification. The Roadman with the help of the chief drummer sings the midnight water song calling for water, followed by three more songs of the Roadman's choice. He then blows the eagle-bone whistle four times. The fireman brings in a pail of water. Kneeling next to the pail, the fireman rolls and smokes a cigarette and prays for all, especially for those who are ill. The cigarette is passed to the Roadman, chief drummer, and cedarman, who do the same. Cedar is continually placed on the fire so the ritual items and all the people continue to be purified. The water is placed in front of the Roadman, who may take the opportunity to speak to everyone again on the purpose of the meeting. He then draws crisscross lines in the water with the eagle-bone whistle, indicating the four directions. This is followed by dipping the feather fan into the water and sprinkling it toward the four directions, on to the ritual instruments, and toward all present, especially the ill, as a blessing. The pail of water is now passed clockwise for everyone to take a sip. When everyone has done so, the fireman takes the pail outside. The Roadman then goes outside and blows the eagle-bone whistle four times to each of the four directions. Upon his return he may speak to everyone and give others the opportunity to speak. At this time, individuals may also go outside for a short break if necessary.

The Cross Fire service does not include a midnight water ceremony. At midnight, however, the singing stops, and the Roadman offers a sermon based on a biblical passage. The Bible may be placed within the altar; sometimes Grandfather Peyote is placed on top. The Bible is treated as other ritual instruments in that it is cedared-off for purification. There may be other biblical references during the night, such as Christian interpretations of the ritual items, that is, the Roadman's staff, which usually has a cross carved on top, may be described as Jesus' walking staff. If healing is part of the Peyote service, references are made to the healing power of Jesus.[57]

After the midnight activities, the singing and drumming continue as before, with each person singing four songs. Peyote is also distributed again. In the period after midnight, the congregation becomes even more prayerful and solemn. Individuals now can use their personal fans and rattles. Many hold their feather fans in front of their faces, deeply in prayer. Care is taken all through the night not to pass between a person praying and the fire, so as to not interrupt the prayer's path to the fire and upward with the smoke. It is the same with the singing and drumming, as all the songs are prayers. During these hours, the cedarman will add more cedar to the fire and circle the tepee, rapidly waving his eagle wing fan and bringing incense toward those who are praying. Through the late hours as well, the fireman cares for the fire, keeping the burning wood arranged in the appropriate manner, sweeping the area, and continuing to shape the ashes into a variety of spiritual symbols. If healing is part of a particular Peyote service, it occurs after the midnight ceremony.

For example, around 3:00 A.M., the Roadman will speak about the ill person, possibly offer some details, mention the family's love and prayers for him or her, and ask all to pray. The patient may be seated in a special place for the doctoring. The Roadman offers Peyote to the patient and proceeds to vigorously fan the body of the patient with the eagle-wing fan. The patient is deeply in prayer. The Roadman is not considered a healer, only a facilitator. The healing comes from the Creator's gift of Peyote, from everyone's praying, and from the continual drumming and singing of healing songs. It is significant to note that healing takes place not only for physical ailments but also for psychological ones. When the doctoring is completed, the singing and drumming continue around the circle until it is time for the morning ceremony.

As dawn breaks the fireman leaves to get the Morning Water Woman. The Roadman blows the whistle four times for her to enter with a pail of water. She sits on the ground inside the door with the bucket between her and the fire. The woman is an essential part of the service as she represents the woman of the Peyote origin narratives. The woman is usually, though not always, the wife of the Roadman. Cedar is placed on the fire for all to be cedared-off again. The Roadman sings the morning water song, followed by three more songs. When he is finished, the drum and the ritual items are placed on the altar cloth. The Morning Water Woman kneels in front of the water. She begins with a talk about the purpose of the meeting, thanks the sponsors, mentions any sick persons in attendance, and gives blessings and hope of renewal for all. She rolls a cigarette in a corn husk, the fireman helps her light it, and using the smoke, she begins to pray either in English or her Native language. While praying she blows smoke toward Grandfather Peyote and the water. She may also use a feather to disperse the smoke. When her prayer is finished, the cigarette is passed to the Roadman, the chief drummer, and cedarman. Each takes four puffs and prays. When they are finished, the fireman places the water in front of the Roadman, who blesses it again and passes it clockwise for all to sip from a special cup. It is a powerful communal experience. As the water is being passed, individuals may speak and offer words of a prayerful or thankful nature. When the water has completed the circle, the woman leaves with the pail. Singing and drumming resume.

When the sun rises, it is time for the closing ceremony. The four sacred foods, water, corn, fruit, and meat, are brought in. They are placed in a straight line between the east door and the fire. The Roadman sings three songs, followed by a fixed closing or quitting song. These songs are sung with extra vigor. It has been a long night of prayer, and the sun is rising as a symbol of a new beginning. Everyone is energized. When the Roadman finishes the closing songs, the water drum is untied and passed around the circle. This gives each person a chance to sip the water from the drum now considered sacred as all the evening's prayers have passed through the water. Some put a finger in the water and touch their heads and hearts as a blessing. The remaining water is poured alongside the crescent mound. The Roadman now puts away his ritual instruments and is ready for the sacred food.

More cedar is added to the fire to bless the four foods, which are consumed for spiritual sustenance. The water is passed around first. As it moves slowly from person to person, the corn is passed, followed by the fruit, and then the meat. Each person ingests a small amount of each food. It is a very reverent and prayerful end to the Peyote service. When the food completes the circle the Roadman adds remarks and thanks all who helped and participated. In the Cross Fire service, the Lord's Prayer is recited at the closing. Everyone rises and shakes hands with the others and goes outside to greet the new day. There is a strong communal and spiritual bond as people mingle and talk. Within the hour, the sponsors provide a quick breakfast with plenty of fresh coffee. After the breakfast some may go and freshen up but soon return to wait for dinner (at noon). The time between breakfast and dinner is a very important for the Peyote community. People renew acquaintances and make new friendships with people from other communities. There are discussions about family, church business, or local politics. People exchange phone numbers and email addresses as important contacts are made. After several hours of such interaction, everyone gathers as a large dinner is served. The food includes Indian-style soup, several meats, vegetables, fry bread, various types of salad, plenty of desserts, and a limitless supply of coffee. There is more than enough for everyone with leftovers for the elders to take home. Before eating, the Roadman gives an inspirational talk, blesses the food, and offers a prayer. The elders are asked to line up first; everyone else follows. After the dinner many of the people linger about and continue to talk and invite each other to future Peyote services. This type of interaction has been going on for more than a century as a network of Peyotists is reinforced and a nationwide Peyote community continues to strengthen its bonds. This sense of community among Peyotists has been a source of strength in the never-ending struggle against the longstanding opposition to the Peyote faith.

CHAPTER THREE

The Assault on Peyotism

In October 1918, while the anti-Peyote legislation was pending in the U.S. Senate, the Oklahoma Peyotists applied for and received a state charter as the Native American Church of Oklahoma. This success by the Peyote community did not reduce the assault on the Peyote faith. The Bureau of Indian Affairs continued the attack. State legislatures throughout the West were debating the prohibition of Peyote. So-called humanitarian groups, determined to "save the Indian," continued to oppose Peyotism as did various Christian groups that had missionaries on many reservations. The latter believed that the Peyote faith was a threat to their Christianizing efforts. Through an informal alliance, these groups worked together to suppress the Peyote faith.

Peyote usage on a reservation was first reported to federal authorities in 1886. The BIA labeled it an intoxicant and a narcotic and issued an order to prohibit its usage. In 1890, they ordered that Peyote buttons be seized and destroyed. The emergence of the Peyote faith challenged the federal government's policy of weakening and eventually eliminating American Indian religions and cultures. By the turn of the century, there were Peyote communities on many reservations in the southern and central plains. In the face of this continued growth, the government expanded its efforts at suppression and began seeking federal anti-Peyote legislation. The BIA's policy of disruption and suppression was led by Chief Special Officer "Pussyfoot" Johnson. With a hundred deputies, he confiscated as many Peyote buttons as he could find. In addition, the BIA convinced other federal agencies to support its efforts. For example, the bureau convinced the Department of Agriculture ban the importation of Peyote from Mexico.

In the first decade of the twentieth century, as the Peyote faith spread into the central plains, particularly South Dakota and Nebraska, the reservation superintendents took the issue into their own hands. The superintendent on the Yankton Sioux Reservation, for instance, jailed several members of the local Peyote community. His superiors in Washington ordered the Peyotists' release, as possession of Peyote was not illegal. Yet the superintendent continued his harassment and confiscated Peyote buttons and ritual instruments such as the water drum. Like other reservation officials, he also began lobbying Congress for legislation outlawing Peyote. By 1916, a coalition of private groups and public officials were pressuring Congress to ban Peyote. Meanwhile, various individuals and organizations were distributing a steady stream of anti-Peyote literature to arouse public opinion against the Peyote faith. These materials labeled Peyote a dangerous narcotic, extremely harmful to the health of American Indians. No consideration was given to the religious or constitutional issues involved. Those opposed to the Peyote faith argued that the use of Peyote was cloaked in a religious context as an excuse for taking drugs and avoiding legal sanctions. As described in chapter 1, anti-Peyote bills were introduced in Congress in 1916, 1917, and 1918, but all failed to pass. Nevertheless, the Bureau of Indian Affairs continued to push for new legislation, while also developing additional strategies to suppress the Peyote faith.

FEDERAL GOVERNMENT

The strategies that emerged after the defeat of the anti-Peyote bills included further attempts by the federal government to influence public opinion, to pressure Congress and state governments in the West before submitting another anti-Peyote bill, and to encourage secular organizations and missionaries to work with the BIA for the suppression of Peyote. In 1919, the BIA intensified its campaign to demonize Peyote and its users. The bureau's literature described Peyote as a harmful narcotic that led to addiction, immorality, and indolence, which would hinder American Indians' "progress" toward "civilization." One of the BIA's strategies in the campaign was to collect as much negative information as possible, including testimonials from missionaries and medical doctors, and use it to discredit Peyotism. Agents began the systematic collection of data on the use of Peyote from anyone who had contact with American Indians on the reservations where the Peyote faith was practiced. All negative accounts were printed and disseminated. It is important to note that all this activity occurred at the high point of the Prohibition movement. Congress adopted the Eighteenth Amendment in December 1917, and by 1919 it was ratified by the states. Even though the new amendment prohibited only "the manufacture, sale, or transportation of intoxicating liquors," the BIA hoped it could be applied to Peyote as well. Many of the groups that lobbied for the prohibition of alcohol, which was already illegal on reservations, also lobbied for the prohibition of Peyote. Cato Sells, the commissioner of Indian Affairs (1913–1921), was active in the Prohibition movement.

The BIA developed a questionnaire, Circular #1522, and addressed it to "Superintendents, Inspecting Officials, Physicians," and all other reservation personnel. Missionaries who worked on the reservations were also requested to fill out the questionnaire. The questionnaire sought information on the extent and depth of Peyote use. It asked about the "moral, mental and physical effect of peyote," and whether the Indians who use Peyote were less "civilized" than those who did not. The questionnaire also asked a respondent to indicate what "opportunity you had to observe the use and effects of Peyote" and whether "you believe the plea that Peyote is used as a religious sacrament is genuine or a cloak." The questions, sent to 115 western agencies, seemed designed to elicit negative information. As a result the tone of the answers, from the 28 agencies that reported Peyote usage, was almost always negative. Respondents claimed that Peyotists were indolent, dirty, shiftless, and less industrious than other Indians and that their use of Peyote lowered their moral and mental efficiency. Some agencies said that under the influence of Peyote the men engaged in immoral relations with women. Some of them compared Peyote to liquor; others claimed it was worse. For example, the superintendent of the Pine Ridge Reservation compared Peyote to opium, which he claimed led to "mental depression." On the question of whether Peyote was legitimately used as a sacrament, the answer was virtually unanimous that the religious explanation was a cloak to prevent legislative action against Peyote. Some of the respondents feared the continued growth of the Peyote faith. However, none of the respondents, according to their own admissions, had ever been to a Peyote service. One rather shocking comment came from Superintendent Leech on the Yankton Sioux Reservation. In a cover letter, he wrote that the

"Indians of this reservation who are addicted to the use of Peyote are an indolent, dirty, bloated class, and if anything could be said in favor of its use it would be that it would probably result in the extermination of those who use it."[1] The BIA acquired the material it was looking for, as the answers on the questionnaire conformed to the BIA's view of Peyote and Peyotists.

Upon closer analysis, however, the answers are instructive about the state of Peyotism in 1919. It is clear that Peyote communities were functioning on many reservations, although a number of members still feared interference by authorities as some were holding their services in secret. Nevertheless they held regularly scheduled services attended by men, women, and children. These communities were able to acquire sufficient amounts of Peyote for their needs and received a regular supply by rail, by parcel post, or by individual travel to other reservations or to southern Texas.[2]

Some of this information from the questionnaires appeared in a series of BIA publications, such as the one titled *Concerning Peyote*, which appeared in 1919. It was compiled by Edgar B. Merritt, the assistant commissioner of the BIA, who had been the leading coordinator of the bureau's effort to get Congress to pass anti-Peyote legislation. The pamphlet included information on Peyote that was alarming and misleading, repeating all the arguments that "the devil's root" was evil, addicting, and debilitating.[3] At the same time, Merritt assisted several members of Congress with a new anti-Peyote bill, but like the earlier legislation, the 1919 bill failed. Additional bills were introduced in 1922, 1924, 1926, and 1937. They met the same fate. With each legislative failure, the BIA vigorously renewed its other efforts to suppress Peyote. In 1921, the BIA hoped to have the congressional Indian appropriations and expenditures bill describe Peyote as a drug so funds could be allocated for its suppression. The House of Representatives did so, but the Senate removed the wording on Peyote as Senator Robert Owen of Oklahoma said Congress had never labeled Peyote a "deleterious drug." The BIA still hoped the wording in the bill for the "suppression of traffic in intoxicating liquor and deleterious drugs" could be applied to Peyote.[4]

Throughout 1922, the BIA continued attacking the Peyote faith. In his 1922 annual report, Charles H. Burke, the new commissioner of Indian Affairs and a former congressman from South Dakota, proposed legislation to control what he claimed was the growing and harmful habit among the Indians of using Peyote. He dismissed the idea that Peyotism was a religion, claiming that the Peyote community exploited this argument to prevent Peyote's prohibition.[5]

One may wonder why the BIA went to such lengths to prohibit and eliminate Peyote given that the number of American Indians active in the Native American Church was not very great. According to BIA figures, only 4 percent of American Indians were active Peyotists, yet the bureau expended tremendous energy in trying to stop Peyotism. Even if the 4 percent figure was low, it is hard to imagine why the BIA saw Peyotism as such a threat except their fear that Peyotism, with its integration of American Indian culture and language, might threaten the successful completion of their acculturation programs. The old maxim "kill the Indian, save the man" was threatened by Peyotism. There were, after all, similar campaigns under way to eliminate traditional marriage ceremonies and to ban or limit Indian dancing. Commissioner Burke and other BIA officials were part of the old guard, still determined to implement and enforce assimilation policies that began with the Dawes Act of 1887. This viewpoint was obvious in the bureau's 1922 annual report dealing with "Indian Custom Marriage and Divorce." The commissioner wrote: "I think it not untimely to suggest the need of legislation subjecting all Indians to the laws of civilization respecting their marital relations. . . . The vicious practice of Indian custom marriage and separation is deplorable." Burke referred to "loose marital relations of barbaric origin" and added that a decent family life was needed before there can be "progress toward civilization."[6] A similar argument was applied to certain Indian dances. In 1921 and 1923, Burke issued orders to suppress those dances and to threaten individuals participating in them with fines and jail. This same attitude extended to Peyote, which had to be eliminated because it was retarding "progress." The BIA's actions were supported by considerable lobbying by various nonsectarian and church groups for the suppression of Peyote. Peyote communities felt very threatened by the continuing assault on their faith.

In 1922, Congressman Carl Hayden introduced yet another bill to criminalize Peyote, which ultimately failed. Since legislative and judicial efforts had failed, there were only two options left to the BIA: continue to pressure western states to criminalize Peyote use and rekindle a public relations campaign to stimulate new interest in federal anti-Peyote legislation. Part of this plan was the BIA's distribution in 1922 of a thirty-eight-page pamphlet titled *Peyote*, prepared by Dr. Robert E. L. Newberne, chief medical supervisor of the BIA. The government printed three thousand copies and distributed them to reservation personnel, to libraries, and to anyone who had an interest in legislation to stop the use of Peyote. It was reprinted in 1925, again widely distributed, until it was withdrawn from circulation in 1934 by Commissioner John Collier.[7] The information in the pamphlet came from the BIA's 1919 questionnaire. *Peyote* also included reports and testimonials from medical doctors and missionaries drawn from bureau's "peyote files." It attacked Peyotism in every conceivable way. The harshness of its language and its Social Darwinian ideas seem out of place, even for the 1920s. Every social, moral, economic, and even biological argument was used to discredit Peyote, although it began with a scientific tone giving a botanical description of the plant, describing its geographic distribution, and commenting on its history in Mexico. Various strategies were used to attack Peyote including one that employed a biological imperative argument or a so-called "cell craving" by Indians for stimulants.[8] Other lines of argument claimed that Peyote was a drug, leading to the downfall of its users, and that the idea of Peyotism as a religion was a mockery. This was followed by a series of testimonials from scholars, medical doctors, and missionaries. It reviewed the writings of Spanish and American missionaries who saw Peyotism as "pagan" worship. The language used to attack Peyote was based on a good versus evil paradigm: Christianity versus paganism, the "power of a drug" versus the "elevating influence of the Cross." The pamphlet attacked Peyote communities that were considering incorporation as churches, arguing that these actions were fraudulent, simple ploys to gain First Amendment protection for drug usage. In a mocking tone, Newberne wrote that having a "Peyote Christian Church is as incongruous as it would be to recognize the Opium Christian Church, or the Cocaine Society of Christians." He described Peyotism as "hopeless slavery to a merciless, powerful, habit forming drug." The testimonials that followed were from the missionaries and medical people who supposedly had direct contact with Peyote communities. They were consistent in viewing Peyote as a habit-forming, intoxicating drug with none of the medicinal value proclaimed by Peyotists, except, according to Newberne, that it had the potential to lead to the ultimate healing: "the last sleep from which there is no awakening until the day dawns for the dead to give their testimony in the courts of eternity." Others who were quoted in the pamphlet claimed that instead of having positive, medicinal properties, Peyote had negative effects on the mind, body, and soul, causing heart failure, hemorrhage, brain disturbance, laziness, and inertia.[9]

Another common theme throughout the pamphlet was that Peyote led to sexual promiscuity. Expressions such as "lust of the flesh," "orgies," and "scenes of unbridled libertinism" were typical. One interesting comment from a medical doctor concluded that Peyote "produced imperfect coordination of movement."[10] Not one of the authors said that they had attended a Peyote meeting, where they would have witnessed the coordination of rapid drumming, gourd rattle shaking, and singing. Newberne concluded that Peyote was such an evil that only restrictive legislation would protect American Indians. The BIA's goal, in issuing the pamphlet, was to influence people who had no direct knowledge of the Peyote religion to support anti-Peyote legislation. In 1923, the BIA had a small victory when Congress added to the Indian appropriations bill $25,000 for the "suppression of traffic in intoxicating liquors and deleterious drugs, including peyote." That provision remained in the federal budget until 1934.

The pamphlet *Peyote* nevertheless contained important data. It included the questions from the 1919 circular and summaries of the answers. The written responses reflected and reinforced the BIA's view of Peyote as an unmitigated evil, but the respondents also sent in considerable data on the number of Peyotists and the geographic distribution of the Peyote faith. Table 1 lists agency (an agency is a federal administrative unit that may encompass more than one reservation and several Indian groups), Indian tribes, total population, number "affected by Peyote," and percentage of Peyotists in the Indian population. This data provides a snapshot of the extent of Peyotism in 1920. The majority of agencies reported no Peyotists within their jurisdiction. Table 1 shows the agencies and the percentages of Peyotists reported for them.[11]

Table 2 lists the number of Indians "affected by peyote" by state and the percentage of Indians who were Peyotists within a state. The data shows that in 1920 Peyotists were primarily located from the southern plains to the northern plains and between the Rocky Mountains and the Mississippi River. There are no Peyotists listed for Arizona, California, Nevada, North Dakota, Oregon, and Washington State. The states with the highest percentages of Peyotists, beginning with Nebraska, are listed in table 2 below. The BIA counted 13,345 Peyotists, or about 4 percent of the 316,008 American Indians (344,303 in 1923).[12]

The data from Oklahoma is somewhat misleading, especially as it is the home of the Peyote religion in the United States. The large majority of American Indians in Oklahoma were members of the so-called Five Civilized Tribes, very few of whom were Peyotists. The 7 percent figure for Oklahoma is 8,255 Peyotists out of 116,494 Indians. That figure represents the highest number of Peyotists in any state. In comparison the Omaha Agency lists 90 percent Peyotists, but the actual number is 1,239. Nebraska with 1,652 Peyotists (67 percent of the Indian population) has the second highest number of Peyotists. South Dakota is third with 1,030 Peyotists, and most of them Yankton Sioux, who had the highest number of all Sioux groups. The Peyotist part of population at the Pine Ridge

Table 1
Percentage of Peyotists by Agency

Agencies	Tribes	Percentage of Peyotists
Cantonment	Arapaho, Cheyenne	90 percent
Cheyenne and Arapaho	Cheyenne, Arapaho	75 percent
Grand Rapids or Wisconsin Rapids	Potawatomi, Winnebago	35 percent
Kickapoo	Iowa, Kickapoo, Sac and Fox	40 percent
Kiowa	Many groups	75 percent
Omaha	Omaha	90 percent
Osage	Osage	50 percent
Otoe	Otoe and Missouri	50 percent
Pawnee	Pawnee	20 percent
Ponca	Kaw, Ponca, Tonkawa	60 percent
Sac and Fox, Iowa	Sac and Fox	30 percent
Sac and Fox, Oklahoma	Sac and Fox	30 percent
Seger	Arapaho, Cheyenne	80 percent
Tongue River	Northern Cheyenne	35 percent
Uintah and Ouray	Uinta, Utes	50 percent
Winnebago	Winnebago	38 percent
Yankton	Yankton, Santee Sioux, Ponca	20 percent

Reservation is listed as 5 percent, at Rosebud as .07 percent, and other South Dakota reservations as 0 percent. It is difficult to assess the accuracy of the statistics. There is little corroborating data. There was a tendency of reservation officials to exaggerate the difficult conditions they were working under, and it was in the interest of the Peyote communities not to bring attention to themselves, especially in the early 1920s when Peyotists were still facing harassment and arrest.[13]

In spite of positive developments for Peyote communities, such as successfully incorporating to gain constitutional protection for Peyotism, opposition did not disappear. Harassment continued, mostly in the form of confiscation of Peyote, since the U.S. Postal Service still prohibited its passage through the mails. Nor did the Bureau of Indian Affairs stop its publishing. In 1923, they issued yet another document attacking Peyotism, a thirty-four-page typescript titled *Peyote*, which was sent to reservation officials, church groups, and nonprofit organizations concerned with American Indians. It was similar to other

TABLE 2
Percentage of Peyotists within Each State

State	Percentage of Peyotists
Nebraska	67.0 percent
Utah	34.0 percent
Iowa	30.0 percent
Kansas	27.0 percent
Wyoming	8.0 percent
Oklahoma	7.0 percent
Montana	5.0 percent
Wisconsin	5.0 percent
South Dakota	4.5 percent

BIA publications in its description of Peyote's damaging effects. What was different is that it claimed to offer "scientific proof" that Peyote was harmful. It included seven studies, written by doctors and scientists reporting on laboratory experiments with humans and animals who were given Peyote buttons or synthesized compounds of the chemicals in Peyote. By today's standards, these experiments were unscientific, and they sometimes gave conflicting results. One study claimed Peyote excited the passions; another said it left the user in a stupor. There was an interesting disclaimer in the introduction to these studies concerning firsthand knowledge of Peyote ceremonies. It stated such observation was not possible because the presence of "white investigators" changed the ceremony, that the Peyotists excluded the objectionable features of Peyotism and made it appear to be a religious service when outsiders were present. Whatever the merits of the studies, which were questioned by many scholars even at the time, the pamphlet was another example of the BIA's assault on Peyote. Today's medical studies show that Peyote has no toxicity, is not habit forming, and has no harmful effects.[14]

Throughout the remainder of the 1920s, the BIA sought outside help for its anti-Peyote campaign by quoting "scientific studies" and seeking support and recommendations from nongovernmental groups and individuals. However, despite the bureau's efforts, studies were appearing that did not support the contention that Peyote was harmful. One of these, published in *The American Journal of Psychology* in 1926, stated that Peyote produced mild auditory and visual enhancement, but nothing harmful, and its prohibition was unnecessary. Anthropologist Ruth Shonle, in her influential article on Peyote, claimed

Peyotism was a "pagan ceremony" and spread because it induced visions; however, she did not describe Peyote as harmful or call for its suppression.

The first book-length studies on Peyote also appeared at this time. Alexandre Rouhier, a pharmacologist, in 1927 published the first monograph focusing on the physiological effects of Peyote. The following year, Heinrich Klüver, a psychology professor at Columbia University, published a study focusing on the psychological effects of Peyote. Rouhier argued that Peyote was not habit forming and did not create a physiological dependence as opium, cocaine, heroin, and alcohol did. He also concluded that Peyote had no known pharmacological uses. Klüver analyzed the visual effects of Peyote and concluded that it did affect one's visual perceptions but had a lesser impact on the other senses. For example, in addressing the issue of promiscuity among Peyotists, he said Peyote had no effect, either way, on one's sexuality. Both studies analyzed the chemical substances in Peyote but did not place it in its total cultural context of a religious service. Most important, and the reason why these works affected the debate on Peyote, is that they did not claim that Peyote was harmful, nor did they call for its suppression. Studies such as these were weakening the BIA's case for anti-Peyote legislation.[15]

Another example of a changing perspective inadvertently came from the Department of the Interior. In 1923 the new secretary of the Interior, Hubert W. Work, appointed an Advisory Council on Indian Affairs, commonly known as the Committee of One Hundred. It was a blue-ribbon panel of one hundred men and women that included scholars, politicians, missionaries, and other prominent Americans. The committee members included the perennial presidential candidate William Jennings Bryan; General John J. Pershing; historian William Allen White; John Collier, future commissioner of the BIA; G. E. E. Lindquist of the Protestant Home Missions Council; and nine anthropologists, including Alfred L. Kroeber, a well-known scholar of American Indian cultures. Several prominent American Indians, such as Charles Eastman and Arthur C. Parker, were also committee members. The committee's charge was to study federal Indian policy and make recommendations. The members submitted a series of resolutions, including one on Peyote. They recommended that the National Research Council of Washington, D.C., undertake a study on the "effects of peyote" and only if that study found Peyote harmful should legislation be recommended "to prohibit its use, sale, and possession." This was a blow to the BIA, who all along operated on the assumption that Peyote was dangerous. Now a high-level advisory group questioned that assumption. Six months later, the secretary of the Interior wrote in his report on the Committee of One Hundred that neither the National Research Council nor the Department of the Interior had the funds to undertake such a study. Thus the recommendation came to naught, which contributed to the slow reevaluation of Peyote.[16]

By the mid-1920s, the BIA seemed to be paying less attention to Peyote, but only because there were so many other problems with federal Indian policy. Even the $25,000 allocated for the suppression of liquor and Peyote was spent on restraining bootleggers from selling alcohol to Indians. On the reservations, health, housing, and land issues were paramount. Living conditions and nutrition were poor, and the overall economic outlook was grim; they would worsen during the Depression. There was a health care crisis. Tuberculosis, trachoma, influenza, and childhood diseases and illness were rife. American Indians were still wards of the state, not withstanding the granting of U.S. citizenship in 1924. Citizenship status changed very little as voting rights were left up to the states. Five states required a voter to be "civilized" to vote; six others required a voter to be a taxpayer; three states did not allow residents of reservations to vote. A Jim Crow–style system in many western states restricted the rights of American Indians. Full voting rights were decades away.

The BIA continued to hope Congress would respond to its pleas about restricting Peyote even with a slow turning of the tide concerning the harmfulness of Peyote. Superintendents in the field were still encouraged to suppress or at least discourage Peyote use. The bureau also tried, once again, in 1924 and 1926, to introduce anti-Peyote legislation in Congress, but to no avail.

During Commissioner Burke's last years, he continued to pursue assimilation policies, but now with less governmental and nongovernmental support. In 1926 he attempted, unsuccessfully, to have a bill introduced again in Congress to outlaw traditional American Indian dances and wedding ceremonies. The BIA continued to distribute anti-Peyote literature. They were able to have Peyote listed, for the first time, as a narcotic in the Narcotic Addict Farm Act, but this did not have any noticeable effect on the acquisition and transporting of Peyote. Burke, however, was besieged with demands from inside and outside of the government to investigate and reform federal Indian policy. The BIA's advisory Board of Indian Commissioners encouraged a study of reservation living conditions. The board, established in 1869, comprised a group of prominent private citizens, who advised the Department of the Interior on Indian policy. Board members had always been a powerful voice supporting assimilation policies. Since 1912 they had been part of the anti-Peyote campaign and supported its suppression. Now in the mid-1920s they were calling for an investigation into conditions on the reservations. Congress authorized a similar investigation. Outside groups such as the Indian Rights Association and American Indian Defense Association, led by John Collier, called for investigations. In 1926 the Board of Indian Commissions recommended that the BIA employ the private Institute for Government Research (Brookings Institution) of Washington, D.C., to conduct a broad analysis of federal Indian policy and make recommendations. Lewis Meriam led the investigation team. After two years' work, the report was completed and submitted to the secretary of the Department of the Interior. It became known as the Meriam Report.

The data that was collected, much of it based on fieldwork, became the basis for its conclusion that federal Indian policy was in chaos and in need of drastic reform. The report laid the groundwork for the reforms of the next decade. The investigators did not spend much time on Peyote. They wrote that the "Peyote Church" was flourishing and that there was no evidence that Peyote was habit forming, even though `another part of the report referred to "peyote addiction." Most important, the Meriam study did not call for the suppression of Peyote.[17]

In this changing atmosphere, the Peyote faith had a lower priority at the BIA. With the recent criticisms of federal Indian policy and the election of Herbert Hoover as president, reform was in the air. Hoover appointed new leadership to the BIA. Charles J. Rhoads, former president of the Indian Rights Association, was appointed commissioner of Indian Affairs. He initiated a change of direction in certain areas but did not waver from the ultimate goal of assimilation. In his first Annual Report, he stated that his goal, though very difficult, was for the American Indian to develop into a "white citizen." He added, however, breaking from the viewpoints of his predecessors, that in the process "what is best in his traditions, arts, [and] crafts" should not be destroyed. There was no mention of Peyote throughout the annual report except that pamphlets on Peyote were still available.[18] During the four years of Hoover and Rhoads there was a transition in federal Indian policy. There were some changes based on the Meriam Report, such as increased funding for food, clothing, health care, and education on the reservations, but major structural changes did not occur. Federal policy was still geared toward turning American Indians into "white citizens." As the BIA eased its frontal assault on the Peyote faith, there were fears among the Peyotists that state governments would attempt to suppress Peyote.

STATE GOVERNMENTS

State governments became involved in the anti-Peyote movement for the same reasons as the Department of the Interior and the BIA. State legislators held similarly negative views of American Indian cultures and supported the assimilation policies, especially the policy of allotment that turned some reservation land into profitable private property as destitute Indian families sold their land to non-Indians. States were also under pressure from the BIA, missionary groups, prohibition organizations, and private groups such as the Indian Rights Association to pass legislation making the possession, sale, and transportation of Peyote illegal. As Congress had failed to pass an anti-Peyote bill, and since most courts would not prosecute Peyotists, the BIA turned to state legislatures to advance its goals. Many western states had less concern than Congress about violating the constitutional right to the free exercise of religion.

In the heat of the 1916 and 1917 anti-Peyote hearings in Congress, three states, Colorado, Nevada, and Utah, with small, but growing Peyote communities, made the possession of Peyote illegal. Kansas followed in 1920. The state legislatures were aware of the arguments against Peyote and given their predilections about American Indians, sided with the anti-Peyote forces. At the local level, the legislatures were lobbied quite heavily by groups that supported federal assimilation policies. In the late teens and early 1920s, there were very few voices calling for First Amendment protection for the Peyote faith. In spite of state laws, however, very few Peyotists were prosecuted successfully. States had no jurisdiction on reservations. In addition some prosecutors may have recognized that since Congress did not pass an anti-Peyote bill, state laws might be unconstitutional under the First Amendment. The uncertainty of the laws was reflected in the fact that while state legislators were prohibiting Peyote, state governments were issuing incorporation charters to Peyote groups, which ostensibly gave them legal protection.

Colorado was the first state to pass restrictive legislation. There were some Peyotists among the Southern Utes, although the BIA reported in 1916 that there were no Peyotists in Colorado. The law, passed in February 1917, prohibited the use of Peyote in the state. This did not affect reservation land, but it prohibited the shipping of Peyote and possible arrest of Peyotists who had Peyote in their possession off the reservation. The campaign in Colorado began in the midst of the 1916 Peyote hearings in Washington. In January 1917, Gertrude Bonnin went to Denver to lobby for an anti-Peyote bill. She gave a series of lectures, distributed anti-Peyote literature, and met with a number of women's organizations, such as the Women's Christian Temperance Union, the National Congress of Mothers and Parent-Teacher Associations. She was a strong proponent of the Colorado anti-Peyote bill.[19]

Back in Utah, Mrs. Bonnin continued her lobbying. The reservation superintendent, Albert H. Kneale, reported to the BIA that 50 percent of the Northern Utes were practicing Peyotists. Bonnin was in close association with the local Catholic, Protestant, and Mormon missionaries. Federal officials, the superintendent, Bonnin, and the missionaries were determined to stop Peyotism. Bonnin wrote to S. M. Brosius of the Indian Rights Association about the evils of Peyote. He published an article, *"The Ravages of Peyote,"* which included Bonnin's writings. She claimed, in an unverified statement, that twenty-five Utes had died from Peyote. The article and other anti-Peyote writings were sent to Colorado and Utah legislators. Gertrude Bonnin seemed to be a voice of authority. She was an American Indian and had worked among the Utes for many years. Superintendent Kneale gave all the anti-Peyote material to Utah state senator Dan Colton, who in turn gave it to the governor and the state pharmacist, who recommended Peyote be added to state's list of prohibited narcotics. The state legislature passed the bill in February 1917. In the same month, Nevada followed suit. Peyote was added to a state statute on the sale and use of poison and was prohibited except by prescription.[20]

In 1923, Arizona, Montana, North Dakota, and South Dakota banned Peyote. South Dakota was a typical example. The leader of the South Dakota effort was Representative Harvey L. Gandy, already known to Peyotists as the author of the anti-Peyote Gandy bill, which had been introduced into the U.S. House of Representatives. With the failure of this bill, Gandy turned his attention to his home state. He had a very experienced and capable ally: Gertrude Bonnin, who was back home on the Yankton Sioux Reservation continuing her lifelong crusade to abolish Peyotism. The activities of Bonnin and her husband, Raymond, who had lobbied legislators in other states, disturbed local Peyote communities. In 1921, her notoriety increased with the publication of her second book, *American Indian Stories,* under her Dakota name Zitkala-Ša (Red Bird). It was a collection of autobiographical stories that had appeared twenty years earlier in *Harper's Magazine* and the *Atlantic Monthly.*[21] Because of her years living and lobbying in the nation's capital, her position as secretary of the Society of American Indians (until 1919), and her position as the editor of its publication *American Indian Magazine,* she had a platform from which to expound her views. She used the journal to campaign against Peyote. In one issue, she claimed that Peyotists were nothing more than drug dealers. With the publication of her book, her ability to publicize her views on Peyote through the media was significant. She became an investigator for the Indian Welfare Committee, a branch of the General Federation of Women's Clubs. On their behalf, she traveled and spoke to women's groups, urging them to support anti-Peyote legislation as they had supported the prohibition of alcohol. In South Dakota, Bonnin and Gandy orchestrated the process of criminalizing the possession of Peyote. In January 1923, legislation was introduced in the South Dakota House and Senate "to prohibit the traffic in and the possession of Peyote." During the debate on the bill, Bonnin brought in twenty anti-Peyote Sioux to testify for its passage. No one testified against the bill. It was sent to the Committee on Food and Drugs; they recommended passage. The bill was then amended with the addition of penalties. The maximum punishment was a $500 fine and/or one year in jail. It was no surprise that the bill passed easily: forty-one to one in the House, ninety-seven to zero in the Senate. Possession of Peyote was now a criminal offense. However, in cases in which Peyotists were arrested, the charges were usually dropped or reversed on appeal. Buell Jones, the attorney general of South Dakota, tried a unique approach. He asked the South Dakota secretary of state to void the articles of incorporation of the various Native American Churches and not issue any new ones as their purpose was to engage in an activity that was now illegal. This line of reasoning found no support.[22] State authorities could not interfere on reservations, but they could arrest or harass people for transporting Peyote and in that process could confiscate Peyote.

Gertrude Bonnin's influence with state legislatures was significant as she proved in Colorado and Utah. In 1926, the Bonnins founded the National Council of American Indians (NCAI). This gave them another platform on which to expound their views of Peyote. They made very little headway in convincing federal officials to revisit the Peyote issue but had some success in lobbying state officials. By the time Gertrude Bonnin died in 1938, thirteen states (not including Oklahoma, which repealed its anti-Peyote legislation in 1909) had outlawed Peyote. In discussing these state laws, Omer Stewart wrote, "I am ready to give Mrs. Bonnin the major credit."[23]

After four states outlawed Peyote in 1923, Iowa followed suit in 1924, New Mexico and Wyoming in 1929, Idaho in 1935, Texas in 1937, California in 1959, and New York in 1965. Legislation to outlaw Peyote was introduced in

Oklahoma in 1927, but it was voted down. In Utah, anti-Peyote legislation was declared unconstitutional and repealed in 1935. Several states, such as Idaho and Iowa, amended their laws to allow the religious use of Peyote. The trend toward states' amending anti-Peyote legislation by making exemptions for the NAC continued into the 1950s and 1960s, although Peyotists were still arrested in various places. As a result, they did not believe that they had the full protection of their constitutional right to the free exercise of their religion. State restrictions on Peyote did have one significant effect: it convinced Peyote communities to incorporate.[24]

NONGOVERNMENTAL ASSAULTS ON PEYOTISM

Church groups and nonsectarian philanthropic organizations opposed the Peyote faith since its origins. These groups supported the federal government's assimilation policies that were designed to weaken American Indian cultures and replace them with the Anglo-American value system, such as replacing communal traditions with American-style individualism. These groups considered themselves "friends of the Indian."

Sectarian Assaults

With the establishment of the reservation system, Christian churches sent missionaries to work among Indian people. Their goal was to convert Indians to their particular denomination. Based on the belief that "civilizing" and "Christianizing" went hand in hand, the missionaries were allies of the BIA from the 1870s to the early 1930s. Notwithstanding the separation of church and state, there was close cooperation, if not partnership, between missionary groups and the BIA. Federal government support for missionary enterprises included the allocation of reservation land for churches, rectories, schools, and cemeteries. Fiscal subsidies were also provided to missionary groups from federal Indian trust funds and missionary schools on federal land were allowed to conduct religious education. Charles Burke, commissioner of Indian Affairs (1921–29), issued an order requiring school children in government boarding schools to attend Sunday school and church services. In return, church groups lobbied for federal policies supported by the BIA. It was a symbiotic relationship. The goal was to replace the Peyote Road with what missionaries described as the "Jesus Road." On most reservations, missionaries had a significant voice in determining local practices. They were active in both sectarian and federal schools; they provided relief services in difficult times; they had direct contact, and sometimes influence, with local BIA officials. They supported the policies to eliminate certain traditional dances, religious ceremonies, clothing, and hairstyles as well as traditional American Indian marriage and divorce. The one policy that enjoyed universal support from church groups was the BIA's campaign to suppress the Peyote faith. Even after the failure of the anti-Peyote legislation, church groups did not lessen their efforts. As others began to modify their views on Peyote in the mid-1920s, the missionary community continued its crusade.

The cooperation between the BIA and missionaries was openly acknowledged by federal officials. Commissioner Burke wrote the foreword to a very influential book by Reverend G. E. E. Lindquist, one of the leading anti-Peyote crusaders. Burke welcomed the cooperation of the churches in supporting assimilation policies. He praised their work in helping to reconstruct the "Red Race."[25] Hubert Work, secretary of the Interior (1923–29), made similar comments in an official government document. He said the "Christian missionary was the pioneer of civilization among the Indians . . . more than 600 missionaries of all denominations are now actively cooperating with Government activities."[26] Reverend Lindquist was one of the most prominent Protestant church leaders of the anti-Peyote crusade. He served as field secretary for the Home Missions Council of the Federal Council of Churches and as missionary-at-large for the Society for the Propagation of the Gospel among Indians. In these capacities he was able to travel and speak throughout the nation for many years. In 1923, Lindquist published *The Red Man in the United States*. It brought him fame and a platform to express his views. The book was a classic "Save the Indian" statement, by which he meant the destruction of American Indian cultures and the imposition of Anglo-American values. He claimed in classic social Darwinian mode that weaknesses in the Indian were the result of "certain racial traits." He argued that the traditional "medicine man" was the old enemy; the new enemy was the "insidious cult of peyote (the Indian's cocaine)." Lindquist devoted a section of his book to the "drug mania." He referred to Peyotists as evil, facing death, and worshipping "false gods." He claimed Peyotism was spreading at an alarming rate and was responsible for 100 percent of the cases of insanity on one reservation. He called for prompt and united action to stop the so-called menace.[27]

Although Lindquist was very influential, he was just one part of the missionary crusade. Many other groups, including Baptists, Catholics, Episcopalians,

Methodists, and Presbyterians, were determined to eliminate traditional American Indian religions, including the Peyote faith. By the late 1920s, and especially in the 1930s, the missionaries, though not a threat to the existence of the NAC, were a severe irritant and a potential threat to the church's growth. One strategy the missionaries used was to paint Peyote people with a negative brush to make them appear evil. Peyotists were called lazy and irresponsible. It was said that they were drug users in league with the devil. They were called derogatory names such as "peyote eaters." The missionaries hoped to deter others from joining the Peyote faith by turning the Peyote community into outcasts. Or to put it another way, they hoped to marginalize a group of people already within a marginalized group. Missionaries also used highly acculturated Christian Indians to speak out against the Peyote faith and to discourage others from socializing with Peyotists or participating in Peyote services. Christian Indians were also useful as "Indian voices" to help convince non-Indians, particularly legislators, to support anti-Peyote campaigns. On occasion missionaries were able to get reservation Christians to write letters. For example in 1916, ninety-two Yankton Sioux sent a petition to Congress urging legislators to support the anti-Peyote bill sponsored by Representative Gandy. The close cooperation between church and state in regard to federal Indian policy ended in the 1930s as the BIA under John Collier revised the bureau's assimilation policies and openly supported cultural autonomy and religious freedom. The church groups continued to oppose the Peyote faith, but now attacked the BIA and Collier for the new policies. Lindquist believed Collier's policies would destroy Indian "progress" and threaten the Christianization process.

The missionaries continued to disseminate publications that carried negative information on Peyote. *The Catholic Sioux Herald* often disparaged Peyotists. In 1940, under its new name, *The Catholic Indian Herald*, the newspaper put out a special issue devoted to attacking Peyote. The paper used inflammatory language, describing Peyotism as a "cancerous growth" that caused insanity and death and Peyotists as "sexually immoral." The paper described the incorporated Native American Church as a mask for drug use and profits for drug dealers. This type of assault was common in the 1920s, but by 1940 had become an anomaly.[28]

Collier and the new BIA policies helped create unity among missionary groups. Collier was the common enemy. They claimed his policies not only slowed their work but also threatened a return to "tribalism" and "paganism."

They lobbied against the new policies of religious freedom and cultural autonomy. Collier was not the sole enemy; many missionaries also opposed President Franklin Roosevelt and most of the New Deal programs. The missionaries felt they were being marginalized, and it is true that missionary influence was waning. Their allies in the Prohibition movement had virtually disappeared with the ending of Prohibition (1933). In addition, the separation of church and state in federal Indian policy was becoming a reality.

Nonsectarian Assaults

Since the implementation of assimilation policies by the BIA in the 1880s and 1890s, various nonsectarian organizations had worked to support these policies. In the second decade of the twentieth century, groups such as the Indian Rights Association, the National Indian Association, the Society of American Indians, the YMCA, the Lake Mohonk Conference, the Women's National Indian Association, the two-million-member General Federation of Women's Clubs, and various prohibition organizations lobbied federal and state governments for the suppression of Peyote. Most of the above groups were active in supporting the congressional anti-Peyote legislation of 1916, 1917, and 1918. After the failure of these bills, most of these organizations turned to state legislators to pass restrictive legislation. In this arena they had some success.

The Indian Rights Association (IRA) was the most active of these groups. The IRA issued a continuous stream of anti-Peyote literature. Its president, the influential Herbert Welsh, lobbied throughout the country. In 1919 IRA members supported another anti-Peyote bill in Congress. Their arguments remained the same: Peyote led to sexual immorality; it retarded progress toward "civilization"; and with the enactment of the Eighteenth Amendment prohibiting alcohol, they argued that Peyote was being used as a substitute for alcohol. When questions arose in the mid-1920s about the true effects of Peyote, the IRA lost interest in opposing it although they continued supporting other assimilationist policies. The Society of American Indians continued its attack on Peyote, but with less intensity as the organization was torn by internal dissention, particularly after the 1920 election of Thomas L. Sloan (Omaha) as president. He supported the Peyote faith and the recently incorporated Native American Church. The organization ceased publishing *American Indian Magazine,* and Gertrude Bonnin and her husband resigned. Mrs. Bonnin continued to travel widely, speaking to many groups, and to lobby state governments to prohibit the possession and use of Peyote.[29]

There were other assimilationist groups such as the newly formed (1922) American Indian Association with its slogan "Americanizing the Original Americans." Mrs. Bonnin, however, was the major force in the anti-Peyote activities in the 1920s. In 1925, she joined with John Collier of the American Indian Defense Association in publicizing poor conditions on reservations and calling for reform. She and Collier had many views in common, but religious freedom for the Peyote community was not one of them. In 1926, the Bonnins founded the National Council of American Indians (NCAI), with offices in Washington, D.C. She was president of the NCAI until her death in 1938. She used her organization not only to try to develop an Indian voting bloc but also to encourage state and federal officials to suppress the Peyote faith. In her capacity as president she lectured on Peyote and encouraged local people to organize and lobby their elected officials. The NCAI did not attract many members, or much public support, but Bonnin was nevertheless determined to continue her activism. Using elegant-looking NCAI letterhead, she began a letter-writing campaign to publicize her views. As president of an American Indian organization, she had the notoriety and a platform from which to speak out.[30]

Mrs. Bonnin continued her intense opposition into the 1930s, when most groups, except for the missionaries, no longer attention paid much attention to the Peyote faith. In 1932, she wrote to a U.S. senator to try to revive federal legislation by stating her continued opposition to Peyote. She claimed it was a money-making scheme by certain individuals and that the use of the Bible in some Peyote services was to perpetuate the subterfuge. She believed Peyote damaged the mind and affected learning. The new scientific evidence to the contrary did not change her opinion in the least. Her greatest influence was with state legislators as she mobilized public opinion, but with changing federal Indian policies her influence declined in her later years. She was a complex person who struggled against the injustices toward American Indians but would not support First Amendment rights for the NAC. She was a committed activist for Indian rights but an uncompromising opponent of Peyotism.[31]

THE DEFENSE OF PEYOTE

As Peyotism expanded throughout the West in the early decades of the twentieth century, the opposition grew. It came from the executive branch of the federal government, from state governments, and from many Christian groups. Opposition also came from a significant number of acculturated American Indians who considered themselves devout Christians and saw the Peyote faith as hindering their progress toward "civilization." Many of these groups formed alliances to eradicate Peyotism. The response to this opposition took several forms. Secrecy was one strategy. Peyote meetings were held in private homes, and Peyotists publicly downplayed the expansion and significance of their faith. This was not a practical or effective strategy as secrecy was difficult to maintain. Another strategy was to focus on the Christian elements that were in the Cross Fire ceremony. Or, if Christian elements were absent from Peyote meetings to add several to the service. Peyotists hoped that by incorporating some Christian elements into the service, such as the use of the Bible, opposition would subside. They developed theological interpretations to parallel Christian theology; they also gave Peyote ritual paraphernalia a Christian interpretation. For example, Peyotists used biblical passages to justify using Peyote as a sacrament; and they compared the ingestion of Peyote as the body of God to the Christian communion of bread and wine as the flesh and blood of Jesus Christ. There were claims that the fire in the center of a Peyote service represented God in the Old Testament saying "let there be light." Blowing the eagle-bone whistle to the four directions became symbolic of announcing the birth of Jesus. The fireman shaped the ashes into a heart or cross to symbolize Jesus. Or one could claim the Peyote Road represented Jesus' road. A Peyote fan with seven feathers was said to represent the Old Testament's seven days of creation, or a twelve-feather fan represented the New Testament's twelve apostles. Whether some of these were contrivances to mute opposition, or whether they were sincerely held beliefs, it made no difference; they had little impact on the opposition to Peyote. There was another option to counter the opposition to Peyotism: seek constitutional protection, particularly the free exercise of religion clause of the First Amendment.

As described in chapter 1, the Oklahoma Peyote community incorporated in 1918, adopting the name Native American Church. The name is significant in that it implies indigenous roots for the Peyote faith. Their charter states: "this corporation is formed to foster and promote the religious belief of the several tribes of Indians in the State of Oklahoma, in the Christian religion with the practice of the Peyote Sacrament." By claiming they were a Christian religion and choosing the word church as part of their official name, they hoped to convince Congress that they deserved First Amendment protection. The use of state-issued charters and incorporation was an effective defensive strategy with nationwide implications. Incorporation in one state was recognized by other states, unless specifically outlawed by a state. The wording of the charters was significant for what they said or did not say. They focused on the elements of Peyotism that were most compatible with Anglo-Christian values. In most charters the term *Christian religion* was common; the word "Peyote" was usually not used. For example, the Oklahoma charter mentioned Peyote, but almost all the other charters written in the 1920s made no mention of it. In 1914 Jonathan Koshiway named his Peyote group the First Born Church of Christ, an obvious biblical reference. The description of its purpose was clearly Christian; Peyote was not mentioned. Koshiway later told two anthropologists that he sought advice from a lawyer on how to gain legal protection for his church.[32]

There was an interesting parallel development mentioned above. As state legislatures were criminalizing the possession of Peyote, Peyote communities were acquiring charters through the offices of secretaries of state. By the end of the 1920s, at least thirteen Peyote groups had incorporated: two in Oklahoma and Nebraska; one each in North Dakota, Montana, Colorado and Idaho; and five in South Dakota. Following Oklahoma, Winnebago Peyotists in Nebraska incorporated in 1921 with the name Peyote Church of Christ. They used a significant Christian reference in their name, but they also referred to Peyote. The charter said they believed in sacramental bread and wine, but since the latter was prohibited to Indians, they adopted Peyote. After some internal debate, they changed their name the following year to Native American Church of Winnebago, Nebraska, following the Oklahoma model. Their neighbors, the Omahas, also incorporated, as the Omaha Peyote Historical Society. Nebraska did not have an anti-Peyote law. Omaha and Winnebago Peyotists have always been active in the defense of their faith and lobbied extensively in Nebraska to protect it.[33]

In South Dakota, Peyotists from the Pine Ridge Reservation took the lead. They perceived a very real threat as the state legislature was debating restrictive legislation. In October 1922, the Peyote leadership filed incorporation papers under the name Native American Church of Allen [County]. However, they amended their charter in 1924 under the new name Native American Church of South Dakota. They did not mention Peyote in their articles of incorporation, but made it clear that they were a "Christian" organization. This was not a theological issue; it was a pragmatic response to a threatening situation. Through the 1920s none of the South Dakota groups mentioned Peyote in their official documents. One can only guess at the debate over the wording in the charters and bylaws. One view was that Peyote, as a gift of God and the central sacramental element, should be included in the wording as demonstrated by the Oklahoma Peyotists who referred to themselves as a "Christian religion with the practice of Peyote sacrament." An alternative view was that the purpose of incorporation was constitutional protection and the muting of opposition, and thus Peyote should not be mentioned. The pragmatic viewpoint won out as the trend toward incorporation continued; however, Peyote was added to the charters by the mid-1930s.

The question that emerges is whether these Christian elements were a strategy to acquire protection and mute opposition or a sincere reflection of the Christian beliefs of the members within the context of the Peyote religion. This is a difficult question to answer; most likely both motives were operative. Certainly incorporation was to gain First Amendment protection, yet there is no evidence to claim that the inclusion of Christian elements was hypocritical. If one attends a Cross Fire meeting today, or reads earlier accounts, one would not question the sincerity of the commitment to Peyote, the Bible, and Jesus Christ. Reviewing all the evidence, as sparse as it is, there is no reason to doubt either motive. The articles of incorporation, their language, their integration of Christian elements were to seek constitutional protection as well as to express a spirituality based on Peyote and the Bible, but all proclaimed the primacy of Peyote.

The writing of articles of incorporation was a significant development for the Peyote faith, not only as a legal defense, but as a process to develop a national organization. Peyote communities developed closer ties as communication was essential in preparing for incorporation. The charters and the church structures they outlined resembled each other as most were based on the 1918 Oklahoma charter. They were now "official" organizations with the structure of nonprofit corporations. Bylaws were written, officers elected, committees established, dues collected, resolutions passed, and minutes taken. Business meetings were held on a regular basis and were run by Robert's Rules of Order. An organizational framework was developing from the ground up, based on local and state charters, ultimately becoming national and international. As the Peyote community was organizing to defend itself, a "new era" was emerging in the nation's capital.

REVERSING COURSE: COMMISSIONER JOHN COLLIER, 1930S

The election of Franklin D. Roosevelt to the presidency in 1932 initiated a new era for American Indians. The president appointed Harold Ickes as secretary of the Interior and John Collier as the new commissioner of Indian Affairs. Together they would reverse a half century of federal Indian policy. Collier had been advocating reform for a decade. He wanted to replace the assimilationist model with a program he called *cultural pluralism*—a term in common usage today. His program, dubbed the "Indian New Deal," included securing the reservation land base, promoting economic growth, developing limited self-government, supporting cultural autonomy by funding the study of American Indian languages and the arts, and protecting religious freedom. Collier was a dynamic and controversial figure. He faced opposition from both ends of the political spectrum. He had opposition from land developers and missionaries and those who still advocated the assimilation of American Indians. He was also criticized by those who advocated the abolition of the BIA and who condemned the idea that Collier or any other federal official knew what was best for the American Indian.

From the perspective of the NAC, Collier's appointment was welcomed as he supported First Amendment protection. In January 1934, he issued Circular #2970, which was sent to all reservation officials, ordering them to end interference with religious and cultural activities. Collier wrote: "No interference with Indian religious life or ceremonial expression will hereafter be tolerated." After this pronouncement, NAC articles of incorporation that were written or amended included references to the sacramental use of Peyote. With these changes in federal policy, the Oklahoma Peyotists revisited their charter. They had functioned as the informal leaders of the nationwide Peyote community and wanted to make their roles more formal. They also concluded that a national organization would be the best defense of their faith. In 1934, they amended their charter to make it possible for groups outside of Oklahoma to legally affiliate with them as part of their Central Council. In the amended version they proclaimed, as in the original 1918 charter, Peyote as a sacrament, but they added that Peyote was a teacher that embodied an ethical system based on "morality, sobriety, kindness and brotherly love for all mankind." There was no mention of Christianity as there had been in the 1918 charter. They also added a reference about "our relationship to our forefathers," reinforcing the indigenous roots of Peyotism.[34] This marked the beginning of a national organization with openly expressed spiritual beliefs.

This did not mean that all opposition suddenly disappeared. Aside from opposition by some state and local officials, there were two sources of internal opposition to Peyotism on the reservations. Some members of the oldest generation remembered, valued, and still secretly practiced the spiritual traditions of their parents and grandparents and opposed Peyotism. To some of them, Peyotism was new, not part of their specific ethnic heritage. This group included some traditional spiritual leaders. The other group in opposition to the Native American Church was the younger generation, sometimes products of Indian/white marriages or relationships, whose members had been to boarding school, belonged to a Christian denomination, spoke mostly English, had an acculturated lifestyle, and were active in local tribal politics. They saw Peyote as a step backward that hindered "progress" in the contemporary world. The internal opposition was in some cases expressed by tribal councils that put restrictions on Peyote.

There were two situations that illustrate this opposition: the Siçangu Lakota, Rosebud Reservation, South Dakota, and the Taos Pueblo of New Mexico. In 1937, the tribal council in Rosebud passed a resolution requesting that the state attorney general cancel the charter of the local Peyote community. Council members argued that Peyote was illegal in South Dakota and should also be illegal on the reservation. They also passed an ordinance requiring Peyote Roadmen and traditional healers to apply for a license and pay a five-dollar annual fee. This was not applicable to Christians. The action of the Rosebud tribal council was a cause for alarm, especially since BIA policy supported religious freedom. Jim Blue Bird, an official of the South Dakota NAC, wrote to Harold Ickes, secretary of the Interior. Blue Bird wanted to know why the tribal council was allowed to do this since religious practices now had constitutional protection. He asked, "[I]s it just because we are aborigines that we are not entitled to First Amendment protection?"[35]

The situation in New Mexico was more complex. The leadership of the Taos Pueblo was concerned with the growth of Peyotism. In the 1920s, Peyote use was noted on the reservation. The Taos Pueblo group was the only Pueblo group to have an organized Peyote community. The members faced opposition from traditional leaders and the Catholic Church. The tribal council tried to block the use of Peyote on the reservation, arguing that New Mexico had declared the possession of Peyote illegal. Local Peyotists appealed to the NAC in Oklahoma for help. They in turn asked Commissioner Collier to intercede and protect their First Amendment rights. In 1936, the Taos tribal police arrested fifteen Peyotists. They were fined $100 each, and when they could not pay, several were jailed and others forced to cede some of their land. Both Ickes and Collier intervened in the case, leading to a compromise in 1937. The tribal council claimed it still opposed Peyotism, but it stopped making arrests and returned the confiscated land while the Peyotists quietly continued to have religious services. Out of this fiasco emerged another attempt by several U.S. senators to reintroduce legislation in Congress that would prohibit the interstate transportation of Peyote.[36]

New Mexico senator Dennis Chavez, an opponent of the Peyote faith, was upset by the turn of events with the Taos. He called for hearings on Peyote. During the hearings witnesses from each side testified, but most of the material submitted came from the 1918 congressional hearings, which included all exaggerated claims about the evils of Peyote. This time things were different. Whereas the BIA supported the prohibition of Peyote during the earlier hearings, the bureau now opposed Senator Chavez's bill to restrict Peyote. The bill died a quiet death.[37] Collier followed this success by getting the Department of Agriculture to rescind its prohibition on the importation of Peyote, and in 1940 he had the U.S. Postal Service lift its ban on shipping Peyote through the mail.

There was another significant turn of events related to the Taos Pueblo and the Chavez bill. Commissioner Collier brought in group of young anthropologists to testify in favor of the Peyote faith. The group included Weston La Barre, Richard E. Schultes, Vincenzo Petrullo, and Omer Stewart. La Barre and Schultes both had done fieldwork with the Kiowas. La Barre had just finished a PhD dissertation on Peyote; Schultes, from Harvard, had become one of the world's most renowned botanists; Petrullo in 1934 published the first book on Peyote in the United States; and Stewart, studying Peyote groups at the time, spent most of his life defending the Peyote faith. All four young men were active scholars doing fieldwork with Peyote communities, including participating in Peyote services. Petrullo, who conducted fieldwork among the Delawares of Oklahoma, testified against the Chavez bill and went on to write about Peyote for *Indians at Work*, a BIA publication. He downplayed the chemical or physiological effects of Peyote and claimed that its real value was its role as a teacher, unifier, and purifier. He believed American Indians could reestablish harmony with God by traveling the Peyote Road, not just as religion, but as a way of life.[38] These individuals not only testified in support of the Peyote faith but also played a role in convincing the public that Peyote was not dangerous. Schultes, for example, wrote such articles for popular magazines. He also provided valuable aid to the NAC and Commissioner Collier by offering to help defeat the Chavez bill and support the sacramental use of Peyote. In addition to his fieldwork with the Kiowas, he also spent time with the Kickapoos, Wichitas, and Quapaws. He attended Peyote meetings and participated in the sacramental ingestion of Peyote. He then spent one and a half years reviewing the literature on Peyote. He claimed no investigator found evidence suggesting that Peyote was habit forming. He also read the missionary literature and concluded that it was written by uninformed or deliberately malicious individuals.[39] For the next fifty years, Schultes defended the Peyote faith. Omer Stewart followed a similar path. He went on to defend Peyotism in the courtroom, in public forums, in scholarly works, in magazines, and in newspapers.

In spite of state laws and restrictions on some reservations, Peyotism continued to grow, and as long as proper procedures were followed, states could not deny Peyotists the right to incorporate. During the Collier years, with new BIA policies along with the persistence of the Peyote community, attitudes slowly changed. Federal opposition to Peyote had declined and many of the groups opposed to Peyote became neutral or indifferent. Close cooperation among Peyote communities became the norm as they clearly shared a common purpose: to defend their right to practice their faith according to their beliefs.

CHAPTER FOUR

The Expansion of Peyotism

In 1955, the Native American Church of the United States, which had incorporated in 1944, reincorporated as the Native American Church of North America. This meant that Canadian Peyotists could now freely affiliate with their American counterparts in the new international organization. The church, and the Peyote faith, had come a long way since incorporation at the state level in Oklahoma in 1918; it was now an international organization, spanning two countries, as well as a national one covering two dozen states. From an organizational perspective, this was an exceptional development. After 1955, the church operated on multiple levels: international, national, state, county, and local. Not all Peyotists belonged to the larger bodies, but the majority did. This put the church in a stronger position to lobby federal and state officials and to enter court cases in which Peyotists had been arrested under various state laws. As a large organization, with legal assistance, more available funds, and public outreach, the NAC could defend its right to practice its faith within the framework of the First Amendment to the U.S. Constitution.

EXPANSION: NORTHERN PLAINS, GREAT BASIN

From the mid-1920s to the 1950s Peyotism expanded rapidly throughout the western part of the United States. Many factors, such as the increasing ease of travel and communication, contributed to this growth. The West was being crisscrossed by roads, highways, and railroads. This allowed for more contact between Peyote communities and reinforcement of personal friendships. There was considerable cooperation between communities, especially in South Dakota, Nebraska, and Oklahoma, in the preparation of articles of incorporation and the sharing of information on potential threats from state authorities. It became quite common for people from different reservations to attend each other's Peyote services. Paths between Winnebago, Omaha, Ponca, Yankton, Rosebud, and Pine Ridge reservations in South Dakota and Nebraska became well beaten. The same was true in Oklahoma, Utah, and Nevada, and eventually in Arizona and New Mexico. The ease of travel facilitated proselytization. In the 1920s and 1930s, Peyotism spread beyond Oklahoma and the southern and central plains, and into the northern plains, the Great Basin region of Utah and Nevada, and into Arizona, New Mexico, California, and Canada. New Peyote communities emerged among the Bannocks and Shoshones of Idaho; the Crees, Chippewas, Blackfeet, and Assiniboines of Montana; the Sioux of North Dakota; the Wind River Shoshones of Wyoming; and the Crees, Chippewas, Blackfeet, and Sioux of Canada. Peyote groups also emerged among the Southern and Northern Paiutes and Washoes of the Great Basin, and the Gosiutes and Western Shoshones in Utah and Nevada. Peyotism also expanded on to the Navajo Reservation and by the mid-1950s had grown tremendously there.[1]

The expansion of Peyotism also increased the demand for Peyote. The growing transportation network facilitated access to the Peyote Gardens in southern Texas and northern Mexico. As oil companies built roads for their industry, access to untouched Peyote cacti became easier. A group of Mexicans and Mexican Americans, known as *peyoteros*, harvested and sold Peyote buttons wholesale to retail companies, or they traveled and sold the buttons directly to Peyotists; or Peyote could be purchased by mail order. As early as 1909, the firm L. Villegas and Company of Laredo, Texas, was selling and shipping Peyote at three dollars per thousand buttons. Upon receipt of the money, they guaranteed immediate shipment of any amount.[2] Another example, from 1927, a peyotero from Oilton, Texas, traveled to Oklahoma with 38,000 Peyote buttons, which he sold for two dollars per one thousand. Omer Stewart reported in 1938 that Peyote buttons sold for two or three cents apiece in Utah. More typical in the 1920s and 1930s, Texas shipping companies sent thousands of dried Peyote buttons to Oklahoma every year. It was shipped en masse to Oklahoma since Peyote possession was legal in that state. One such company, Wormser Brothers of Laredo, Texas, shipped one thousand Peyote buttons for ten dollars. In 1950 in Wisconsin, Peyote was purchased via the mail at a cost of twenty dollars per one thousand for high-grade sun-dried Peyote buttons and ten dollars per one thousand for oven-dried buttons. Federal law prohibited the shipment of Peyote to states that had outlawed it, so many of the Peyote people used the new highways and rail lines to travel to Oklahoma to purchase their Peyote. Others traveled south to Texas to buy Peyote directly from the peyoteros.[3]

Another factor that facilitated the spread of Peyotism was the personal friendships that had developed among many young American Indians who had attended boarding schools. After returning home, some of the students were attracted to Peyotism. They communicated with old school friends. The influence of this group of young people, especially the graduates of the Carlisle Indian School and Haskell Institute in Kansas, remained instrumental in creating and maintaining a network of Peyotists. With widespread contacts and opportunities for proselytizing, the diffusion of the Peyote faith proceeded quite rapidly.

Once the Peyote faith was introduced on a reservation, a local Peyote community developed and soon it would legally incorporate as a church or join an already incorporated group. The people who joined had a sense of being part of a wider Peyote world, especially after 1918, when the majority of Peyote communities took the name Native American Church. Peyotism spread with a relatively unified doctrine and ritual, but with an organizational structure that allowed for local autonomy. Local groups chose their own leadership as the national church did not sanction Roadmen. Leaders emerged based on personal qualities such as integrity, spirituality, charisma, knowledge, lifestyle, compassion, and commitment. Beyond leadership, the local group developed its own administrative structure under the requirements of state incorporation laws. This meant elections and governance through bylaws, in addition to prayer meetings, baptisms, marriages, and funerals, without oversight or veto by a higher body. With such a structure, Peyotism functioned very well in spite of some differences in ritual in terms of the degree of Christian influence. Peyote groups shared a common theological framework that allowed an individual to feel comfortable attending a Peyote meeting anywhere in the country. By the 1920s and 1930s, even though no national organization existed, Peyotists believed that they were part of a nationwide community.

The Lakotas/Dakotas (Sioux) fit this pattern. In 1924, they joined together and incorporated as the Native American Church of South Dakota, followed by the establishment of the Native American Church of North Dakota; however, they remained incorporated groups on the local level. Participating in or taking leadership positions on the state and national level did not infringe on local autonomy. The large state and national bodies reflected the sense of unity, but more important they functioned as a defense against those forces trying to restrict or prohibit Peyote. The above factors in the diffusion of Peyote are external, yet the internal values reflected in the belief structure are the real essential elements in the spread of the Peyote faith. Peyote, viewed as a sacred plant, existed within a familiar cosmological framework that allowed Peyotism to serve people's spiritual, aesthetic, and social needs. In addition, when a person became part of a Peyote community, his or her tribal identity was not weakened in the least. Peyotists argued that their faith strengthened an individual's tribal identity and helped him or her cope with the reservation environment, which *was* a threat to one's identity. Being a member of an American Indian tribal group and being a Peyotist were not conflicting identities. The new elements, such as Peyote itself, even the Christian elements that were absorbed into Peyotism, were invested with values that resonated with the traditional meanings of life. An essentialist center of life was reinforced in a dynamic way to serve basic human needs. Not all American Indians saw Peyotism in this light, but a significant number did accept the faith as an inherent part of an indigenous spiritual heritage.

As Peyotism expanded to the southwest, west, and north in the 1920s and 1930s, it followed a pattern of expansion similar to that earlier in the twentieth century, but now the Peyote faith had fewer state and federal enemies. It continued to be perceived by many American Indians as an ethical system that not only offered a better life on earth but also offered a spiritual means of healing the body, mind, and spirit, thus rebalancing one's life. This new expansion was very significant as it occurred in the 1920s, a time of severe economic dislocation and serious health concerns that worsened in the following decade as the Depression deepened. Peyotism had an appealing message as it expanded from individual to individual, from family to family, and from group to group. There were many dozens of Peyote Roadmen who crisscrossed the West during this period. They included Jim Blue Bird and Sam Lone Bear and the well-traveled Albert Hensley and Jonathan Koshiway. Ben Lancaster and Franklin Mack (Washoe), brothers George and John Anderson (Caddo), Truman Dailey (Oto), Fred Lookout (Osage), William Wash (Northern Ute), Charley Knight (Ute Mountain Ute), Gilbert Jack (Bannock), and Clifford Jake (Southern Piaute) made significant contributions to the expansion of the Peyote faith.[4] In addition,

Yankton Sioux Peyotists Sam Necklace and Johnson Goodhouse made regular trips to North Dakota to introduce the Peyote faith to the Sioux on the Devil's Lake (called Spirit Lake today) Reservation and to Canadian Sioux at Griswold, Manitoba. Other Peyotists also traveled to nearby groups, although the distribution was very uneven. Some members of the Three Affiliated Tribes (Mandans, Hidatsas, Arikaras) on the Fort Berthold Reservation became Peyotists. The same happened with a number of Ojibwas (Chippewas) on the Turtle Mountain Reservation in North Dakota and the Leech Lake Reservation in Minnesota, and the Crees on the Rocky Boy Reservation in Montana.

There was also a small Peyote community among the Menominees in Wisconsin. They were introduced to Peyote early in the twentieth century by Mitchell Neck (Potawatomi) and neighboring Winnebagos. Although only a small number, approximately 3 percent, of Menominees were Peyotists, they are one of the most studied groups as well as having one of the first court cases testing the legal right to the sacramental use of Peyote. Anthropologists Sidney Slotkin and George and Louise Spindler spent considerable time with the Menominees, having been invited by the local Peyotists to record their history and culture. The anthropologists attended Peyote services and conducted extensive interviews with Peyotists that are published verbatim in their works. Slotkin conducted his fieldwork 1949–51; the Spindlers did theirs in the mid-1950s.

The Menominees had a difficult time with local authorities. In 1914, Mitchell Neck was arrested by a U.S. marshal for carrying Peyote onto the Menominee Reservation. He was taken to federal court in Milwaukee and charged with violating the 1897 federal statute against the possession of intoxicants on an Indian reservation. The judge acquitted him on the grounds that Peyote was not covered by the 1897 statute and that the BIA did not have the right to interfere with the shipment of Peyote. The Menominee Peyote community remained strong, practicing mostly the Half Moon. They referred to themselves as "The Peyote Club," held annual conventions, and elected officers. In 1946, they became involved with Oklahoma Peyotists and sent representatives to the NAC national convention. In spite of the growing popularity of Peyotism, there were few, if any, Peyotists before the 1950s on the Crow Creek, Standing Rock, or Sisseton Reservations in South Dakota.[5]

Even with a more favorable climate for expansion, there were clouds on the horizon. Then, as today, Peyotists feared that somehow they could be denied access to their "sacred medicine." For example, in the late 1930s, the U.S. Congress reevaluated the country's narcotic laws and in 1938 passed the Food, Drug and Cosmetic Act, which listed Peyote as a narcotic even though there was no new evidence that it was habit forming or harmful. (The Harrison Narcotic Act of 1914 had not included Peyote.) As several states revised their narcotic laws, they also classified Peyote as a narcotic. Although the John Collier administration protected the religious use of Peyote from persecution by federal and state authorities, Peyotists were concerned, since they could not predict the future action of Congress, state legislatures, or aggressive prosecutors, sheriffs, or police. Given the history of the previous decades in regard to Peyote, the Peyotists' feeling of insecurity was not unfounded. After all, individuals were still being arrested for Peyote possession, and in the 1940s, there was a renewed anti-Peyote campaign in Nevada as well as a continuing spate of anti-Peyote articles in popular journals. There was also the issue of internal opposition to Peyotism on several reservations.

As the Peyote faith expanded into new areas, local opposition among the American Indians, sometimes very bitter, surfaced. For instance, some Western Shoshones described Peyote as a narcotic and tied it to witchcraft. Although Peyotists argued that their faith was traditional, other American Indians claimed it was not the way that their ancestors had worshipped. Sometimes the opposition was led by traditional spiritual leaders who felt threatened by a loss of power.[6] Some individuals, influenced by missionaries, looked down on Peyotists and avoided socializing with them. However, by the 1950s, much of this internal opposition had declined, and eventually many American Indian non-Peyotists supported the Peyote faith as a religious freedom issue.

During the 1920s and 1930s, the two variants of the Peyote ceremony, the Cross Fire and Half Moon, were well established. Individual Roadmen taught one or the other. Peyotists considered themselves Half Moon or Cross Fire, but felt comfortable attending either type of service. As with many groups, such as the Crows on the northern plains of Montana, they practiced both variants of worship. Peyotism entered their reservation in the late 1920s. The Northern Cheyennes and Northern Arapahos introduced Peyote to the Crows. In addition they were visited by Kiowa Roadmen and the two famous travelers Albert Hensley and Sam Lone Bear. Peyotism became quite popular as it was tied to healing. It also seems that local opposition was minimal as Peyotists rapidly grew in numbers and became involved in local politics. By 1960 more than half of the Crow population were Peyotists. It is interesting to note that the increasing impact of Peyotism on Crow society has not decreased Crow ethnic identity. They are still intensely Crow in their cultural worldview, with many individuals still speaking Crow and participating in Sun Dances, vision quests, and sweat lodge ceremonies. Some Peyotists are also practicing Christians and participants in traditional ceremonies.[7]

As Peyote faith spread northward, it also expanded westward into the Great Basin, a large area between the Rocky Mountains and the Sierra Nevada mountain range in eastern California. This includes all of Nevada and parts of California, Oregon, Idaho, Wyoming, and Utah. Within the Great Basin there are many commonalities: Almost all of the American Indian groups have Peyote communities practicing both the Cross Fire and Half Moon services; many individuals practice multiple faiths, including Peyotism, traditional spirituality, and Christianity. They all maintain a strong ethnic identity as well as a sense of belonging to a nationwide Peyote community.

Originally introduced from outside the region, Peyotism spread from group to group. The Ute living on three reservations in Colorado and Utah were one of the earliest groups in the Great Basin to adopt Peyotism. They were introduced to Peyotism by the Southern Cheyennes and Arapahos of northwest Oklahoma. The Ute involvement with Peyote varied considerably, indicating the complexity of analyzing the dissemination of Peyotism. The Utes on the Uintah Ouray Reservation in northeast Utah were the first to adopt Peyotism. They were visited by Southern Cheyenne Roadmen who introduced the Half Moon ceremony. By 1919, 50 percent of the Utes on the reservation were Peyotists. The Southern Ute and the Ute Mountain Ute located in southern Colorado and Utah had very different experiences with the Peyote faith. Although there were some early Peyotists in this area, a 1919 BIA report indicated that there were none; however, by 1938, when Omer Stewart visited the Ute Mountain Ute, he found 90 percent of them were Peyotists; he found only 5 percent among the Southern Ute. Explanations for the difference are not obvious, except that the Ute Mountain Utes had extremely harsh reservation conditions and minimal opposition from tribal leaders. Some investigators claim that Peyotism provided the Ute Mountain Utes with social solidarity and that it was perceived as a traditional form of healing.[8] However, Peyotism grew rapidly on the Uintah Ouray Reservation in spite of intense opposition from Ute Christians, missionaries, and federal and local officials. Since Utah had outlawed Peyote in 1917, officials confiscated Peyote and broke up Peyote meetings. As a result, Peyote had to be smuggled onto the reservation and Peyote meetings held in secret. The Peyotists in Utah were not able to worship openly until the 1930s. Even under these circumstances, they were able to disseminate Peyotism to their neighbors and to other Utes in the south.

The Utes influenced the Gosiutes, who were closely related to the Shoshones and lived on the Gosiute Reservation along the Utah/Nevada border. Sam Lone Bear introduced them to the Cross Fire ceremony and was credited with curing several ill people; however, during the early 1930s the Utes introduced the Half Moon Way to the Gosiutes. By the end of the decade, the majority of Gosiutes were Peyotists. As with many other groups, the Gosiutes did not have an exclusivity of religious commitment. Some were Peyotists and practicing Mormons at the same time. They also attended whatever type of Peyote service was available. When one person was asked why he attended both the Half Moon and Cross Fire services, he replied, "[I]t's the same herb [Peyote]."[9]

Much farther to the west of the Gosiutes, on the Nevada/California border below Lake Tahoe, is the Washoe Reservation. The introduction of Peyote to the Washoes occurred at the same time as it did among their more scattered neighbors, the Northern Paiutes, who lived on several reservations in the western part of the Great Basin. The Cross Fire Way was introduced by Sam Lone Bear in 1929 and Raymond Lone Bear (Uintah Ute) in 1932, but it grew very slowly until the arrival of Ben Lancaster in 1936. He was a Washoe living with the Southern Cheyennes in Oklahoma. He returned home in 1936 and introduced the Half Moon Way. He ran Peyote meetings for the Washoes, Paiutes, and Shoshones. Lancaster, with his charisma, colorful personality, and reputation for doctoring, and with the support of his relative Sam Dick, who was a traditional medicine man, was able to expand Peyotism. About 14 percent, or approximately 300 of 2,257 inhabitants, had become Peyotists by the end of the 1930s.[10] Lancaster was a larger than life figure whom people praised or resented. He called himself Chief Gray Horse from his younger years when he was a traveling salesman selling Chief Gray Horse's Indian Herbs. He gave up this trade when he became a Peyotist. Living in Oklahoma, he learned the Cheyenne/Kiowa-style Peyote service. To some Washoes, Peyotism seemed to be the answer to alcoholism, poverty, and apathy. One Peyotist said: "This medicine was give [sic] to us Indians to save our life. . . . It is against alcohol because it is the booze that just about wiped us out. The Herb goes in there, inside a person, and fights the booze."[11] Lancaster's success aroused considerable hostility among Washoe traditionalists, missionaries, and medical professionals. The hostility grew so intense that the Peyote community was forced to hold religious services in secret. Lancaster was such a dominant figure that he alienated some Peyotists. He was also controversial because he encouraged women to attend Peyote meetings at a time when many groups did not allow women to attend except for doctoring and serving as the Morning Water Woman. In addition, women in Lancaster's services were allowed to sing while holding the Roadman's staff and gourd rattle and upon occasion women served as chief drummer. Women attending meetings at this time was not typical, and singing during the services was extremely rare. (By the second half of the twentieth century, women's attendance would become universal.) Lancaster was also under suspicion by local authorities. When Nevada revived its anti-Peyote law in 1941, he was arrested in Reno, but the following year a judge dismissed the charges against him.

After a period of decline, Washoe Peyotism expanded in the late 1940s and 1950s, and with the help of the NAC national leaders, the Washoes, along with Shoshones and Paiutes, incorporated in 1958 as the Native American Church of Nevada. Peyotists in eastern California incorporated the same year as the Native American Church of California. In recent decades, Washoe Peyotists have become part of the mainstream of Washoe community life, participating in the recent cultural and economic revival.[12]

SOUTHWEST: DINÉ (NAVAJO) NATION

The Diné (their name means "The People") are the most numerous American Indian population in the United States. They number almost 300,000 and account for the largest number of Peyotists, as most estimates put the number at almost 50 percent of the Diné. They live on the large Diné Reservation, approximately 29,000 square miles, or two-thirds the size of Ohio. It is located mostly in northeastern Arizona with parts of the reservation in southern Utah and northwestern New Mexico, in the so-called Four Corners area. It is part of their traditional homeland and is bounded by what they believe are four sacred mountains. The land is arid to semiarid plateau, with canyons and stands of evergreen, pine, and oak trees. Some of the land is suitable for farming, but it is used mostly for grazing as the Diné have accumulated large herds of sheep, goats, and horses. The present Diné Reservation (Diné Bikéyah) was established by treaty in 1868. As with many other Native nations, the Diné have had a difficult time with the U.S. government. Prior to the treaty, they struggled against

U.S. military forces for several decades. In 1864, they were attacked by a force led by Kit Carson. As part of his plan to drive the Diné from their homeland, he destroyed their crops and livestock. They were forced to march the Long Walk for several hundred miles to Fort Sumner in New Mexico, where they endured a terrible time. Under these circumstances, they signed the treaty and returned to a reduced homeland, where they slowly resurrected their economic base. Years later, in 1923, the Navajo Tribal Council was established. Unfortunately, the impetus for its establishment was the Department of the Interior, whose goal was to use the council for its own ends. The council was not meant to protect, benefit, or govern the Diné people, but to approve leases for corporations to exploit natural resources such as oil. Nevertheless, the council was the first step on the long road to self-determination.[13]

The Peyote faith came late to the Diné people. In 1919, the BIA noted the absence of Peyote on the reservation. The first known involvement with Peyote occurred in the northeast corner of the reservation close to the Ute Mountain Ute Reservation. In the late 1910s, several Diné attended Peyote services with their Ute neighbors in Towaoc, Colorado. Charles Tso, from Shiprock, New Mexico, claimed he attended Ute Peyote meetings in 1918. Through the 1920s, other Diné also attended services with the Utes, and Ute Roadman Charley Knight traveled among the Navajos running Peyote meetings. Tso was possibly the first Diné to become a Roadman, conducting services on the Diné Reservation beginning in 1930. From that point Peyotism began to spread, although very slowly at first. After 1933, many Diné worked on Civilian Conservation Corps projects on the Ute Mountain Ute Reservation, thus having more contact with Peyote people. By 1935, there were several Diné Roadmen conducting services in the northeastern part of the reservation around Shiprock, New Mexico. By the late 1930s, Peyotism had spread to the southeast corner of the reservation in the Fort Defiance and Window Rock area. This occurred during the most difficult decade for the Diné in the twentieth century.[14]

The Depression and the federal government's response had a devastating impact. The Diné region normally has low rainfall; however, during the 1930s annual rainfall declined, water resources dried up, animal forage disappeared, and the soil dried out and blew away. The subsequent soil erosion compounded an already difficult situation. The BIA and Commissioner Collier blamed overstocking of sheep, goats, and horses for the soil erosion. Their answer: a systematic program of livestock reduction. Collier initiated a program that caused the Diné much pain and suffering and has left a bitter legacy. Collier, criticized by many for his top-down style of leadership, thought he knew what was best for the Diné. He acted arbitrarily and imposed his will on them. Collier and other officials did not understand the social and cultural significance of the livestock. They were intrinsic to the Diné sense of spiritual well-being and to their status in the community. They were part of one's extended family with a significant impact on women, who had the major responsibility for the goat and sheep herds. Collier wanted immediate approval from the Tribal Council and threatened to withhold other funds if it was not forthcoming. Under considerable duress, the council gave their approval. Federal officials demanded that the farmers surrender part of their herds. Given the Depression there was no market for animal products. As historian Peter Iverson wrote so poignantly, "[T]he federal men would seize animals, take them over a hill or down into a canyon or into a corral, and shoot them and leave them to rot." People were in mourning as the culling of the herds continued until the end of the decade. They considered their livestock sacred. Howard Gorman, a Tribal Council member said, "Livestock was a necessity and meant survival. Some people consider livestock as sacred because it is life's necessity. They think of livestock as their mother." It is impossible to describe the anguish caused by the livestock reduction program. Some individuals refused to cooperate and resisted federal officials. The Diné have never forgiven Commissioner Collier. Some Diné claimed that the BIA turned a self-sufficient people into a dependent people who had to rely on charity to survive.[15]

In this atmosphere Peyotism expanded very slowly. It has been tempting for scholars to explain the growth of Peyotism as a response to the livestock reduction crisis. Anthropologist David Aberle, who was hired in the 1949 by the BIA to study Diné Peyotism, espoused this viewpoint. He applied "relative depravation theory" to explain the attraction of Peyote. He claimed the livestock reduction and the growing poverty made Peyotism attractive. The application of this theory to the Diné in the 1930s is problematic since during the worst years of the Depression and the livestock reduction, only a small number of the people became Peyotists and those only on the northern part of the reservation. The great expansion of the Peyote faith came later, in the decades after World War II. In fact, Aberle claimed that by 1951 only 12 to 14 percent, or 8,000–9,000, of the Diné were Peyotists. By 1965, those numbers had jumped to 35 to 39 percent, and by 1972, to 40 to 60 percent. One reason for the slow growth of Peyotism in the 1930s may have been the tremendous opposition it faced. Arizona had criminalized the possession of Peyote in 1923, and New Mexico in 1929, but that was only a small part of the problem. A large majority of the Diné opposed Peyotism in its early years. This included traditional spiritual leaders, members of the Tribal Council, and Diné who were practicing Christians. There was also a strong Christian missionary presence that encouraged the opposition. The controversy over Peyote created factionalism and bitterness. Some Diné argued the Peyote was not part of traditional spirituality; others argued that it would retard economic and social progress; some claimed it was harmful.[16]

In 1938, two Peyotists were arrested on the reservation and charged with possession of "dope." They were convicted and sentenced to sixty days in jail. Soon after, Senator Chavez of New Mexico, still smarting over the failure of his 1937 anti-Peyote bill, asked the superintendent of the Navajo Reservation for a full investigation of Peyote usage. Following the investigation, the Tribal Council, in June 1940, held a hearing to consider Peyotism. Jacob C. Morgan, the chair of the Tribal Council and an ordained Methodist minister who had attended boarding school at Hampton Institute, was a strong advocate of acculturation and an opponent of Peyotism. He was also a member of the American Indian Federation, a right-wing group that was established to oppose the "Indian New Deal." They associated Collier's Indian policies with Communism as some of Collier's programs seemed to support communal traditions. In addition, the Tribal Council was still reeling from the livestock reduction program and was not about to support any Collier policy even if it involved religious freedom. The council members who spoke used old BIA documents to claim that Peyote caused physical harm, led to sexual excesses, insanity, and upon occasion, death. The idea that Peyote could be a medicine was ridiculed. The only Peyotist on the council was Hola Tso. He asked for medical reports that proved Peyote was harmful. He then described his own beneficial experiences with the Peyote faith. His efforts were to no avail. The council voted 52–1 to prohibit the introduction, sale, or use of Peyote on the reservation, with offenders subject to a jail sentence up to nine months, a hundred-dollar fine, or both. The resolution stated that Peyotism was "not connected with any Navajo religious practice and is in contradiction to the traditional ceremonies of the Navajo people." Even though Collier opposed the resolution and knew very well that Peyote was not dangerous, he approved it on the basis of protecting the right of the Diné to legislate for themselves. On several other occasions, Hola Tso tried unsuccessfully to get the council to reconsider the resolution. During the following years, enforcement of the ban on Peyote by tribal authorities was sporadic. Nevertheless, throughout the late 1940s and early 1950s, almost one hundred Peyotists were arrested each year and had their Peyote ritual paraphernalia confiscated. In addition, there were reports of vigilante activities by private individuals who broke up Peyote meetings and seized ritual items. For the most part, however, authorities were not able to stop the shipment of Peyote to the reservation or put a stop to Peyote meetings in the vast rural areas of the reservation. The Tribal Council did not rescind its ban on the religious use of Peyote until 1967.[17]

In the 1940s, Diné Peyotists became part of the wider Peyote community; they visited other reservations while being visited by Peyotists such as Truman Dailey (Oto) to run services for them. In 1946, with the help of the Oklahoma Peyotists and with the influence of neighboring Peyotists, the Diné incorporated as the NAC of the State of Arizona. The NAC of New Mexico and the NAC of the State of Utah had incorporated in 1945. The Arizona situation was an anomaly. Both the state legislature and the Navajo Tribal Council had banned the use of Peyote, yet the secretary of state issued the NAC a charter of incorporation.

In spite of the opposition, Peyote grew rapidly in the 1950s and 1960s. This growth is not easy to explain as the Diné consider themselves a traditional people, and as some pointed out, Peyote was not traditional. There were other factors such as poverty, but that is only a small part of an answer since poverty was not a universal characteristic of Peyotists. Many Osages, for example, were Peyotists even though they had considerable oil wealth. Thus one cannot assert a correlation between poverty and the growth of Peyotism. The Diné did not claim they were drawn to Peyotism because of visions. Many claim to have never had a vision even after decades of involvement with the NAC. There were changes on the reservation caused by World War II and its aftermath. There were more roads and railroads and more people had cars or trucks. Many individuals had been wage earners during the war, working on railroads, in factories, and on farms. There was also a significant expansion of educational opportunities. In addition, in the 1950s the Tribal Council asserted itself and collected more royalties from companies exploiting their natural resources. Self-determination was in the wind. There was considerable change, but it cannot be considered a major factor in the acceptance of Peyotism. The changes affected almost all Diné, yet many did not adopt Peyotism. There is also the complicating factor of the relationship between internal opposition on the reservation and the growth of Peyotism. In some cases one could argue that stiff opposition from elders and tribal leaders stifled the religion's growth as with the Diné in the 1930s, yet there are cases in which opposition could be a catalyst to the growth of Peyotism, as it was among the Winnebagos in Nebraska in the early twentieth century. This begs another question. Does Peyotism expand when local opposition declines? The answer is a guarded yes, with exceptions such as the Siçangu Lakotas on the Rosebud Reservation. By the 1940s and 1950s, the older generation of Diné, with roots in pre-reservation spirituality, was passing away, eliminating what had been a significant source of opposition.

Deprivation and change may have been important factors, but there was a more essential reason involved in the spread of Peyotism, such as the reputation that Peyote acquired as a healer able to cure a variety of conditions. This takes into account the viewpoint of the Diné that their traditional belief system was able to accommodate the Peyote faith. As described in chapter 2, healing is one of the most essential elements in Diné spirituality. Their cosmology or worldview is based on the concept of *Hózhóoji*, or *Hózhó*, which means that the purpose of life is to travel the path of beauty and harmony in a universe where everything is sacred and interrelated. The goal is to have a good life and live to an old age. Diné spiritual practices are meant to restore Hózhó when one's life is out of balance, thus spirituality and associated ritual have an essential restorative quality. There are many reasons why one's life may be out of balance; two major factors are psychological and physical illnesses. Once the negative reputation about Peyote as harmful began to change to a belief in its efficacy as a curative, more Diné began to explore Peyotism. There is almost universal agreement among contemporary scholars and Diné Peyotists that the healing power of Peyote was the major factor in its acceptance. This was especially the case in the late 1940s when health issues and declining federal support for health care created a crisis. There was an epidemic of tuberculosis, serious malnutrition, and a high rate of infant mortality. Part of the health care crisis included a growing problem of alcohol abuse and its devastating impact on families. In the midst of this crisis the debate over Peyote continued. Some Diné considered it divisive, even within families. Others felt the opposite. One Navajo Peyotist, Dick Clark, argued that traditional Navajo medicine was not effective in combating alcoholism and that Peyote had a reputation for healing the disease of alcoholism. In addition, many Diné were now giving personal testimonials to Peyote's effectiveness.[18]

Slowly, Peyotism became more acceptable as people realized the horror stories about Peyote were not true. Even those who were not drawn to Peyotism stopped opposing it. What helped make this possible was the parallel with the traditional Diné spiritual beliefs and practices and the "genius of adaptability" of Diné society.[19] Adaptation and incorporation is an essential characteristic of Diné culture. One can point to the incorporation of domesticated animals, particularly sheep, goats, and horses that were introduced by the Spanish, as well as the incorporation of some ceremonial practices from the Hopis and Pueblos. Peter Iverson has written that throughout their history, the Navajos have brought in "new people, new ideas and new elements, and over time made them Navajo."[20] This helps explain the slow but steady acceptance of the Peyote faith as more and more Diné saw it as another way to restore balance, harmony, and good health to one's life. This fit well with traditional Diné spirituality, in which the main purpose of religious ceremonies was to communicate with the Holy People (Gods), so that they might aid in the healing and restoration of a harmonious life. Now one might also pray to the Holy People through the sacramental use of Peyote.

There are other significant parallels between traditional Diné faith and Peyotism in addition to the holistic approach to healing. Neither has an organized priesthood, but both have trained specialists that learn by observation, experience, and practice as they watch and are taught by other specialists. And both consider singing, which is prayer, as essential to healing. In the final analysis, however, the key to understanding the dissemination of Peyote is that the Diné have made Peyotism a part of their spiritual world. The various elements of Peyotism have been placed within a Diné cultural framework. Peyote religious services, which are mostly Half Moon, do not differ in any significant way from those held elsewhere in America, with the exception of the use of the Diné language. Nevertheless, as mentioned previously, the Diné came to perceive Peyotism as Diné. They did not change Peyotism but saw in it a spirituality that paralleled their traditional faith. This happened as Peyote acquired a more positive image as some saw its impact in reducing alcohol and substance abuse.[21] As many scholars have pointed out, Diné Peyotists are intensely Diné. It has not affected the traditional sense of identity or ethnicity; in fact one could argue that Peyotism has reinforced Diné identity. One additional but very significant point is that as Peyotism expanded in the1950s and 1960s, women were active participants in Peyote services. Peyotism expanded as whole families became involved and went to the services together. In photographs of

Navajo Peyote meetings from this time, women are among the congregants. The women at first sang softly along with the men, but eventually some women held the staff and rattle and sang on their own as is common today.

Another essential factor that helps explain the Diné's acceptance of Peyotism is that they did not have to give up one faith for another. Peyotism does not demand or expect exclusivity. When one begins to participate in the NAC, giving up other faiths is not required. One can practice multiple faiths without a sense of contradiction. Many Peyotists continue to be practicing Christians, and many continue to participate in traditional Diné spiritual ceremonies. The practice of multiple faiths is most obvious in healing as many scholars and studies have noted and many Diné openly discuss. The Diné view good health and healing as holistic in nature. When help is needed, it is not unusual for an individual to seek it by attending a Peyote service, a traditional healing ceremony, and a western doctor, hospital, or clinic. Many studies have demonstrated how the Diné use all three healing systems when faced with a difficult health issues. Although western medicine has become more commonplace, it does not offer the cultural, psychological, and holistic elements of Peyotism and traditional Diné healing.[22]

THE NATIVE AMERICAN CHURCH: A NATIONAL ORGANIZATION

Early in 1955, Allen P. Dale, president of the Native American Church of the United States, reflecting on the previous decade, wrote in the *Quarterly Bulletin of the Native American Church*: "The aim of our organization is to protect our way of worship." Protecting the free exercise of their faith was the motivating force that led to the establishment of a national organization in 1944. The impetus to organize on a national scale reflected the growth of the Peyote faith as well as concerns about continued opposition in the form of harassment and arrest under a variety of inconsistent state laws. There was still missionary opposition as Reverend G. Lindquist was still active in supporting an anti-Peyote agenda. There was no significant threat to Peyotism from the federal government, although Congresswoman Frances Bolton of Ohio proposed anti-Peyote legislation in 1944. In fact, in 1940 the U.S. Postal Service lifted its ban on shipping Peyote through the mail. There were still articles in the popular press claiming Peyote was a harmful narcotic, yet there were a number of prominent anthropologists who were now defending Peyotism. By the mid-1940s, the Oklahoma Peyotists had concluded that a broader organizational structure was needed to coordinate the activities of the chartered Peyote groups in the western states.

The year 1944, like 1918, was a watershed year for the NAC. Oklahoma Peyotists were the unofficial leaders of the NAC. In addition to providing leadership for the Peyote communities in Oklahoma, they helped other Peyote groups throughout the West, for example, assisting Peyotists to incorporate in Wisconsin in 1939 and in Iowa in 1943. By 1944, eight states had incorporated Peyote groups. The need for a coordinated approach to the wide range of legal restrictions on Peyote in most western states was deemed essential. This was considered the best way to protect the constitutional rights of NAC members. This had been planned at least a decade earlier and had been discussed as early as 1923, when a federal charter was proposed. Attorneys told the NAC leaders that this was highly unlikely as there were no federal charters for churches or religions. It was not pursued any further at that time. In 1934, under President Ned Brace (Kiowa), the Oklahoma NAC charter was amended to allow out-of-state Peyote groups to affiliate, but the timing was not right. Given the Depression and the difficulty and expense of travel, the plan did not succeed, but the idea for a chartered national organization was alive. In 1944, the time was right. The charter of the Oklahoma NAC was amended and a new name adopted: "Native American Church of the United States."[23]

The introduction to the amended charter is explicit on the constitutional rights of American Indians, claiming the "inherent right to protection in the free exercise of their religious beliefs in the unmolested practice of the rituals under Amendment I to the Constitution." The charter is also explicit on "the use of peyote as a sacrament," as well as reiterating the ethical basis of the Peyote faith: "to promote morality, sobriety, industry, charity, and the right living and to cultivate a spirit of self respect and brotherly love." There are references to an almighty God, but no mention of Christianity. The charter sets up the NAC as a nonprofit corporation controlled by five trustees with headquarters in El Reno, Oklahoma. Membership was available to Peyote groups who could appoint voting delegates. Mack Haag (Southern Cheyenne) was elected president and Frank Takes Gun (Crow), the only non-Oklahoman in the leadership group, vice president.

The NAC of the United States had a stable leadership that helped put the organization on a firm footing. The first president, Mack Haag, had been an important leader of Oklahoma Peyotists for many decades. He was one of the original signers of the 1918 articles of incorporation in Oklahoma. Allen P. Dale (Omaha) was the second president, 1946–54. He claims to have attended his first Peyote meeting in 1908, when he was twelve years old. He went on to Haskell Institute, where he made many contacts that aided the future expansion of Peyotism. In 1917, he joined the U.S. Army and served in World War I. He became active with the Oklahoma Peyotists and played a major role in the discussions leading to a national organization and helping it develop into a major force in the defense of religious freedom. He was elected as a delegate-at-large in 1945 and president in 1946.

The controversial Frank Takes Gun was vice president from 1944 to 1954. His major responsibility was dealing with legal issues and assisting Peyote groups that wanted to incorporate. For example, he assisted Peyote groups in New Mexico, Utah, Arizona, Colorado, and Texas to incorporate. He also specialized in legal issues and traveled to assist Peyotists who had been arrested. Another important official was Truman Dailey, who served as secretary, 1944–50. He traveled widely, teaching about Peyotism and running Peyote meetings from New Mexico and Arizona to California and Idaho. These three men, and others, provided solid leadership for a new organization in a period of rapid expansion of members and incorporated groups.

In 1944, the organization held its first national convention. Such events were not new; for example, Peyotists from Oklahoma and South Dakota had been having statewide conventions since the 1920s. In the early years, the national conventions were held in Oklahoma, an indication of the influence of the Oklahoma Peyotists. On average, members from eight to ten states were represented at the conventions. Legal issues were the most commonly debated topics. These included the concern over the transportation of Peyote from state to state, the quilt-work pattern of conflicting state laws concerning Peyote, and the continuing arrests for possession of Peyote. Everyone agreed that the solution was to encourage all Peyote groups to incorporate as it was believed to be the only way to gain legal protection.[24]

The one controversy that emerged was the dissatisfaction of some Oklahoma Peyotists, who preferred their old state organization to a national organization that paid less attention to Oklahoma issues. By 1946, there was dissension within the national NAC between members who had a national outlook for the church and those who wanted an organization with a focus on Oklahoma Peyotism. Those favoring the latter obtained the original 1918 Oklahoma charter, which they amended in 1949, using the name NAC of Oklahoma. The 1949 amended Oklahoma charter was virtually the same as the original 1918 charter. It also reaffirmed the commitment to the sacramental use of Peyote. Some local Peyote communities remained with the Oklahoma organization and did not affiliate with the national group. The NAC that was chartered in 1944 continued as the national organization, but reincorporated in 1950 to be certain to maintain the distinction between the national group and the Oklahoma group. In spite of this division, it was Peyotists from Oklahoma who continued to provide most of the leadership for the national organization.

Other events made the time more appropriate to launch a national organization. Commissioner John Collier had been a supporter and defender of the Peyote faith for several decades, which he reaffirmed with his call for religious toleration and cultural autonomy in 1934. Three years later, he defended Peyotism in congressional hearings over Senator Chavez's proposal to ban the interstate shipment of Peyote. However, in late 1930s and early 1940s, Collier's influence and power were waning. He was under attack by many members of Congress as well as by various citizen groups. During World War II, Indian affairs were given minimal attention. In 1942, BIA headquarters was moved to Chicago to make room in Washington for war-related office space. The reform aspects of the Indian New Deal slowed to a crawl, contributing to Collier's resignation in January 1945. Given the above, both Peyotists and American Indians in general felt the need for national organizations given the scope of national problems.

At the same time the NAC of the United States was established, an intertribal organization, the National Council of American Indians (NCAI), was founded. It was an advocacy group dedicated to protecting treaty rights, supporting land claims, and defending cultural and religious practices. The establishment of the NCAI was in response to the threat of the U.S. government's abdicating its responsibilities to federally recognized tribes. The NCAI was significant for the NAC, as more and more American Indians who were not Peyotists were defending the constitutional rights of all American Indians, including NAC members.

The new national NAC has been described as a "loose confederacy." It had a congregational-style structure that allowed regional and local autonomy. It also included working with and supporting Peyote communities that chose not to become officially affiliated with the national NAC. The leadership of the latter was elected by delegates from affiliated groups. The leaders administered the organization according to their bylaws. They passed resolutions, held business meetings, collected dues, set up sub-committees when needed, planned annual conventions, and coordinated the defense of the Peyote faith. They did not establish an "official" theology nor did they interfere with the way Roadmen conducted religious services around the country, nor did they sanction or approve of who became a Roadman.

Below the national organization, there were state-chartered groups, and within states there were local Peyote groups that incorporated either regionally, by county, or by ethnic group. There were also smaller Peyote communities that did not incorporate. The state and local chartered groups voluntarily affiliated with the national NAC. They were required to pay a small annual fee that went toward administrative costs. They sent delegates to the annual national conventions (which have continued to the present day). The conventions were essential to the stability of the organization. It was a time one could meet Peyotists from the wider community. Friendships were renewed, members enjoyed the sense of community from the religious services that were held at night, and legal and public relations strategies were discussed in the face of continuing opposition.

In the late 1940s and early 1950s, the public debate over Peyote reemerged as part of a national campaign against narcotics. In 1949, the reputable *Journal of the American Medical Association* published an article that condemned Peyote and described it as habit forming and harmful and called for its prohibition. The article cited no new research. It repeated outdated sources on the evil effects of Peyote. This controversy and the continuing arrests led the BIA to hire David Aberle to conduct a thorough study of Navajo Peyotism. The result was his highly recognized work *The Peyote Religion among the Navaho*. He also became a lifelong defender of the Peyote faith. *Time* magazine followed with an article "Button, Button . . . ," repeating old orgy stories such as "men hopped up on peyote are likely to grab the closest female," and claimed that one-third of the Navajo population were "addicts."[25] These quotes were credited to Christian missionaries on the Navajo Reservation. The articles provoked a response from anthropologists who had attended Peyote services, had interviewed Peyotists, and had studied the Peyote faith. In a letter to the editor in *Time*, Omer Stewart and David McAllester attacked the "Button, Button . . ." article and defended the Peyote faith. In *Science*, five anthropologists signed a statement protesting the anti-Peyote propaganda and defending the NAC as a legitimate religious organization that deserved constitutional protection. They wrote:

The belief is that God put some of his Holy Spirit into peyote, which he gave to the Indians. And by eating the sacramental peyote the Indian absorbs God's Spirit, in the same way that white Christians absorb that Spirit by means of sacramental bread and wine.[26]

The national NAC was concerned about these attacks on Peyote, fearing it could lead to greater restrictions. This was a major agenda item at the annual conventions. For example, in Texas in 1953, a peyotero was arrested and charged with violating a narcotics law even though the Texas Department of Agriculture had allowed Peyote to be harvested, sold, and transported for sacramental use. President Dale retained a lawyer to defend the accused man. A grand jury refused an indictment, and the charges were dropped. This led to the deletion of "peyote" from the Texas Narcotic Drug Act. It was this type of situation that was discussed at the national conventions. Everyone was reminded that vigilance was needed to protect the church's constitutional rights. There were also discussions about the Diné Reservation and several other reservations, including Cheyenne River Reservation, where Peyote was still prohibited. President Dale received reports that Diné Peyotists were denied jobs on the reservation. He asked members to try to get affidavits attesting to the denial. Even with the absence of federal restrictions, state laws and some tribal council restrictions posed a serious threat to Peyotism. The one area that the national NAC leadership avoided was interfering with NAC state and local groups. For example, in 1953 a delegate from South Dakota asked for help in sorting out complications and tensions between the statewide NAC of South Dakota and local incorporated groups. President Dale responded that he had no authority to intervene in such issues.[27]

The last convention as the NAC of the United States was held in Tama, Iowa, in 1954. It was only the second one to be held outside of Oklahoma. The previous year the Omahas had hosted the national convention in Macy, Nebraska. This last convention was crucial for the future of the NAC, as the decision was made to become an international organization. It was also quite unusual when J. Sidney Slotkin, the University of Chicago anthropologist, was nominated and elected as one of three members of the board of trustees. As discussed earlier, Slotkin had done considerable fieldwork and publishing on Menominee Peyotism. He had been made an honorary member of the local NAC, and on that basis he was nominated for the board. Once elected, he offered to edit a newsletter and to coordinate efforts to establish a membership list. As part of the leadership, he assisted in the transition to an international organization.[28]

Part of the reason for the decision to expand into an international organization was based on the growth of Peyotism in Canada and the need to recognize and support the continued ritual use of Peyote in Mexico. Small Peyote communities emerged in Canada in the 1920s, and by the early 1950s had grown significantly. In 1953, Canadian Crees attended the NAC's national convention. The following year, Canadian Peyotists incorporated as the Native American Church of Canada. There had always been a back-and-forth relationship between American and Canadian Peyotists. NAC officials, including the vice president, Frank Takes Gun, had traveled to Canada in 1953 and probably assisted them in their incorporation. In 1955, Takes Gun and Slotkin traveled to Canada to discuss the establishment of an international NAC. The purpose was to establish effective communication among Peyotists in North America. It was believed that only by collaboration and a unified effort could Peyote be protected for Native North Americans.[29]

The Peyote faith had grown considerably from the days of Quanah Parker to the mid-twentieth century. There were now Peyote communities in eighteen western states and two Canadian provinces. The distribution was uneven but encompassed a large number of American Indian groups. Peyotism grew in memberships as more and more individuals participated in the sacramental use of Peyote; it also grew institutionally from local community groups to an international organization. From the very beginning of Peyotism, Peyote people had interacted with each other, traveling widely, teaching, learning, and worshipping together in each other's services. By mid-century most observers and participants would agree that except for the differences between the Half Moon and Cross Fire forms of worship, there was uniformity to the Peyote faith. Wherever one attended a Peyote meeting, he or she would be totally familiar with the structure and ritual of the service. The commonalty also extended to the church's music and art. Both are very distinctive and easily recognizable. They are an integral part of Peyote spirituality. The music, in the form of voice, drum, and rattle, is the essential form of prayer. The artwork plays a special role that reflects the symbolism of the Peyote faith. Both art and music are created within the context of Peyote spirituality and are essential elements in unifying the Peyote community.

CHAPTER FIVE

Peyote Art and Music

The spiritual power of Peyote is expressed through a rich array of musical and visual arts. Their development corresponds with the emergence of Peyotism in the late nineteenth century. Although artistic styles and techniques have evolved, the arts' forms and functions, along with the Peyote ceremony and ritual, have remained relatively constant for more than a century. These arts are considered sacred. They are integral parts of a spiritual continuum with theological, ceremonial, aesthetic, and social significance. The artworks and music unite the Peyote community across time and space. They help sustain the Peyote community in difficult times as they are restorative and protective and meant to reestablish harmony and balance. Together with the spiritual power of Peyote, the arts function as instruments of prayer and tools of communication. Every Peyote song, every work of art is imbued with spirituality and sacredness to generate and harness power to protect, to teach, and to heal.

One may study art and music separately, but in Peyotism they function together inside the cosmological framework of the Peyote faith. They are produced and used for ceremonial purposes by members of the Peyote community who have been inspired by their spiritual experiences. These sacred arts are inseparably intertwined with Peyote theology and incorporate a commonly understood iconography.

When objects made for ritual purposes in a spiritual setting are not in use, they are stored away. When one is in the home of a Peyote family, one rarely sees Peyote ritual objects on display. Although a great deal of Peyote art is not used in

Peyote meetings, that art is still considered spiritual as it expresses the belief structure in symbolic and iconic forms. For example, since the late nineteenth century, various Native American Church artists have produced paintings and drawings that express spiritual values and use Peyote symbolism. The same is true with Peyote-inspired jewelry; it may be worn to a Peyote meeting, but it is also worn as an everyday item as a Christian wears a cross on a chain. It is common for Peyotists to give such iconic and ritual items to each other as gifts.

Peyote visual arts were not originally made to be collected, displayed, or sold. It was unusual to find a non-Peyotist producing Peyote art. This has changed in recent years, however, as one can now purchase these items from commercial establishments. Such commercialism is a growing concern. Recent legislation, written by Diné Peyotists and passed by the Diné Nation Council in 2005, "prohibit[s] the unauthorized commercial production and sale, use of sacred instruments, and to prohibit the unauthorized recording and sale of sacred songs." The bylaws of the NAC of South Dakota list the same restrictions, as do the bylaws of the NAC of North America, which "do not condone the practices of either pawn or sale of religious prayer instruments."[1]

Art historians, anthropologists, and ethnomusicologists have tended to study American Indian arts on a regional basis using broad categories such as Woodlands, Plains, Southwest, or Northwest; or by individual groups such as studies of Hopi music, Zuni pottery, or Diné weaving. This approach does not fit an analysis of Peyote art and music as the content, form, and style, in spite of local variation and individual creativity, conforms to the theology, ceremonialism, and aesthetics of the Peyote faith. More than a century of interaction and communication among Peyotists, including the constant travel and teaching by Roadmen, account for the geographic diffusion and continuity of Peyote art and music.

PEYOTE VISUAL ARTS

Daniel Swan states in his important study that Peyote art is a distinct genre of American Indian art.[2] It is historically and stylistically unique and encompasses a wide range of media using specific iconic features that represent elements of Peyote theology. The artwork includes paintings, drawing, and prints; beadwork; feather work; jewelry; fabric arts such as appliqué work on shawls, vests, and pillows; and carving on drumsticks, Roadmen's staffs, and Peyote boxes (sometimes called gourd boxes). Sacred symbols are painted or incised on Peyote boxes, rattles, and buckets used to carry water into a Peyote meeting. The artwork described above can be divided into three categories in terms of usage. First are items created for ceremonial use in Peyote services, such as feather fans, water drums, drumsticks, gourd rattles, Peyote boxes, and the Roadmen's staffs. The second category includes nonritual items that may be worn or carried into a Peyote service such as jewelry; appliqués on clothing, shawls, blankets or pillows; and beadwork on moccasins, vests, belts, and bolo ties. The third category encompasses artwork that is not used or displayed in Peyote meetings, such as paintings, drawings, and prints, as well as jewelry, beadwork, and appliqués on various items.

Regardless of the particular function, all of these works reflect distinctive Peyote iconography. The most ubiquitous symbols are the Peyote button, the tepee, and the waterbird. They appear on almost all artworks and represent the essential core of Peyotism as Peyote is the sacrament, the tepee is the house of prayer, and the waterbird is a messenger that carries prayers skyward. Other common symbols and icons depicted in artworks include water drums, drumsticks, gourd rattles, feather fans, eagle feathers, fire and ashes, altars, Roadmen's staffs, eagle-bone whistles, sage, cedar, and various birds. The iconography of the Cross Fire Way also includes Christian symbols and icons such as crosses, hearts, and images of Christ. For example, a Roadman's staff may have a cross carved on top. Another example is *Indian Religion,* a painting by Tennyson Eckiwaudah (Comanche). It depicts Jesus emerging from the top of a tepee filled with silhouetted Peyotists in prayer. These symbols and icons demonstrate the power of prayer and reinforce the spiritual beliefs of the NAC.[3]

Artworks are portrayed in two ways. There are the actual three-dimensional objects, such as gourd rattles, Peyote boxes, drumsticks, and feather fans. They are decorated very elaborately and must conform to certain iconic and aesthetic values. These same objects and others also come in two-dimensional form as these images appear in jewelry and beadwork, in paintings and drawings, and in appliqués. For example, feather fans and gourd rattles are depicted in many paintings and drawings.

OBJECTS CREATED FOR CEREMONIAL
USE IN PEYOTE CEREMONIES

Objects created for specific ritual use hold a special place for all Peyotists: they are sacred and essential for prayer. After they are made, they must be blessed in a Peyote meeting and are blessed again each time they are used. The blessing is a purification process where the item, such as the Roadman's staff, is cedared off or smudged, by passing it through the smoke of smoldering cedar that has been sprinkled on the fire. The item may also be rubbed with sage as part of purification. The same is true with rattles, fans, and water drums. The Peyote that will be ingested is also purified in the same manner. Before tying the buckskin to the drum, a prayer is offered. After the drum is tied, it is purified. The drum becomes sacred, as does the water inside it. When the drum is untied at the end of the service some of the individuals may sip the water, which has become powerful as the prayers of the singers and the sound of the drum have passed through the water all night. As a special blessing for all, the remaining water may be poured along the crescent mound that represents the Peyote Road, the path all should follow for a better life.[4]

Ritual instruments are placed in Peyote boxes. They are universal as virtually all church members use them to carry the special items that are taken into religious services. Besides being a cornucopia of potential power, the Peyote boxes are works of art. Originally Peyotists carried their ritual items in leather satchels, tool boxes, tackle boxes, or old suitcases. By the early to mid-twentieth century, elaborate boxes, usually made of cedar, became essential for Peyotists. They vary in size, but usually they are approximately twenty-four to thirty-two inches long, eight to ten inches wide, and six to eight inches deep, with a hinged lid and a handle on top, and sometimes with a removable drawer. Elaborately decorated, the boxes are either carved or painted with designs depicting the symbols of the faith, such as Peyote buttons, feathers, rattles, water drums, tepees, sacred fires, waterbirds, or feather fans. There may also be depictions of sunrises, stars, and rainbows. A Peyote ceremony or the Morning Water Woman may also be illustrated. Some boxes have inlaid material or items glued on such as a cross. The symbols may also reflect whether the owner is a follower of the Cross Fire or Half Moon Way. The inside of the Peyote box may be painted or lined with felt cloth. However they are designed, these boxes are extremely special to their owners. An excellent example is the Peyote box of the late Adam Sitting Crow (Yankton Sioux) made in the 1960s. An eagle feather is carved on top and a horseshoe-shaped mound showing the Peyote Road with Grandfather Peyote in the center is incised on the back. (See figure 6.)

All Peyote boxes contain the basic items needed for a Peyote service, such as Peyote for the congregants, a special pouch or box for Grandfather Peyote, rattles, feather fans, drumsticks, rope and small stones to tie the buckskin to

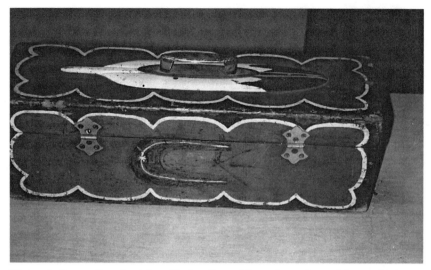

Figure 6. Peyote box, by Adam Sitting Crow. Photo by author with permission of family.

the drum, a leather cedar pouch, sprigs of sage, tobacco and dried corn husks for rolling prayer cigarettes and a fire stick to light them, an eagle-bone whistle, and an altar cloth. For the Cross Fire ceremony, individuals may have a Bible and other Christian-inspired items. Many personal items are carried in Peyote boxes, such as family photographs, religious medals, depictions of Jesus and Mary, Peyote-style jewelry, and NAC membership cards.[5]

Ritual instruments are essential to harness the power of prayer; this is especially true of the fire and the ashes. At dusk, when the altar is prepared and the fire is started, the Roadman carries his Peyote box into the tepee or hogan and sits to the west of the fire. He opens the box, lays out an altar cloth, carefully removes each ritual object, and purifies it four times by passing it through smoke from the smoldering cedar that has been sprinkled on the fire by the cedarman. It is a powerful moment of purification that will help everyone receive blessings throughout the night. The sacred fire is a central focus for all. It is the locus for another form of sacred art that is essential to Peyote meetings: the creation of symbols with the ashes from the fire. This is an ephemeral art form as it is created and re-created throughout the night by the fireman, who uses two pieces of firewood to shape the hot ashes into iconic

Figure 7. Painted water bucket. Photo by author.

forms such as eagles, crescent-shaped mounds, waterbirds, stars, hearts, and crosses. The forms act as empowering agents, giving strength to the prayers by creating a more efficacious environment for the transmission and answering of those prayers.

Another type of painting occurs on the buckets used to transport water into the Peyote service at midnight and dawn. These are special containers employed only for this purpose. The water they carry is used to bless the ritual instruments and the congregants. Using acrylics, artists decorate these stainless steel or enamel water buckets with Peyote iconography. (See figure 7.) The design may incorporate a complete tepee resting on a large Peyote button, messenger birds, eagle feathers, or other ritual objects. When carried into the service, the bucket and water are purified with cedar smoke. The Roadman then dips an eagle feather into the bucket, touching the water at each of the four directions. He does this four times, while flicking the water toward all as a blessing. The bucket is passed around for each person to take a sip. The painted water buckets demonstrate again the integrated nature of Peyotism. Peyote and the ritual instruments are essential to harness the power of prayer.

The Roadman's staff is also an essential ceremonial object. It is the symbol of authority to conduct a Peyote meeting. The staffs are made of wood, approximately thirty-six to forty-eight inches in length and constructed in two or three parts joined by a screw-in socket so they can be unscrewed and carried in a Peyote box. Some Peyotists claim the staff was originally a bow; the Delawares refer to the staff as an arrow; some call it a staff of life. The Roadman's staff is decorated with Peyote symbols incised in the wood. Small bands of beadwork surround the upper part of the staff, and horse or deer hair is attached on top. It may also have other items attached to it, such as feathers or sage. The staff is a powerful ceremonial object, as it is held in the hands of each singer throughout the night, collecting and transmitting all their prayers.[6]

The gourd rattle is another essential item in Peyote meetings. Two singers, one with the rattle, the other with the drum, sing Peyote songs. The rattles are crafted by Peyotists with precision and care. (See figure 8.) They are made from pear-shaped gourds (*Lagenaria* spp.) approximately three inches in diameter. After the gourd is dried, rubbed smooth, and polished, a wooden handle about twelve inches in length is inserted into the end of the stem. It protrudes about two inches out of the other end. The handle is held in place by a wooden stopper that fits tightly into the gourd. Pebbles or beads are placed inside to produce the desired sound. The handle is removable so the number of pebbles or beads can be changed to modify the sound in conjunction with the singer's voice. A good sounding rattle is a treasure. These rattles have been part of Peyotism since its origins as shown in James Mooney's 1892 photograph (see figure 3, chapter 2). The same year he wrote a detailed description (including a photo) of a Kiowa Peyote rattle. It has a partially beaded handle with leather fringes on the bottom. A woman is painted on the gourd. She represents the Morning Water Woman who is described in the Peyote origin narratives. Gourd rattles are also depicted in the hide paintings and ledger book drawings of Silver Horn (Kiowa) at the turn of the twentieth century. Many of the old rattles have painted motifs or incised patterns on the gourd. Sometimes designs are incised and filled with paint. The motifs may incorporate humans, animals, or objects such as tepees or Peyote buttons. For example, an early Arapaho gourd rattle depicts a messenger bird flying skyward. Among the Winnebago, gourds may be painted with images of Christ, crosses, or other Christian symbols. Most contemporary gourd rattles are not incised or painted.[7]

Gourd rattles vary from artist to artist, but they maintain a definite style and structure. The handles are fully beaded, or partially beaded and carved. The beads are brightly colored with many reds, yellows, and blues. On the top of the rattle are strands of horse or deer hair, in natural color or dyed red. Some Peyotists claim it represents the soft tuft on the top of the Peyote button; others say it represents the rays of the sun.[8] Attached to the handle are strands of leather fringe. Viewed as a whole with gourd and handle, horsehair top and

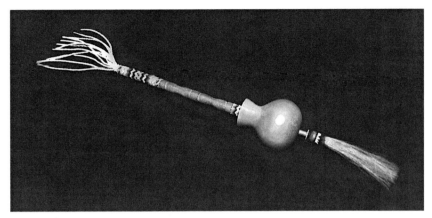

Figure 8. Diné Peyote gourd rattle. Photo by David Gentilini.

fringed bottom, the rattle gives one a sense of harmony and balance. Gourd rattles are essential instruments of prayer as are feathers and feather fans.

Peyotists consider feather fans among their most sacred objects. The feathers come from a variety of birds and are considered to be messengers that carry prayers and blessings. People especially prize feathers from eagles and hawks. There are four types of fans. One is flat and rigid, one is loose and flexible, a third is made from the wing of an eagle, and a fourth type is made from a single eagle feather. The flat fan is usually made from the tail feathers of a single bird, while the loose fan has more feathers from several bird species. In both of these types, the quill end of the feathers, which may be wrapped in leather or beaded for the loose fan, are placed in a leather socket, wrapped tightly, and attached to a beaded wooden handle with leather fringes on the bottom (see figure 9). The feathers on the loose fan are attached in a flexible manner so they can be spread out to make a wider fan. The eagle wing is made into a fan using leather strips to tie it to a beaded wooden handle.

This fan is an essential part of the Roadman's ritual equipment. During Peyote services, the fan is passed around with the Roadman's staff for the singer to hold while singing his or her four songs. The Roadman also uses the eagle-wing fan to purify and bless the congregants by fanning cedar smoke on them. The fan is also used in healing in the same manner, as the Roadman waves the fan very vigorously across the body of the ill person. With the ingestion of Peyote in conjunction with fanning, the spiritual power to heal is transmitted to the sick person. The fans made from a single eagle feather have the quill end bound

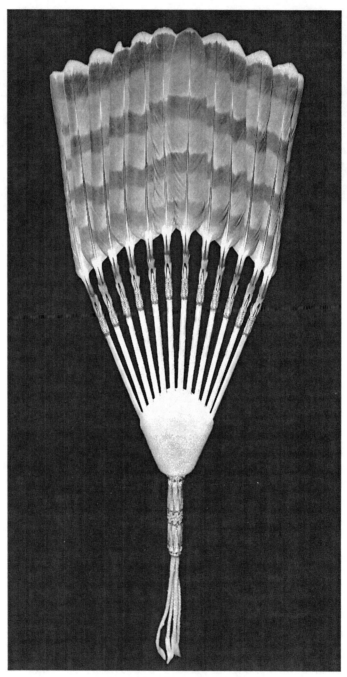

Figure 9. Peyote feather fan. Photo by David Gentilini.

with leather and beaded, with leather fringe attached to the bottom (see figure 10). Peyotists carry their own fans; however, during the Peyote ceremony, the fans are only brought out after midnight for individual use. One uses the fan to draw cedar smoke toward oneself, as it offers spiritual protection, and uses the fan as an aid to prayer. The fan may be held in front of one's face, allowing full concentration while praying. According to Diné Peyotists, the fan is employed "ritually to transfer the power of the cedar smoke, the fire and Chief Peyote to participants as they hold the feathers toward these elements and bless themselves by patting their bodies with the feathers."[9]

It is considered bad form to walk between someone who is praying and the sacred fire, as it may interrupt the passage of prayer from the individual to the fire and upward. Joseph W. Rice (Kiowa), a well-known artist, reflected on the sacred nature of the feather fan. "Each fan is like a person to me. . . . Once, I was planning a fan, and I had seven feathers hanging on the wall. I was watching them, opening and closing, moving, imagining what they'd be used for. These feathers are guardians, helpers, protectors. When you fan somebody off with cedar, it's good medicine. The fans have a spirit, a life of their own."[10]

Almost all of the ceremonial instruments previously described are decorated with beadwork that has the same spiritual, iconic, and aesthetic importance of other artworks. Beadwork requires technical skills and the ability to visualize and conceptualize patterns, colors, and space. This is especially difficult with wraparound beadwork. The stitching of beads one at a time on a cylindrical object, such as a feather fan handle, gourd rattle handle, and staff was an innovation of Comanche and Kiowa Peyotists in the late nineteenth century. This stitching became known as the "Peyote stitch" or "gourd stitch" from beadwork on gourd rattle handles. It can also be applied to flat surfaces. The motifs and colors represent Peyote symbolism and iconic conventions, with individual artists adding creative touches. The patterns may represent Peyote, various birds and feathers, the sacred fire, a tepee, a heart, or a cross. The patterns and colors symbolize a wide variety of phenomena such as sunrises, sunsets, rainbows, lightning, and water. In one pattern, four rows of colored beads represent dusk, midnight, daybreak, and sunlight, symbolizing the entire Peyote service from beginning to end. It should be pointed out that the motifs and colors may be interpreted differently by different individuals or groups over time. In addition to beadwork on ceremonial items, Peyote-style beadwork is added to jewelry, moccasins, belts, buckles, bolo ties, women's shawls, and other items of clothing.[11]

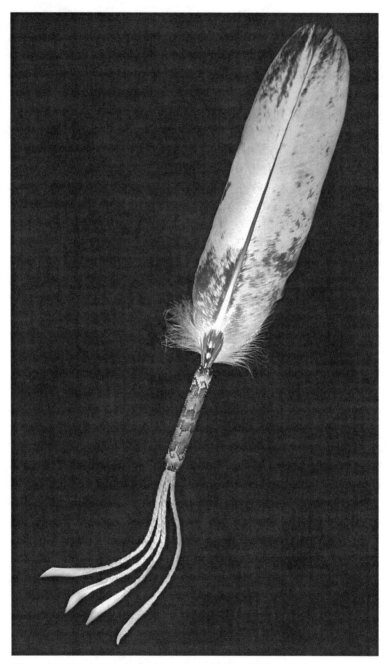

Figure 10. Beaded eagle feather. Photo by David Gentilini.

NONRITUAL PEYOTE ART

Peyote artworks not used as ritual objects are still considered spiritual, but they are not regarded with the same degree of sacredness as the items used in Peyote services. Swan's study illustrates the wide variety of Peyote art. Swan also shows how this art is integrated into the belief structure of Peyotism. The art also integrates aesthetics and theology. Nonritual art also includes three-dimensional objects such as jewelry and beadwork as well as a significant amount of two-dimensional work, such as paintings, drawings, and prints. The display of the nonritual items as symbols of faith reinforces one's identity as a member of the Peyote community.

Peyote-style jewelry is not part of the ritual equipment used in Peyote meetings; however, Peyotists may wear the jewelry during a service, or at any other time as a personal, religious, or aesthetic statement. Peyote jewelry began to appear after 1900 but did not become widespread until the 1920s and 1930s. Today it has become an extremely common personal adornment worn by Peyotists and non-Peyotists. Metal jewelry and beadwork are the most common forms. Metal jewelry is made from sterling silver, silver coins, brass, and German silver (nickel, tin, and copper alloy). The Diné are renowned for their silversmithing, a skill learned from Mexican silversmiths in the mid-nineteenth century. In the mid-twentieth century, the silversmiths who became Peyotists incorporated Peyote iconography into their jewelry; this jewelry is now being produced in significant amounts. The Diné, and many others, especially from Oklahoma and South Dakota, craft jewelry and beadwork into earrings, hair stays, bracelets, rings, necklaces, broaches, pendants, bolo ties, scarf and tie slides, buckles, stickpins, and tie clips. Three examples of Diné silver pins, shown in figure 11, illustrate the basic Peyote iconography used on metal jewelry. The piece on the left combines a waterbird and a Peyote button. The middle piece is a replica of a flat feather fan, and the right piece is a tepee resting on a Peyote drum base with a waterbird carrying prayers skyward. Today this style jewelry is commonly worn by Peyotists. Beads are also stitched on to vests, shawls, moccasins, belts, and barrettes. Originally the jewelry was not produced for sale, although it was and still is common to give Peyote jewelry as gifts to other NAC members. The jewelry, both metalwork and beadwork, is fashioned into the symbols of the Peyote faith. A messenger bird, Peyote button, and tepee are the most common motifs, but also feathers, feather fans, rattles, and drums are

Figure 11. Diné Peyote-style silver jewelry. Photo by David Gentilini.

used. For example, silver earrings can be made into the shape of a Peyote button, or tie clips can be crafted with a silver tepee and feathers. Some Peyote jewelry reflects the Cross Fire Way and employs Christian imagery.[12]

ARTWORK CREATED AND USED
OUTSIDE A CEREMONIAL CONTEXT

As Peyotism diffused through the southern plains, artists began illustrating the beliefs, practices, and symbols of the Peyote faith in painting and drawings. The ritual objects mentioned in the early literature and portrayed in photographs were illustrated in two-dimensional artworks. The earliest known Peyote drawings were produced in ledger books by Silver Horn in 1883, although the bulk of his work was produced after 1891. Ledger book drawings emerged during the early reservation era and in POW camps such as Fort Marion in Florida. These drawings are a narrative art form using the pages of account books or similar bound pads of paper acquired from non-Indian sources. The Peyote drawings grew out of the pictorial tradition of the Plains tribes, who recorded personal exploits, tribal histories, and calendars of annual events on tepee coverings, shields, and animal hides. Silver Horn is an important figure in Kiowa history. He is known as an artist who worked in a variety of media and also as a keeper of one of the Kiowa's sacred medicine bundles. More than one thousand of his drawings in pencil, crayon, and ink are extant. He produced artwork on paper, hide, and muslin for four decades. Some of these he created for sale. He was also a silversmith and known for his feather work. Fifty-two of his drawings depict various aspects of Peyotism. His son James claimed that Quanah Parker introduced Silver Horn to Peyote. One of Silver Horn's 1883 drawings shows Parker emerging from a tepee holding two feather fans as if he is welcoming the sun. Silver Horn became an active Peyotist. The importance of his art is reflected in his belief that Peyotism and traditional Kiowa spirituality were not incompatible. He linked Sun Dance and Peyote imagery. For example, he used a rainbow in both Sun Dance and Peyote drawings to symbolize the path to spiritual power. He helped integrate Peyotism into the Kiowa traditional belief system.[13]

Silver Horn's Peyote ledger book drawings are narratives of the all-night Peyote ceremony. In a series of four sketchbooks produced in 1891, he included fourteen drawings illustrating the sequence of ritual events from the setting up of a tepee before the opening at dusk to the closing at dawn when a woman brings in the four sacred foods. He portrays a Roadman, his assistants, ritual paraphernalia, individuals in prayer, and various aspects of the service, such as the midnight and dawn water ceremony. His drawings show great detail, such as the Peyote Road incised along the top of the crescent-shaped mound. Silver Horn also illustrates both men and women worshipping in a tepee.[14]

Silver Horn painted on animal hides as well. At the turn of the century, James Mooney commissioned the artist to produce a large hide painting for display in the Louisiana Purchase Exposition of 1902. It is one of Silver Horn's most striking works (fifty-seven by twenty-eight inches). With vivid colors and a more naturalistic style, it shows he had moved away from the Plains pictorial tradition. His new style was a precursor of the work of future Peyote artists. The hide painting depicts a Sun Dance and a Peyote ceremony, giving them equal significance. The hide is divided into sections with the lower right depicting the Roadman and his three assistants carrying ritual paraphernalia into the tepee. On the left side of the tepee are two Peyotists with their ritual equipment spread out on the ground. Above the two men, sitting outside the tepee, is the Morning Water Woman with a water bucket, preparing to enter at dawn. The top right is Silver Horn's most complete depiction of a Peyote ceremony. It is portrayed as if one is looking down on the service with the tepee cover removed. The Half Moon altar, fire, and firewood are in the center. The Roadman is in front of the altar holding the rattle, staff, and eagle-feather fan while singing. To his right the chief drummer is striking a three-legged water drum. To the left is the cedarman; the fireman is next to the entrance. One of the congregants has four Peyote buttons in front of him, praying before he ingests the first one. Another person is praying while holding a feather fan in front of his face just as one would find today. There is a woman among the participants. Most of the iconic and symbolic images of later Peyote artworks are present in Silver Horn's work with the exception of the messenger bird, which appears later in the Peyote painting of others. The hide painting as a whole portrays two narratives: the procession of ritual events of the Peyote service, and the implicit transition from the days of the Sun Dance, outlawed by the time this painting was created, to the era of Peyotism.[15]

Silver Horn had contemporaries in Oklahoma who were producing Peyote paintings and drawings. Carl Sweezy (Arapaho, 1881–1953) and Earnest Spybuck (Shawnee, 1883–1949) produced Peyote artworks in the early twentieth century. Both had attended Indian boarding schools, were active Peyotists, and became professional artists commissioned by anthropologists to produce artwork for their respective institutions. These artists worked mostly in watercolor depicting themes from everyday life, spiritual activities, and events they experienced, including portrayals of Peyote ceremonies. Sweezy produced several fine pieces of Peyote art, as exemplified by his *Indian Religion*, a watercolor portrayal of a Peyote ceremony with seventeen people, inside a tepee with altar, fire, Roadman, and chief drummer in the midst of drumming and singing, congregants, including three women praying with feather fans. Spybuck also was an accomplished watercolorist. His work shows great precision, giving the viewer an intimate look at the internal activities of a Peyote ceremony. One is struck by the detail in his *Delaware Peyote Religion*, which places the tepee amid trees and stars, giving the piece an in-depth perspective lacking in the work of others. Silver Horn, Sweezy, and Spybuck proved to be very influential among young artists.[16]

The influence of Silver Horn extended beyond his paintings and drawings. He was a role model and teacher for the next generation of Kiowa Peyote artists. A group of young artists, known as the Kiowa Five, emerged as his protégés—all acknowledged him as their teacher. One of the five, Stephen Mopope, was Silver Horn's grandnephew. Mopope along with Spencer Asah, James Auchiah, Jack Hokeah, and Monroe Tsatoke produced a significant body of art in the 1920s and 1930s. They emerged from the tradition of Silver Horn's art but also studied art in a variety of schools, including the University of Oklahoma in 1926–27. In their training, they were influenced by the modernist movements in art, yet remained rooted in their Kiowa heritage. Their emphasis on the waterbird and cormorant as messenger birds became such a prominent part of their imagery that these images, along with the tepee, have been incorporated into the logos of many NAC groups. The two aquatic birds are especially tall, thirty to thirty-six inches, and have very long necks. The waterbird is sometimes called a water turkey because of its size. Artists depict these birds with their neck stretched out, beak pointing upward, wings outstretched, giving a sense of speed and a powerful upward thrust toward the sky. In some renderings, the Peyote button is depicted as the force propelling the birds upward.[17]

Works by Silver Horn's protégés are powerful evocations of the Peyote faith. As time passed, their imagery became more stylized with many of their works focusing on the messenger bird. For example, in his *Peyote Design* (1940), James Auchiah depicts rays exploding from a Peyote button and propelling a cormorant skyward, carrying prayers to the Great Spirit.[18] Tsatoke developed the messenger bird into an elaborate motif, which influenced later Peyote artists to give the messenger bird, along with the tepee, central prominence in their imagery. Tsatoke added movement to his birds, not only upward, but inside the tepee, where the birds are intertwined with smoke from the sacred fire, gliding through the tepee gathering prayers for their eventual journey. In an important study, *The Peyote Ritual: Visions and Descriptions of Monroe Tsatoke*, fourteen of his paintings are reproduced along with statements he made about his faith and his art. Of the fourteen reproductions, seven have a central messenger bird motif. His titles are: *The Cormorant, The Yellow Hammers, Fire Bird, Song Bird, The Bird of Dawn*, and two titled *Water Bird*. He explained that the birds are

> used in many different ways and designs as the messenger bird who flies in the interior of the tepee, to whom prayers may be trusted, and it

is the only one who can carry the message to the heart of the unknown mysteries. . . . The outstretched wings mean this—the flight into the unknown. The outstretched neck is important. The bird is reaching and swaying. On the shoulders are the symbols of the peyote plant.[19]

Tsatoke wrote that his painting was inspired by a vision he had: "When the prayers begin, the messenger gods begin to weave back and forth. They begin to lay designs, the prayers are designs. Out of the prayers new designs become visible." This imagery of fluid prayers is the basis for his bird motifs and designs as he perceives the birds as an "In Between God." The use of spiritual inspiration for his artwork is characteristic of Peyote artists.[20]

Most reflective of the influence of Silver Horn is the work of his grand-nephew, Stephen Mopope (1898–1974), a prolific artist renowned for his many paintings and drawings of Kiowa daily life, traditional ceremonies, and the Peyote faith. In the late 1930s, the government commissioned him to paint murals in the new Department of the Interior building. Today many museums hold his works. Typical of his Peyote paintings is the finely executed *Peyote Design* (see figure 12). This watercolor contains all the essential elements of a Peyote meeting. In the middle, as the central focus, is Grandfather Peyote on the center of the crescent-shaped mound, which has the Peyote Road etched along the top. In the forefront is the sacred fire, ashes, firewood on each side, and a fire stick used to light prayer cigarettes. Just above Grandfather Peyote is the Roadman, flanked on his right by a water drum and two drumsticks and on the left by a water drum, gourd rattle, and eagle-bone whistle. Above the Roadman are two rows of eagle and cormorant feathers, pointing upward, topped by the Roadman's staff. The overall impression is one of upward motion from the fire stick, through the feathers and staff, carrying everyone's prayers skyward. The painting, with its vibrant colors, evokes a sense of balance and symmetry as well as creating an atmosphere of spirituality for individuals to pray, sing, and seek help to follow the Peyote Road.[21]

As the works of the Kiowa Five became more popular, they were shown in major exhibitions in several countries. Some of their paintings were shown in 1928 at the First International Congress of Folk Arts in Prague, Czecho-slovakia, and later in the Exposition of Indian Tribal Arts that toured the United States in 1930. Throughout the 1930s, these artists were very popular not only for their paintings but also for their dancing and their elaborate Kiowa dance regalia.

Figure 12. Stephen Mopope, *Peyote Design*, 1930s. Courtesy National Anthropological Archives.

There were other painters, all Peyotists, such as Beatien Yazz (Diné), Cecil Murdock (Kickapoo), Archie Black Owl (Southern Cheyenne), Russell Wagoshe (Osage), and Tennyson Eckiwaudah (Comanche). Several of them had formal training and became professional artists. In the 1930s, there was a great expansion of American Indian arts, including Peyote art, encouraged by the establishment of Dorothy Dunn's art studio at the Santa Fe Indian School, the Indian Arts and Crafts Board established by Congress in 1935, and the New Deal's Federal Art Project, which put American Indians to work producing arts and crafts. As a result, several of the Kiowa Five were commissioned to paint murals in public buildings. Peyotist Woody Crumbo (Creek/Potawatomi) was commissioned to paint a Peyote mural on a wall in the Department of the Interior in 1940. The mural contains typical Peyote imagery depicting a stylized and highly energized waterbird carrying prayers skyward after bursting forth from a tepee resting on a base that is a huge Peyote button. After so many attempts by federal officials to suppress the Peyote faith, the painting of a Peyote mural in the Department of the Interior is quite ironic.[22]

This expansion in the arts before World War II was evident in major exhibitions. American Indian art was featured at the Golden Gate International Exposition in San Francisco in 1939. It was followed in 1941 by the well-publicized exhibit Indian Art of the United States at New York's Museum of Modern Art. At the latter exhibition, a Peyote work, *Bird in Flight*, by Kiowa painter Monroe Tsatoke, was included. It may have been the first showing of a Peyote work at such a prestigious institution. The painting depicts a slim-necked waterbird rushing prayers upward. There is a prominent Peyote button on each wing. This is a very special work, as it was his last painting; he died of tuberculosis in 1937, at the age of thirty-three. Along with his paintings, Tsatoke composed a number of poems inspired by spiritual experiences:

A Peyote Thought

The Peyote Man is trying to pray
to the unknown mystery he can only call light.
He prays to The Great Light
to understand the light within himself.[23]

The paintings of Tsatoke and the others of this era have common motifs and iconography. Their artistic styles are dynamic and reflect the era in which the works were created as well as the traditional roots and the individual creativity of the artists. Exhibits such as the ones mentioned above were important as they indicated a changing attitude toward American Indian art. Their works were exhibited as fine art, not as ethnography.[24]

As Peyotism expanded into the Southwest, the Great Basin, and the Northwest in the 1950s, the production of Peyote artworks increased. These works were further fostered during the cultural renaissance of the 1960s, which stimulated an explosion of fine arts, performing arts, and literature, as well as a revival of traditional ceremonial practices. This was a nationwide phenomenon, as a greater and greater number of people participated in the revival of traditional spirituality. In terms of American Indian art, the fact that this spiritual revival corresponded with the revival of the arts can be explained by the integral nature of art and spirituality. This decade brought forward a new generation of artists producing Peyote art. Harding Big Bow, Robert Redbird, and Al Momaday (Kiowas), Alfred Whiteman (Cheyenne/Arapaho), and Rance Hood (Comanche) all made significant contributions.

In the late 1960s and throughout the 1970s, Peyote art became more widely recognized as a distinct American Indian art form. As the renaissance in Native arts expanded and museums began exhibiting more American Indian art, they included Peyote art. One such exhibit was at the Southern Plains Indian Museum, Anadarko, Oklahoma, in 1969–70. After its initial showing there, the exhibit traveled to eight other sites in South Dakota and Montana. Of the fifty-seven items in the exhibition catalog, eighteen were Peyote artworks. These included Tennyson Eckiwaudah's oil on canvas *Native American Church: Peyote Religion*. There were two tempera paintings on mat board, six Peyote feather fans, four gourd rattles, all with carved and beaded handles, a silver waterbird pin, and two beaded pendants with waterbird motifs. The artists were Kiowas and Comanches whose art had been produced in the 1960s. Using the contemporary works of Peyote artists, rather than mounting an exhibit of items that were in anthropological collections, was an important development. This trend has continued as more museums are collecting and displaying Peyote items as works of art. In 1993, the Indian Arts and Crafts Board sponsored an exhibit titled Masters of Beauty: Native American Church Art. There has also been a major exhibit of Silver Horn's work at the University of Chicago, and there was a national tour of Peyote art, Symbols of Faith and Belief: Art of the Native American Church, sponsored by the Gilcrease Museum, Tulsa, Oklahoma, where the exhibition opened in 1999 before traveling for several years.

During the latter half of the twentieth century, there was an increase in the production of Peyote art as well as an expansion of the types of art produced. The production of ritual instruments for use in Peyote services increased in conjunction with the growing number of Peyotists. This was especially true on the Diné Reservation, where Peyotism has continued to expand, creating a demand for ritual paraphernalia and Peyote-style artwork such as jewelry. Daniel Swan estimates that there are ten thousand Diné producing Peyote artwork. Some, such as Patrick Scott, have established reputations as accomplished artists. Until the end of the twentieth century, one did not commonly find ritual items for sale. Dennis Lessard points this out about South Dakota. Swan, in *Peyote Art,* makes the same observation.[25] However, this has undergone change. It is now possible to find such items specifically made for the arts market.

In addition, nonritual Peyote art is being produced in ever-increasing quantities. There are more artists to produce such works, plus there are more Peyotists and non-Peyotists who desire such items as paintings, drawings, and original prints, sometimes signed and numbered. Some of these works are reproduced as posters, sponsored by individual artists, various local or regional organizations, or by commercial enterprises. Peyote-inspired metal jewelry and beadwork is made in larger quantities. This type of nonritual Peyote art expanded in the 1970s and 1980s, and today much of it is available commercially. Peyote art began to adorn the covers of record albums, cassettes, and CDs. One can find printed Peyote iconography on pillows, vests, shawls, and T-shirts. Some of these items are found for sale at powwows or flea markets on or near reservations. The commoditization of some Peyote material, including the music, has upset a number of the older members of the Peyote community, who do not want to see their faith commercialized. Today many ritual items, made for the market, can be purchased in arts and crafts stores and online. One can purchase a matching Roadman's staff and gourd rattle, painted water buckets, water drums made from brass, stainless steel or carbon steel, and a wide variety of feather fans. Some items can be special ordered; the purchaser can request specific types of feathers (excluding eagle feathers) or bead colors. Some of the items are mass produced, and some are made by artists working for the sellers. One can also find computer generated Peyote-style prints for sale. Yet the majority of ritual objects, especially those of the highest quality, which are usually not sold to non-Peyotists, are still made by members of the NAC. In spite of the increase in the production of non-ritual Peyote art, the various works, both two-dimensional and three-dimensional, still reflect the spiritual beliefs and values of Peyotism.

The contemporary artworks of Peyotists reflect their roots in the Peyote faith, but their work is dynamic in that it is influenced by trends in modern art. As American Indian art in general, and Peyote art specifically, has become part of the wider world of art, one can detect the various influences in technique and style rooted in movements such as surrealism, cubism, abstract expressionism, and postmodernism, yet the essential inspiration comes from the artist's faith and culture. *Peyote Visions* by Robert Redbird (Kiowa) is such an example. It is a dynamic, highly energized, personal rendering of a prayer, depicting a person holding a gourd rattle and a feather fan. Smoke is swirling around two messenger birds, while twelve eagle feathers and four Peyote buttons appear to hang in midair. All of the images emanate from a large Peyote button, which is releasing the power to carry the prayers skyward. It is a very contemporary work, yet it contains traditional Peyote symbolism and iconography as well as a cornstalk, which is a Kiowa reference to the power of regeneration.[26]

A large majority of Peyotists are highly skilled artists, singers, and musicians. Many have been recognized for their individual talent as singers, painters, bead-workers, and silversmiths. For the most part, they make their own religious paraphernalia and their musical instruments; they create their own music and compose their own songs. One grows up learning these skills within the social context of the Peyote community. It is not just that Peyote art and spirituality are integrated, but that Peyote art and daily life are integrated as well. The function of Peyote artworks produced for ritual purposes is prayer, as prayer facilitates communication with the spirit world. Whether artworks are pro-duced for ritual or nonritual use, they are created and embellished according to aesthetic criteria, iconography, and symbolism that best express the theology, spirituality, healing, and teaching power of Peyote. As many artworks demon-strate, the utilitarian nature of the items produced for use in Peyote religious services does not mean they are devoid of aesthetic principles; in fact the opposite is the case. They are constructed and decorated with the aesthetic criteria that best enhance the imagery that expresses the beliefs of Peyotism. Employing Peyote aesthetics evokes a feeling of union with the power of Peyote. The primacy of Peyote is demonstrated by its size and central position in paintings and drawings. Form and function are integrated. Swan has written that "the interconnectedness of form, design, and religious experience creates objects of exquisite beauty and powerful emotion."[27] The gourd rattle described previously evokes aesthetic balance and a sense of symmetry. Form and function are one, as the design of the rattle, the sound of the rattle, and the prayers it accompanies glorify Peyote, the sacred herb. It epitomizes the ritual use of Peyote art with the integration of aesthetics, iconography, and spirituality, the same integration that is reflected in Peyote music.

PEYOTE MUSIC

Music is an integral part of American Indian life and culture. It is rich and diverse and touches all aspects of daily life. It is intrinsic to spirituality and ceremony. Music perpetuates culture and community, reaffirms ethnicity, communicates with spiritual sources of power, and validates social institutions. It is also essential in healing in virtually all American Indian societies. Peyote music fits within this framework of traditional American Indian music. Along with visual arts, Peyote music energizes and enables the power of Peyote to teach, to protect, and to heal. In essence, it is sacred music. Prayer, music, and healing function together; they cannot be separated. Peyote songs are not an accompaniment to healing; they are, with Peyote, the essential center for healing. The songs are prayers; they are not elements in themselves, but are vehicles for the journey along the Peyote Road. Learning the music at a young age is essential; excellence with song, drum, and rattle part of the criteria to become a Roadman. (See figure 13.) The music is a significant integrative force. Peyote families practice songs and drumming. Adults encourage the youth to practice; first to listen, then to sing and drum. A father or uncle may be heard saying, "[D]id you catch it, did you catch it?" meaning, did you learn the song? Gerald Primeaux said, "[A]s a child, Grandpa Harry [Primeaux] taught me how to catch a song. I would watch him. We practiced with cassettes, practiced on a coffee can covered with a piece of rubber held on by a rubber band. We tie drum, watch others, experts correct you. By age fourteen I could tie drum."[28] There are several sources for the songs. There is a longstanding tradition of passing songs from generation to generation within families as well as learning songs from other Peyotists. Or, one creates a song by inspiration or by revelation as part of a spiritual experience. Whatever the immediate source, the ultimate origin is the power of Peyote. Concerning the origins of songs, a Comanche Peyotist told David McAllester, "I found this song ['It Is Morning, Arise'] by the power of peyote, like all my songs. When I am eating peyote I feel the power, the song comes to me. I could not find them any other way." Another man said to McAllester, "I think this is an Apache song. I did not make any of these songs. The Comanche now do make songs and they also get them in visions . . . those who look for songs have a peyote meeting. . . . I think I know about fifty songs. It is strange I did not make any of these. I just heard them from other people."[29]

Whatever their origins, the songs are gifts to be shared; there are no proprietary rights. Individuals credit the sources of their songs. Many singers have a large repertoire of songs, some of their own, some they learned from others. This also includes songs from other languages. Reuben Snake said his son "sings all kinds of songs, Kiowa and Comanche, Cheyenne and Ponca, Navajo and

Figure 13. Gerald Primeaux, Sr., and son Adrian practicing, 2006, Yankton Sioux Reservation. Photo by author.

Sioux and Apache. Even though we don't speak those languages, we still know what the songs mean."[30] Most Peyotists also have a collection of Peyote music on cassettes and CDs, acquired commercially, given or traded among each other, or recorded at Peyote meetings. At present-day meetings, there are usually several people taping the songs. It would be a rare occasion today to attend a Peyote meeting with only one tribal group represented. People are invited and readily travel to attend meetings. Given the nature of the interaction among Peyotists, there is always opportunity to share songs. For example, Winnebagos and Yankton Sioux attend each other's services. Roadmen are invited to run meetings for other groups. A Diné Roadman may be invited to run a meeting in Oklahoma or South Dakota. Peyote groups in the Great Basin regularly attend each other's services. This has been the norm since the late nineteenth century.

Peyote music is a powerful spiritual force, but it also has tremendous social significance. The music has helped create "community" and has done so for more than a hundred years. It binds generations and ethnicities and spans geographic regions. Music creates a sense of belonging. It begins at home as children learn from adults, as teenagers practice together. Virtually everyone encourages and reinforces the youth to learn songs, to use the gourd rattle and the water drum. This is part of the process of integrating youth into the Peyote community. When a Peyote meeting takes place, people arrive early; after the service is over, they stay for hours, many times discussing and learning new songs. Several may go listen to a particular song on a car CD player, boom box, or iPod.

In the early years of Peyote music, songs were learned by direct contact with other Peyotists as few owned recording devices, nor could many afford the records that were available. Tape recorders were not affordable until the late 1960s and early 1970s, when battery-powered cassette recorders made it possible for Peyotists to record themselves and others and to listen to tapes at home or in their cars.

In the 1890s, anthropologists began recording traditional American Indian music on wax cylinders. Two of the earliest anthropologists to do so were Francis La Flesche and Alice Fletcher, who recorded Omaha songs. Beginning in 1914, Frances Densmore, ethnomusicologist for the Smithsonian Bureau of American Ethnology, began extensive recording of American Indian music. In the 1930s, she recorded Peyote songs of the Winnebagos of Wisconsin, the Cheyennes, and the Arapahos. In 1927, the famous photographer Edward S. Curtis described the rapid growth of Peyotism he saw in his travels. In addition to taking photographs of thousands of American Indians, he recorded Peyote music and included the transcriptions of the four fixed or standard Peyote songs (discussed below) in volume nineteen of his massive twenty-volume *The North American Indian*. In 1936, anthropologist Martha Huot collected Peyote songs from the Fox of Iowa. In the late 1930s as well, Omer Stewart collected Peyote songs from the Northern Paiutes, the Uintah Utes, and the Washoes. In the late 1940s, anthropologist Willard Rhodes, collecting music for the Library of Congress, began recording Peyote songs of the Kiowas, Delawares, Utes, Navajos, and Sioux. David McAllester was recording at this same time as well as studying the recordings of others. His monograph *Peyote Music* appeared in 1949. He recorded mostly Comanche Peyote songs, but included analyses of the Fox, Washoe, Dakota, Cheyenne, Shoshone, Winnebago, and Pawnee music. He used his own recordings for the Comanches, but he relied on the recordings of Stewart, Huot, Densmore, Rhodes, and other anthropologists for the additional groups. McAllester also published a study of Menominee Peyote music.

In the 1940s, Reverend Linn Paughty, a Kiowa Methodist minister, established his own label: American Indian Sound Chiefs. By the 1950s, he had released a considerable number of 78s and LPs of American Indian music, which included Kiowa, Kiowa Comanche, and Kiowa-Apache Peyote songs. The latter have recently been re-released by Indian House Records. Some of the songs are by well-known Peyote Roadmen such as Nelson Big Bow, Harding Big Bow, James Aunguoe, and Ed Hummingbird (Kiowas). Reverend Paughty is important as he was one of the first producers to consider the American Indian market for his records.

In the 1950s, anthropologist Warren d'Azevado began an extensive collection of Washoe Peyote songs. In 1951, Ray Boley founded Canyon Records, which soon became the largest producer of American Indian music. In the 1960s, Tony Isaacs founded Indian House Records and Oscar Humphries founded Indian Records. All three companies have released a considerable body of Peyote music. What was significant about this growth is that there was now an American Indian market for the music. More recently, other labels, such as Cool Runnings Music, Zango Music, and J & C Music (Diné owned), have entered the market. Zango Music has re-released older Peyote songs from the 1970s, as well as con-temporary songs from Canadian NAC communities.

The market for Peyote music today is extensive. The music is sold by the above companies and distributed widely throughout the country and is sold by dealers at most powwows. There are literally hundreds of commercially produced titles. There is also a demand for re-releasing older songs that were issued on LP albums in the 1970s and 1980s. The popularity of Peyote music has been recognized by the Native American Music Awards (Nammys) and the Grammy Awards. The Nammys were established in 1998. In 2000, the Nammy award for the "Best Traditional Music" went to Peyotists Gerald Primeaux, Sr., and Neulon Dion, Jr., for their *Yankton Sioux Peyote Songs: In Loving Memory*. In the same year, the Grammys added an award for the Best Native American Music Album. To the surprise of many, the award went to a Native American Church recording. Johnny Mike (Diné) and Verdell Primeaux's (Oglala/Yank-ton/Ponca) *Bless the People: Harmonized Peyote Songs* won the award. It was the first NAC music to win a nationally recognized award. These two popular singers have produced more than a dozen CDs. With this recognition, record companies began to produce more and more NAC music. With this additional popularity, the Native American Music Association in 2007 added a new cate-gory to the Nammy awards: Best Native American Church Recording. There were many submissions and six nominees that represented a cross section of Peyotists from the United States and Canada, including Denise Becenti, a female

Diné Peyotist. The winner for 2007 was well-known singer Gerald Primeaux, Sr., for his *Voice of a Dakota: Harmonized Healing Songs.* Primeaux is from a multiple-generation Peyote family. His late father, Asa Primeaux, was a well-known singer and Roadman and part of the group of Yankton Sioux singers who developed harmonizing Peyote songs in the 1970s. His grandfather, Harry Primeaux, was also a well-known singer. His great-grandfather was Sam Necklace, chief priest (1929–49) of the Native American Church of Charles Mix County (South Dakota). As with many other Peyotists, Gerald's roots run deep in the Peyote faith. The 2008 Nammy Award for the Best Native American Church Recording went for the first time to a female singer, Janette Turtle (Southern Cheyenne/Navajo), for her *New Beginning.* Of the six nominees for this award, three were women. Having women as singers in Peyote meetings, while holding the Roadman's staff and sage, and using the gourd rattle, has been a significant development in Peyotism since the 1980s and 1990s. This change occurred locally at different times, but it is quite common today, as it is for women to have their own Peyote boxes with all the items needed to fully participate in a service. This change paralleled women's singing and drumming at powwows and women, such as Wilma Mankiller (Cherokee), taking leadership positions in tribal governments. By the late 1990s, women from various Peyote communities in the United States and Canada were commercially recording Peyote music. Several have established reputations as singers and have been accorded public recognition.

There are also significant private collections of Peyote music. Since the advent of the battery-powered recorders, NAC members have been taping themselves and others, much of it during Peyote services. This is in contrast to the music collected by many anthropologists or recorded commercially. Most of the latter was not recorded in actual Peyote services, but in private homes, for example, where sets of songs were sung specifically to be recorded. Most commercially available music was produced in a studio setting. Many of the recordings owned by Peyotists were taped during actual Peyote services and, as many would say, exude the power of Peyote. There are literally tens of thousands of such recordings in private hands, passed on to the next generation. Some collections have been donated to oral history centers or American Indian Studies centers, where they are usually under restricted use as they are considered sacred music.[31]

Peyote music has a distinct sound and style, easily recognizable from the other types of American Indian music. There has been considerable debate as to the origins of Peyote music. Some researchers have claimed that Peyote music was influenced by Ghost Dance music or by the singing style of Christian hymns. The most likely explanation is a Southwest American Indian origin, such as the Apaches, particularly Mescalero Apaches and Plains Apaches, who were closely involved with Peyotism in its early years. The Apaches used a water drum and rattle in their traditional music. They were also in regular contact with the Peyote complex in Mexico, especially the Huicholes, who use a gourd rattle and a small kettle-like drum in a ceremony that is associated with Peyote. Whatever the origin, Peyote music emerged with the origins of the Peyote faith and was well established by the time James Mooney was describing Peyotism in the early 1890s.

Peyote music is performed by two people: a singer using a gourd rattle and a drummer on the water drum. When blessed, the two instruments are considered sacred. The drum is central to the music as it sets the tempo and rhythm. It is also one of the most depicted symbols in Peyote art. Tying the drum in preparation for a Peyote meeting is a sacred process. Before the all-night service begins, the chief drummer enters the tepee with the fire burning and begins the complicated process of the tying the deerskin head to the drum. Each part of the drum is purified by passing it through cedar smoke. The kettle is partially filled with water, then hot pieces of charcoal are placed in the water (the number varies). The skin is soaked in water, squeezed, and placed over the top of the kettle. Seven stones or marbles are used as anchors to secure the drumhead. A cotton rope is tied around the first stone and wrapped around the bottom of the kettle. The rest of the stones are tied in the same manner by the rope, which is crisscrossed around the drum, pulling the drumhead tightly over the kettle (see figure 14). The drum is tied in such a way that the rope forms a seven-pointed star on the bottom of the drum. A sharp tool, made of antler or wood, can be inserted under the rope and twisted, tightening the rope and making the drumhead tauter. When the drum, which sits on the ground at a slightly tilted angle, is played, the drummer holds it by four fingers on the side and the thumb on top. The drum can be tilted at different angles, moving the water inside, affecting its acoustics. The moisture keeps the drumhead taut and responsive to pressure by the thumb in order to alter timbre and pitch. According to one Peyotist in the 1950s, "[T]he drummer must keep his thumb on just the right place to get a full, round sound. . . . The drummer has to catch the voice of each singer and tune the drum."[32] The combination of thumb pressure, water movement, and rapid beating of the drum enables the drummer to produce the desired sound.

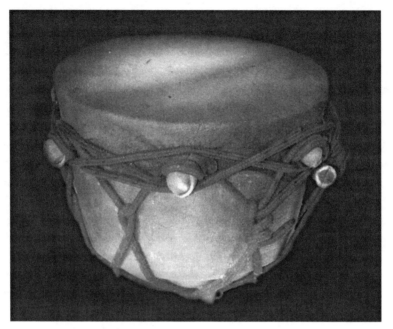

Figure 14. Peyote water drum. Photo by author.

To Peyotists, the drum symbolizes their collective values. Reuben Snake says it represents the heartbeat of your mother, others say the heartbeat of mother earth. Gerald Primeaux describes the drum

> as four elements, the kettle is mother earth, the stretched hide is blue sky, seven marbles are the continents; the water in the drum is ocean, rivers and lakes; the rope ties it [mother earth] all together; the star is the universe; the charcoal represents the spirits of the deceased and those not yet born, the drum beat is the breathing of mother earth . . . with the drum the whole world is in your hands; animal, plant, human.[33]

Peyote songs are divided into two categories: required fixed songs and songs freely chosen by the singer. The fixed are the Opening Song, the Midnight Water Song, the Morning Water Song, and the Quitting or Closing Song, which are usually sung by the Roadman. All other songs are the choice of the singer and can be sung in any order. As the service begins, the Roadman and the chief drummer start with the fixed Opening Song, followed by three songs of their choice. The length of a song varies from one to three minutes. When the

Roadman and chief drummer finish, the rattle, staff, and sage are passed to the person on their left, who asks someone to drum. The drum and the drumstick are passed to that person, as the same drum is used by everyone. Each person sings four songs. Throughout the night, the drum may go around three or four times, depending on the number of persons in attendance. If, for example, there were twenty singers, singing 4 songs each, that would be 80 songs per round, and with four rounds, 360 songs. The singer, who is kneeling on both knees, or sometimes on one knee, holds the staff and sage in the left hand and the rattle in the right. The drummer, who is kneeling on one knee, holds the drum with the left hand and strikes it with the right hand. A single wooden drumstick is used. Drumsticks are made of hard wood and are ten to fourteen inches long and may be incised with designs or decorated with beadwork. They are very special as Peyotists have their own drumsticks. Peyote music sounds different from other American Indian music because of the tempo of the drum. It is much faster, 120 to 150 beats per minute. Most songs begin with a percussive flurry of rattle and drum followed by the singer. This brisk tempo is kept up throughout the song and is accompanied by a vocal delivery of rapidly repeated vocables, words, and phrases. The combination of singers, drum, and rattle, sometimes at the same speed, sometimes at varying speeds, adds to the impression of rapid tempo.[34] Since the 1970s, some Peyotists have added singing in harmony to their repertoire.

Peyote songs have two textual patterns. There are vocables, and there are words and phrases in the vernacular or in English. The vocables are ear-pleasing syllables that have uplifting spiritual significance but do not have a literal meaning. There are short vocables at the beginning and ending of a song and a drop in pitch by the drummer between songs. Some songs, called "straight songs," are all vocables. Within the vocables there is repetition of syllables to multiply the power of the prayer. An example of a line of vocable syllables from a Yankton Sioux song is "*He ya no ho wi da he de yo wa*"; a Washoe example is "*yo wa no hay nay*" or "*no wa nay o na.*" The words in the Yankton songs have many common spiritual themes. The Cross Fire songs have references to Wanikiya, Lakota or Dakota for Savior or Jesus. For example: "*He wanikiya ye yedo o do*, that's what the Savior said." Sometimes the English "Jesus" is used. There are references to the Savior in some Half Moon songs, although Christian elements are generally absent in Half Moon Peyote services. The common themes of the songs include: sinful world, human weakness, individual sin, compassion, taking pity on human beings, giving strength, forgiveness, dawn is coming (new life), everlasting life, and the need for prayer. Many songs are for health and well-being, especially for the children and coming generations, and for a successful journey along the Peyote Road. There are birthday songs, memorial songs, and songs for soldiers such as "God Bless Our Soldier Boys." Requests are made to the Great Spirit, God, Creator, Heavenly Father, Our Lord, and Jesus Our Savior for "life's blessings." There are also references to Peyote: "Our Holy Medicine"; "Peyote, you have seen all the wrong things that I have done. In the name of Jesus, forgive me"; "Eat this peyote with God in mind, and you're going to live"; "I have taken your medicine, so God pity me"; "Peyote pity me. I am trying to be good." Many songs are dedicated to the relatives, past and present.[35]

The music is compelling; words cannot adequately describe it. The combination of rapid tempo and repetition, with two accomplished musicians, makes the music vibrate throughout the tepee; echoes seem to reverberate from everywhere. Other participants may be singing or humming along to support the singer. When a particularly powerful set of four songs has been sung, the Peyote people say it is not just the singers; it is the power of Peyote. It is an all-encompassing experience: the songs are prayers being carried skyward beseeching the Great Spirit to take pity on humble human beings.

CHAPTER SIX

The Struggle for
Constitutional Protection

From its initial incorporation in 1918, the Native American Church grew
steadily, first on the state level then on the national level. Then in 1955, at the
last meeting of the NAC as a national organization, some members proposed
that its charter be revised to encompass a broader range of Peyotists. The proposal passed and the NAC became an international organization, the NAC of
North America. A number of Peyote communities chose not to affiliate with
the international organization—which is still the case today. The purpose of
a broader organization was to mobilize and to coordinate efforts to protect
the religious freedom of its members, and specifically to protect the right to
the sacramental use of Peyote. Although there were no federal restrictions on the
use of Peyote, it was not for lack of trying on the part on several governmental
agencies. In the mid-1950s, Peyotists still worried that federal policy could
change. There was also the problem of state statutes. A number of states protected the religious use of Peyote, but others did not, making the transporting
of Peyote and the possibility of arrest a significant issue. Church members
were also concerned about reports in the popular press about Peyote. Some
outsiders still called it a "cult." In 1951 *Time* magazine reported that sexual orgies
took place under the influence of Peyote.[1]

Meanwhile federal Indian policy was changing. The reform-based Indian
New Deal gave way to the policies of termination and relocation. Federal officials were again proposing policies aimed at assimilating American Indians

and ending the federal-tribal government relationship and the corresponding federal trust responsibility. Dillon Myer, the commissioner of Indian Affairs, actively sought termination of the reservation system. In 1953, Congress passed legislation to carry out this plan. Alongside termination was a relocation program aimed at encouraging American Indians to leave the reservations and seek employment in urban centers. Both programs proved disastrous and were doomed to fail. The federal government backed away from them in the late 1950s and early 1960s. These plans were reminiscent of earlier federal policies and a cause of discomfort to the Peyote community. It was unclear how this would impact the NAC, but changing federal policies created an air of uncertainty.

The severity of the termination and relocation policies provoked a backlash as American Indians who had not been consulted on the new policy initiatives universally opposed them. Charges of "cultural genocide" were hurled at the government. Following termination and relocation to its conclusion meant an end of reservation communities and possible collapse of the social, spiritual, and cultural foundation of Indian life. This possibility provoked an outcry, which contributed to the activism of the 1960s and the determination to take control and preserve the American Indian cultural and spiritual heritage. A political, cultural, and spiritual renaissance emerged that had a significant impact on all American Indian communities. For the NAC one positive consequence was that many American Indians who were not Peyotists now supported the Peyote faith as a religious freedom issue. An unintended consequence of relocation was that a number of Peyotists moved to cities such as Denver, Los Angeles, San Francisco, and Minneapolis and helped establish Peyote communities as part of an activist/urban renaissance.

The issue of religious freedom dominated the concerns of the NAC of North America for the remainder of the twentieth century and continues to do so in the twenty-first century. Peyotists feared the passage of new prohibitive federal and state statutes (California prohibited the possession of Peyote in 1959) as well as unfavorable rulings by local, state, or federal courts in cases in which Peyotists had been arrested for possession of Peyote. There was also a concern about non-Indian use of Peyote. The fear was that the use of Peyote by non-Indians, who sought the same legal right to possess Peyote on religious grounds that the Peyotists had, could result in the loss of such rights by NAC members. There was also a problem in the late 1950s and 1960s about the growing recreational use of Peyote by non-Indians that could lead to a crack-down on "drugs." It was feared that such a crackdown or "war on drugs" could lead to restrictive legislation.

LEGISLATIVE AND LEGAL CHALLENGES

Allen Dale continued as the president of the new international NAC. With the help of the board of trustees, which now included Sidney Slotkin, Dale, and other officers, improved the organizational structure of the NAC and worked to strengthen the lines of communication among the members. Slotkin became a staunch defender of Peyotism in the tradition of James Mooney as scholar/activist. He published popular and scholarly works on Peyote. His major study, *The Peyote Religion*, is still valuable as it contains a history of the legal status of Peyotism, lists of federal and state anti-Peyote statutes, and lists of local- and state-chartered Peyote groups. He also developed a questionnaire to assess the membership and edited the *Quarterly Bulletin*, which was mailed free of charge to all members. The *Bulletin* lasted only three years, but it was a milestone in that it provided a regular means of disseminating information. Slotkin also designed membership cards to help keep track of individual members (see figure 15). The cards could also be shown to law enforcement authorities to prove membership in a bona fide American Indian religious organization, which was entitled to use Peyote for sacramental purposes. The questionnaire Slotkin developed was sent to local Peyote leaders. President Dale wanted to know the extent of the membership. Local leaders were asked to supply information. For example, a questionnaire was sent to Jim Blue Bird, a recognized Peyote leader on the Pine Ridge Reservation. He provided his group's official name and the number of its members: eighty-four men, seventy-eight women, and 168 children. In all, sixty-six groups responded from eighteen states and two Canadian provinces.[2]

The *Quarterly Bulletin* became an essential organ for the NAC to disseminate information. For example it explained how to purchase Peyote. The names and addresses of the peyoteros (Mexican American licensed Peyote harvesters and merchants) were listed as were the prices for Peyote. Members were reminded that Peyote could legally be shipped through the U.S. Postal Service and as of 1957 could legally be imported into Canada. The *Bulletin* listed Peyote communities by state and gave the names and addresses of local leaders. In 1958,

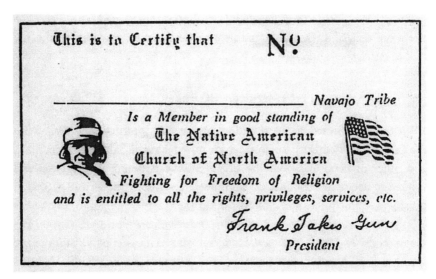

Figure 15. Native American Church membership card.

after three years as editor, Slotkin stepped down over some differences with Takes Gun. Later that year Slotkin died very unexpectedly at age forty-eight.

After a year of organizing and establishing better lines of communication, the NAC met in Scottsbluff, Nebraska, for its annual convention. Frank Takes Gun, the vice president, was elected president, and Hola Tso, the well-known Diné Peyotist, was elected vice president. Takes Gun set two major goals for the organization. First, encourage Peyote communities to incorporate for their own protection. Within the next two to three years he helped groups do so in Arizona, California, Colorado, Nevada, New Mexico, and Utah. His second goal was to challenge state restrictions on the use of Peyote. To accomplish these goals, he enlisted legal help from the American Civil Liberties Union (ACLU).[3]

Frank Takes Gun remained president until 1974. His presidency proved controversial as a number of members accused him of not operating in a democratic fashion. According to some he was a top-down administrator who alienated colleagues by the way he managed policy, flouted the bylaws, and ran the annual conventions. For example, at the 1957 convention, the bylaws were changed so officers, including Takes Gun, could serve six-year terms instead of two-year terms. Some NAC members questioned the process by which the bylaws had been changed, but in 1958 Takes Gun was elected to a six-year term based on the disputed bylaws. Nevertheless, he was an indefatigable fighter for legal rights of Peyotists. Omer Stewart has criticized Takes Gun's leadership style but also credited him with using various legal and political strategies to protect the church on both the state and federal levels. This was in keeping with the stated purpose of the organization: "to protect our way of worship." Takes Gun traveled extensively, meeting with local groups, assessing potential problems with state legislatures, and most important, working on court cases when Peyotists were arrested. His major goal was to have all state restrictions on the sacramental use of Peyote abolished so that wherever one went in the United States, one would have the legal protection to practice one's faith. His area of greatest concern was the Navajo Reservation. Takes Gun sent an open letter to the NAC members in 1957 outlining his concerns. He said he would focus on states that had not exempted Peyote from their substance abuse statutes. He called them "emergency areas." He followed through in 1958 as he helped convince the New Mexico legislature to decriminalize the use of Peyote for religious purposes. Aside from the "emergency areas," he wrote, "foremost among all the trouble areas which we have today is the Navajo Reservation."[4]

The Diné faced a double dilemma. Navajo tribal government as well as the state of Arizona prohibited Peyote, and officials of both governments arrested Peyotists. In each situation the courts responded differently. In 1959, Mary Attakai (Diné), living off the reservation, was arrested in Williams, Arizona, for possession of Peyote. She was defended by the ACLU, with experts such as Omer Stewart and Frank Takes Gun and two psychiatrists testifying for her. ACLU lawyers argued for acquittal based on the free exercise of religion clause of the First Amendment. In Arizona's Superior Court, the judge ruled the anti-Peyote statute unconstitutional as applied to the defendant, whose use of Peyote was part of her religious beliefs. The state appealed the decision to the Arizona Supreme Court, which dismissed the appeal and allowed Mary Attakai's acquittal to stand. The ruling did not affect the state's prohibition of Peyote, but it did set a precedent for the legal use of Peyote as a sacrament. After this ruling, the state of Arizona did not question the religious use of Peyote; however, it remained illegal on the Navajo Reservation.[5]

Although the Attakai case went well for the Peyote community, this was not so in cases involving Navajo tribal authorities. Since the passage of the 1940 ordinance prohibiting the use of Peyote, hundreds of Navajo Peyotists had been arrested. *The Navajo Yearbook* of 1961 lists 768 arrests from 1952 to 1960. In 1956, Mike Kayonnie, a member of the NAC, was arrested and jailed. Since the arrest occurred on a reservation, the case went to federal court. In spite of ACLU lawyers and expert witnesses, the judge ordered the defendant to be kept in jail, thus upholding the Navajos' 1940 ordinance. In 1958, in Shiprock, New Mexico, tribal authorities raided a Peyote service and arrested three Navajo Peyotists. The three were tried, convicted, and sentenced to jail under the 1940 ordinance. The NAC decided to fight this case in U.S. District Court. An appeal was filed, but the U.S. Court of Appeals denied it on the grounds that federal courts had no jurisdiction over tribal laws. The only recourse for the NAC was to challenge the ordinance or to convince the Navajo Tribal Council to reverse its ban on Peyote.[6]

In 1960, with the help of the ACLU, Hola Tso and several other Peyotists sent a letter to the secretary of the Interior requesting that he revoke the 1940 ordinance as a restriction of religious freedom. The letter became part of a class action suit in the U.S. District Court, District of Columbia. The court ruled against the Peyotists. The case went to the U.S. Court of Appeals, which also upheld the 1940 ordinance, claiming the court had no jurisdiction over Navajo legislation. In a final appeal, the U.S. Supreme Court refused to hear the case; thus, the Navajo ordinance was upheld again. At this point the issue was clear: redress through the courts would not work. The only recourse was to convince the Navajo Tribal Council to rescind its 1940 anti-Peyote ordinance.

Through the 1950s and 1960s, the number of Navajo Peyotists grew rapidly. With this growth came collective strength and increased political influence as several Peyotists were elected to the tribal council. In addition, the Navajo Peyotists were organizing as Peyotists had done in other states. In the north, the Northern Navajo Four Corners Area Chapter of the NAC of North America was formed in the 1950s, and in the south, in the Window Rock area, the NAC of Navajoland was established in 1966. A key turning point for the Navajos was when they received support for Peyotism from non-Peyotists. In the early 1960s, Raymond Nakai, was campaigning for the position of chairman of the Navajo Nation. Nakai was not a NAC member, but he was an ardent supporter of civil rights, which included support for the NAC as a religious freedom issue. In return for his championship of its cause, Nakai received the support of the Peyote community and was elected tribal chairman in 1962. Once in office, he stopped the arrests, and along with David S. Clark, the president of the

NAC of Navajoland, began a campaign to have the 1940 ordinance rescinded. With the help of President Takes Gun, Nakia and Clark lobbied the council, trying to convince them that Peyote was not a narcotic but part of a long-standing religious tradition. In March 1967, after two days of debate, the Navajo Tribal Council rescinded the 1940 ordinance by a vote of twenty-nine to twenty-six. The resolution stated: "It shall not be unlawful for any member of the Native American Church to transport peyote into Navajo country, or buy, sell, possess, or use peyote in any form, in connection with religious practices, sacraments or services of the Native American Church."[7] It had been a long struggle, but now on the Navajo Reservation the use of Peyote as a sacrament had legal protection. While the leaders of the NAC had been mostly concerned with the Navajo Reservation, legal problems had emerged elsewhere.

In 1962, three Diné, Jack Woody, Leon B. Anderson, and Dan Dee Nez, were arrested in Needles, California, for the use and possession of Peyote during a religious service. They were tried and convicted; their appeal was denied by the California District Court of Appeals. This case was a major concern for the Peyote community. At the request of the NAC leadership, the ACLU agreed to take the case, which they appealed to the California Supreme Court. The attorneys argued that California did not have a "compelling state interest" case to control illicit drugs, as the defendants had used Peyote in a religious service; thus the use of the compelling-interest standard denied Peyotists their right to the free exercise of their beliefs. The defense also argued that the state could abridge a religious practice only by demonstrating that a compelling state interest outweighed the religious practice. They used the example of the National Prohibition Act of 1919, which banned alcoholic beverages but exempted the use of wine for sacramental purposes. The court concluded that the conviction was an infringement on the defendants' rights. By a five to one vote the California Supreme Court reversed the conviction and acquitted the three men. This was a significant ruling. NAC members were now exempted from California's statute regarding the use of Peyote. Omer Stewart wrote that it had the "greatest national impact." It served as a precedent for later Peyote cases and stood as the standard until *Oregon v. Smith* in 1990, when the U.S. Supreme Court supported Oregon's compelling-interest argument over the NAC's First Amendment right to practice its religion. While these battles were being waged with courts and legislatures, there was struggle within the leadership of the NAC of North America.[8]

LEADERSHIP CONTROVERSY

After the election of Frank Takes Gun in 1958, disgruntled members, mostly from Oklahoma, refused to recognize his election and established an alternative organization, keeping the name NAC of North America. A planning meeting was held in 1964, followed by an annual convention later that year. Emerson Decorah (Winnebago, Wisconsin) was elected president. Frank Takes Gun continued to serve as president of the original group, still leading the struggle for religious rights and seemingly disregarding the reconstituted group. The latter were also upset because Takes Gun had spent so much of his time and resources struggling for the Navajo Peyotists that he was not paying attention to other important issues. The Navajos were grateful for Takes Gun's support but were uneasy about the allegations that he had been elected improperly. As a consequence, segments of the Navajo Peyote community distanced themselves from Takes Gun. By the end of the 1960s, when the sacramental use of Peyote was legalized for the Navajos, they were able to focus on the leadership issues in the NAC.[9]

The final break between the Navajo Peyotists and Takes Gun occurred in 1968, when Takes Gun was re-elected president at a poorly attended national convention in Gallup, New Mexico. The officials of the Native American Church of Navajoland, led by President Clark, rejected the election of officers in the Takes Gun group. In a letter to the *Navajo Times*, they cited voting irregularities. One long-range result of this episode was that the NAC of Navajoland did not affiliate with the NAC of North America; it has remained independent up to the present. The other major Navajo group, the Four Corners Branch, joined the reconstituted NAC of North America, which held its own election in 1968, choosing to ignore the Takes Gun group. There were other smaller Navajo Peyote communities; some, such as the Northern Navajoland Native American Church Association, affiliated with the NAC of North America; other groups remained independent. In spite of this disunity, Peyotists could come together on one issue: protecting Peyote from state and federal restrictions.[10]

By the early 1970s the breach between various Peyote communities had begun to close. In 1972, James Atcitty, a prominent Navajo from New Mexico, was elected by both branches of the NAC, although Frank Takes Gun continued to refer to himself as the president. By 1976, the split had been healed, with both NAC groups being incorporated into one organization. In spite of the confusion with the leadership of the NAC of North America, the state organizations continued to function; for the most part, Peyotists were more involved with their local groups and state organizations than with the national group. The two Navajo groups previously mentioned as well as state organizations in Oklahoma and South Dakota operated effectively, meeting the spiritual and legal needs of individuals and affiliated groups. One of the most effective groups was the Native American Church, State of Oklahoma. In 1966, they revised their constitution and bylaws, reaffirming their commitment to the practice of "Peyote Sacrament" and to the traditional values of Peyotism: charity, industry, morality, sobriety, right living, self-respect, and brotherly love. The state organizations accepted local chapters as members, and with a small annual membership fee, the local members could attend and vote at state conferences.[11]

While the turmoil over the leadership was swirling in the 1960s and the early 1970s, other larger issues were on the horizon in Texas, the source of all Peyote in the United States, as the federal government prepared to crack down on illegal drugs. As previously mentioned, the cultural renaissance had a significant impact on American Indian life. Partially as a result of the renaissance, the American public became more knowledgeable about American Indian culture and spirituality, including the NAC and Peyote. This was not a favorable development for the NAC community as counterculture youth, or hippies, sought out Peyote, believing it contained significant amounts of hallucinogenic properties. Much of this was misinformation, yet many youth began trespassing on the Peyote habitat in Texas or trying to buy it illegally. The NAC was alarmed, as were the federal government and officials in Texas.

The interest of American youth in Peyote goes back to the early 1950s, when members of the beat generation, so-called beatniks, such as Jack Kerouac, Allen Ginsberg, and William Burroughs began experimenting with Peyote. All three had spent time in Mexico, where they had easy access to Peyote. What gave Peyote its notoriety in the 1950s was the publication of Aldous Huxley's *The Doors of Perception* (1954); Huxley was already a cult hero to the beats for his *Brave New World* (1946). The beat generation greeted his new book with great enthusiasm. Huxley reported on his experiments with Peyote and tried to convince his readers that Peyote could open the doors of human consciousness and prepare the way to reach a mystical state. More and more of the beat group began seeking out the cactus. This small group of writers popularized Peyote to others of their generation. For example, in Ginsberg's well-publicized poem "Howl," he mentions Peyote; he recited the poem at poetry readings across the country. The beat generation was certainly familiar with Peyote, but they were a small subculture with limited influence on the wider American youth culture. This would change in the mid-sixties, when the emerging counterculture turned to the beat writers, especially Kerouac and Ginsberg, for inspiration. The significance of the beat generation in this context is that their writings helped introduce youth of the 1960s to hallu-cinogenic drugs in general and to Peyote, specifically.[12] Huxley's *The Doors of Perception* became popular with counterculture youth after the rock group The Doors made it known that their name came from his book. Now that the counterculture was cognizant of Peyote, it became an issue for state and federal authorities and a crisis for the Peyote community, which feared another movement to outlaw their sacrament. In addition to these fears, the growing knowledge of Peyote created other problems, such as the concern over the supply of Peyote. It was not widely available, since it grew only in Texas. The survival of the Peyote cactus was threatened as more and more people sought Peyote buttons.

FEDERAL AND STATE POLICIES

Many state and federal officials believed there was an impending drug crisis and began to take measures to counter the growing use of drugs among America's youth. In 1965, the U.S. Congress passed the Drug Abuse Control Act, which added hallucinogens to the controlled substances list of depressant and stim-ulant drugs. Peyote, even with a small amount of hallucinogenic material, was included; however, an exemption was written into the *Federal Register* for the sacramental use of Peyote by members of the NAC in "bona fide religious ceremonies." In addition, the suppliers of Peyote were required to register and maintain a record of receipts and disbursements. In 1967, Texas made the possession of Peyote illegal, without the exemption. As Texas was the only source of Peyote, the NAC became involved. A group of Peyotists met in El Reno, Oklahoma, to develop a strategy. They decided to test the constitu-tionality of the Texas prohibition. David S. Clark, working with Frank Takes Gun, had himself arrested for possession of Peyote. In 1968, the case went to state court, where Clark's attorney cited the exemptions in other states such and California and Arizona and argued that the sacramental use of Peyote was part of a religious tradition. The court ruled in favor of Clark, stating that the "evidence in this case has shown that Peyotism is a bona fide religion practiced by members of the Native American Church, and that Peyote is an essential ingredient of the religious ceremony." The Texas statute as applied to the defendant was declared unconstitutional. The NAC petitioned the governor and the legislature asking for a statewide exemption. A delegation of NAC leaders testified at the state legislature. Given the testimony and the court decision in the Clark case, the Texas legislature amended its 1967 statute and made an exemption for Peyotists, stating that parts of the law relating to the possession and use of Peyote did not apply to "members of the Native American Church in bona fide religious ceremonies." Two additional requirements were added: the suppliers of Peyote (the peyoteros) had to register with the state and the exemption did not apply to individuals with "less than 25 percent Indian blood." The blood-quantum requirement was specifically included to prevent non-Indians from also seeking an exemption. Although Texas exemption was a major victory for the NAC, some church members had concerns about the blood-quantum requirement and the need to prove church membership.[13]

At the same time, the U.S. Congress was under pressure to revise and toughen federal laws in regard to increasing drug use. In 1970, it passed the Comprehensive Drug Abuse Prevention and Control Act, which consolidated dozens of antidrug laws. Peyote was specifically classified as a hallucinogen in the Schedule I list of controlled substances (divided into narcotics and hallucinogens), which included clearly dangerous drugs such as heroin, LSD, and psilocybin. However, this statute was not aimed at the Peyote use by the NAC; it was aimed at the nonspiritual use of Peyote and the use of Peyote by non-Indians, especially counterculture youth. By this time, attitudes concerning the sacramental use of Peyote had changed—very few voices spoke against it. In fact the reverse was the case. Dr. Robert L. Bergman, a public health physician on the Navajo Reservation, claimed there were no negative effects caused by Peyote. Dr. Bergman, who attended Peyote services and interviewed several hundred Peyotists, stated that very few of the interviewees said they experienced visions or had any ill effects. In line with changing opinions, the Department of Justice wrote a regulatory exemption for NAC members, following what several courts and states had ruled or legislated in the past decade. Under the category Special Exempt Persons, it states that

> the listing of peyote as a controlled substance in Schedule I does not apply to the non-drug use of peyote in bona fide religious ceremonies of the

Native American Church, and members of the Native American Church so using peyote are exempt from registration. Any person who manufactures peyote for or distributes peyote to the Native American Church, however, is required to obtain registration annually and to comply with all other requirements of law.[14]

The federal exemption has one major difference from the Texas statute. There is no mention of a blood-quantum requirement. Furthermore, membership in a federally recognized tribe was not mentioned, although membership in the NAC was mandatory. Several issues emerged from this statute and the exemption. First, some Peyotists were upset that their sacred herb was labeled a "drug." Second, this raised the issue of whether non-Indians could participate in Peyote services, partake of the holy sacrament, and become members of the NAC, and whether non-Indian groups could apply for the exemption as had already happened in New Mexico. In 1963, the Church of the Awakening, a non-Indian group, applied for an exemption from the federal regulations to use psychedelic drugs. Other groups, such as the Neo-American Church, also applied. Both were denied, but the possibility of a non-Indian group's being granted an exemption remained. In any case, by 1970, federal policy allowed for the religious use of Peyote by NAC members, and many states had similar exemptions. Nevertheless the Peyote community remained uneasy, always fearful that governmental policies could change and restrictions be placed on its religious practices.

In 1971, the NAC met in Tama, Iowa, for its annual convention. It was a difficult time as President Leonard Springer (Omaha) had just died and Vice President Walter Wabaunasee (Iowa, Fox) served as the presiding officer. The implications of recent federal and state legislation dominated the convention. As positive as the exemptions were, they raised concerns. The debate focused on membership cards. This was crucial as proof of membership could mean the avoidance of arrest. How to do this with an expanding membership, with many members living in remote areas, would not be easy, and it would be expensive. Earlier attempts to introduce membership cards in the 1950s had had limited success. Some NAC members feared the cards would get into the wrong hands. They settled on numbered cards that would be distributed to affiliated groups, who would then distribute them to their members. As part of this discussion the "hippie movement" was brought up as a threat to the church and the supply of Peyote. This opened up the issue of who should be allowed into Peyote services. The question was asked about the legality of allowing "Caucasian friends" into the ceremonies. Joe Shields (Yankton Sioux) asked whether he could have "some paper to deny anyone from entering our ceremony." Former president Truman Dailey stated that "this religion is for Indians and Indians alone . . . that only Indians should participate in our ceremonies."[15] All these concerns were real and contentious and would remain so throughout the rest of the twentieth century. No less a concern were the possibilities that the exemptions for the NAC could be rescinded or not upheld in court and that non-Indians would be given access to Peyote. This possibility emerged in 1973.

In 1969, in Parks, Arizona, undercover agents from the Department of Public Safety gained access to a Peyote meeting that was being conducted by Diné Roadman Dan Chee. The service was held to bless the marriage of Janice and Fred Whittingham, non-Indians. Once Peyote was distributed, the agents arrested almost everyone. The Diné Peyotists were defended by the tribe's legal counsel and under Arizona's exemption the charges were dismissed. However, the non-Indians were put on trial and convicted of possession of an illegal substance. In 1973, their conviction was overturned by the Arizona Court of Appeals (*State of Arizona v. Janice and Fred Whittingham*), which concluded that Peyote was used during a religious service and thus protected by the U.S. Constitution. Many observers wondered whether this would open the door to non-Indian groups using religious arguments to gain legal access to Peyote. This certainly was a concern, but it would be rectified by new federal legislation in 1978. This case added to *Woody et al.* further established the constitutional basis for a religious exemption for Peyote use. Both of these rulings were cited as precedents in similar cases, such as *Whitehorn v. State of Oklahoma* (1977). George Whitehorn, a NAC member, was arrested for driving with an expired license. He also had Peyote buttons strung on a necklace he was wearing. He was convicted of possession, but on appeal, citing *Woody* and *Whittingham*, the appellate court overturned his conviction, stating that the state did not have a compelling reason to not grant him the exemption.[16]

Yet the possession of Peyote for religious reasons remained a major issue as there were considerable discrepancies among state laws regarding exemptions. Oregon was one of the few western states that did not allow an exemption for the sacramental use of Peyote. Roland Soto, a Peyotist, was arrested in an unusual case. He was stopped for a traffic violation when the officer saw a small "medicine bundle" hanging from the rear-view mirror. Upon investigation the officer found a dried Peyote button. Soto was arrested and charged with possession of an illegal substance. The unusual aspect of the trial was that the judge refused to allow the attorneys to present a religious defense of the charges. Soto was found guilty, and the Oregon Court of Appeals upheld his conviction. This case and other religious freedom issues made the struggle for self-determination more intense.[17]

The struggle for self-determination intensified in the early 1970s as part of the cultural and spiritual renaissance. For a cultural and spiritual renewal to be viable, greater political and economic autonomy were essential. Spurred on by the activities of the American Indian Movement and the National Congress of American Indians as well as many urban and reservation Indian groups, American Indians became more committed to working for change. This commitment was fueled by frustration over unresolved issues, many related to religious liberty. In addition to concerns raised in the Soto case about the admissibility of a religious defense, there was growing anger over myriad unresolved issues, such as the protection of sacred sites. Other issues included the difficulty in acquiring sacred eagle feathers, the rights of prisoners to practice their faith, the looting of Indian cemeteries, the return of thousands of stolen sacred objects, and the vexing issue of repatriation of human remains. There were literally thousands of skeletal remains in museums, universities, and private collections. These issues brought together a diverse group of American Indians seeking federal protection. A bill was introduced into Congress after much lobbying. Hearings were held, testimony was given, and Congress passed the American Indian Religious Freedom Act of 1978 (AIRFA). It reaffirmed the principle of religious freedom, stating: "Whereas the freedom of religion for all people is an inherent right, fundamental to the democratic structure of the United States and is guaranteed by the First Amendment . . . [it is] the policy of the United States to protect and preserve for American Indians their inherent right of freedom to believe, express, and exercise the traditional religions . . . and the freedom to worship through ceremonials and traditional rites." The bill mandated federal agencies to protect the religious freedom of American Indians and to change any federal regulation that impaired the free exercise of beliefs and practices. AIRFA was welcomed and cheered by many American Indians; it brought much-needed attention to the issues, safeguarded some sacred sites, and helped establish the principle of the repatriation of sacred objects and human remains. However, within a year the shortcomings of the bill became obvious. It was a statement of policy that did not establish any rights that could be protected in a court of law, nor did it establish any enforcement procedures. As many said, "It lacked teeth." Peyote and the Native American Church were not mentioned in the bill, but it had been assumed that they would be protected by AIRFA as an American Indian religion. But as a piece of legislation, AIRFA was unfinished business as it was not full-proof protection for the religious liberty issues at hand, as the NAC would soon learn.[18]

THE PEYOTE GARDENS

Since the emergence of the Peyote faith, the supply of Peyote buttons has been an issue. At first the problem was interference by federal and state officials, who tried to stop the harvesting, sale, and distribution of Peyote. It was confiscated and destroyed by federal officials, mailing it via the U.S. Postal Service was made illegal for several decades, and many states passed laws against it. From the 1930s to the 1960s, however, the restrictions on the possession and use of Peyote were lessened, with the federal government and many states exempting the religious use of Peyote from their drug regulations. In the 1960s, the supply of Peyote became a concern. Demand for Peyote grew as the Peyote faith expanded, especially among the Diné and among groups in the Northwest. For example, in the 1970s, three Peyote communities in the state of Washington filed incorporation papers. Virtually all major cities west of the Mississippi River now had Peyote communities. Other threats to the supply included the loss of Peyote habitat and the closing of Peyote growth areas by local landowners, the "invasion" by hippies, and a growing problem of improper harvesting of Peyote. All these factors have threatened the supply, causing a dramatic increase in the cost of Peyote.

As described earlier, the Peyote cactus grows in northeast Mexico and southeast Texas along the Rio Grande. NAC members refer to this growth area as the *Peyote Gardens*, a term of reverence, as it is considered sacred ground, a Garden of Eden. All Peyotists desire to make a pilgrimage to the land of the holy sacrament. They want to see the cactus in its natural habitat and walk on what they believe is holy land. One Washoe from Nevada described the trip:

> We made that trip in a few days. Nobody got tired. We didn't sleep once. Nobody got hungry. We didn't have no [*sic*] flat tires and that old car kept moving as long as we were singing. We kept passing through towns and moving over the road like the wheels wasn't on the ground. We

didn't make dust. We saw people looking at us. . . . We made it. We found where the Medicine grows. We was singing there and had a couple little Meetings there. We prayed all the time on that trip. We prayed to the Medicine where It was growing in that gray sand like they got in Texas.[19]

It is not an elaborate, ritualized pilgrimage like that undertaken by the Huicholes in Mexico, but more of an individualized trip with friends or family to a revered place. While in the Peyote Gardens prayers are offered, sage is used for purification, tobacco may be sprinkled on the ground, and sometimes Peyote services are held at the homes of the peyoteros. As part of this spiritual experience, Peyotists may also harvest a small number of Peyote buttons for themselves.[20]

In the early years of the Peyote faith, Peyote was harvested by individuals, or purchased from landowners or from the peyoteros. The peyoteros eventually came to dominate the trade, turning it into a commercial enterprise. In order for this to become a successful business, a positive interaction among landowners, peyoteros, and Peyotists was needed. This was essential to establish a regular supply of Peyote since the natural habitat of the Peyote cactus is on private property. In the early years, some landowners welcomed the peyoteros and the Peyotists, sometimes making a small profit from the transactions. With permission of the landowners, the peyoteros harvested, dried, and sold Peyote in sacks of a thousand buttons. The peyotero system developed in the late nineteenth century in Los Ojuelos, a small community in the Peyote growth region with access to nearby rail lines. As Peyotists traveled to Texas it was quite easy to purchase dried Peyote. If green Peyote was harvested or purchased, it would take several days to dry, which would increase the cost of the trip. If one traveled long distances with green Peyote, there might be spoilage. The peyoteros provided a service by having dried Peyote ready to sell or mail. The peyoteros, located mostly in Laredo, Oilton, and Mirando City, Texas, saw their role as being more than just running a business. They understood that they were supplying a sacred medicine. Over the years many friendships developed as the peyoteros opened their homes to visiting Peyotists. In some cases the peyotero tradition was passed to subsequent generations, as were the friendships between the two groups.[21]

Amanda Cárdenas and her husband, Claudio, were two of the most well-known peyoteros. Mrs. Cárdenas harvested and sold Peyote for almost sixty-years. She inherited the business from her father who had been a supplier since the early 1920s. From her home in Los Ojuelos she became well known to Peyotists from around the country. She was always referred to with terms of endearment as "mom" or "grandma." In 1957, she moved to the nearby town of Mirando City, a center of the Peyote trade. Her home was a gathering place for NAC members. She had space for people to camp and a tepee and hogan to hold prayer services. Each February, she hosted Peyote ceremonies for the many visitors. In February 1975, for example, she registered 350 guests and had to hold Peyote meetings over several days to accommodate everyone. She was a personal friend of many NAC leaders. She became the first person to be licensed by the state of Texas in 1969 when Peyote merchants were required to register. Cárdenas continued her work into her eighties, but even after her harvesting days were over, her home remained a pilgrimage site. Many Peyotists have fond memories of her. Many wanted to be photographed with her and take mementos home. When individuals left for home, she blessed them, saying, "In the name of the Father, Son, and Holy Ghost, carry these people and sacred medicine home safely." She died in 2005 at age one hundred. She had a Catholic funeral mass followed by an all-night Peyote ceremony to honor her life. Her land with a small Peyote garden, home, tepee, and hogan was divided into five lots. Two of the lots went to her son, Claudio, Jr., and three lots were put in a perpetual trust for the Native American Church.[22]

Since the late1960s, the supply of Peyote has been threatened by a variety of factors. The most notable impact was the large number of Diné traveling from Arizona to the Peyote Gardens. At the same time young people were flocking to Texas (and Mexico) seeking Peyote. This was illegal, but made no difference to hundreds of young people who trampled through the area in search of the small cactus. This was disruptive to the legal Peyote trade. They were trespassing on private property, thus angering many landowners, who began fencing their land and locking the gates. The so-called hippies were seeking a "drug," giving Peyote a negative image by associating it with more powerful hallucinogens such as LSD. By closing their land, the owners also effectively kept out the peyoteros, who had the legal right to harvest Peyote but needed permission to be on private property. Sometimes permission was given, but less so in the 1970s. In the northern region of the Peyote Gardens, there were mostly large land holdings, so just a few recalcitrant owners had a great impact on the supply. In the southern or the lower Rio Grande region, there were mostly small land holdings, so one could more easily find individuals willing to give permission for the harvesting. The year 1972 seems to have been the high point of young people trespassing and causing problems. By 1975 they were mostly gone, but the stigma of Peyote as a "drug" remained. The damage had been done as some angry landowners refused to allow anyone to harvest Peyote on their land. A related consequence is that the Mexican government, equally alarmed by the influx of young Americans, criminalized the possession of Peyote and forbade its export.[23]

There are two other factors related to the reduction of the Peyote natural habitat. In the 1930s, as the oil industry expanded in the region, new roads opened Peyote areas that were difficult to reach, but this access brought inexperienced harvesters into the fields. Even some oil workers made extra money cutting off the tops of Peyote plants and selling them to visiting Indians. Much of this harvesting was done carelessly, causing permanent damage to large swaths of Peyote plants. To ensure regeneration, the top of the cactus must be cut in a specific manner. A short, flat shovel is placed just slightly below the soil surface and pushed horizontally with the ground, slicing off the top of the cactus. If done properly the root regenerates; sometimes multiple tops emerge. If cared for properly, a Peyote field could reproduce itself indefinitely as new tops emerge in about two months. The Peyote cactus is very resilient if harvested properly. Today's peyoteros are not part of this problem. They are licensed, experienced, and very careful as they respect the plants and do not want to harm their livelihood. The second factor that affects the supply of Peyote is root plowing. This is a technique in which the soil is turned over by a tractor pulling large vertical tines that turn the soil and pull up the roots of plants. The natural vegetation is destroyed, and the land is seeded with grasses. This has been undertaken by a number of landowners who want to increase their grazeable land. In the past fifty years or so, thousands of acres of natural Peyote growth have been lost. Given all these factors, the declining supply of Peyote and the increased demand for it have created a vexing problem for the Peyote community.[24]

From the mid-1980s until the present, the supply of Peyote and the legal issues surrounding it have been a major concern to the leadership of all Peyote groups. In July 1982, the NAC of North America held its thirty-third annual convention in Saskatchewan, Canada. In President Emerson Jackson's (Diné) annual report, the supply issue was paramount, particularly in reference to non-Indian groups who wanted access to Peyote. A group called the Peyote Way Church of God had just filed suit against the state of Texas and the federal government challenging the 25 percent Indian-blood-quantum requirement to buy Peyote. If successful this would open the floodgates to similar groups seeking an exemption, thus further threatening the supply. After serving four years as president, Jackson stepped down. Douglas Long (Winnebago, Wisconsin), the secretary for the past four years, was elected the new president. As a result of the concern over the supply, Long appointed an advisory committee to the Texas Department of Public Safety to keep the lines of communication open and make sure the church leaders had input into any change in state regulations. Like some of his predecessors, Long was an activist president. He was a lifelong member of the NAC and former president of the NAC of Wisconsin. He began his presidency with a fact-finding trip to NAC chapters. He continued to travel widely, attending Peyote services and being invited to serve as Roadman for local Peyote communities. He also spent time in the nation's capital, meeting with private and public agencies including the DEA, Surgeon General's Office, Indian Health Service, U.S. Customs Service, and the U.S. Postal Service. He was determined to have full federal protection for the NAC.

Throughout the late 1970s and 1980s, there were still problems. Church members were occasionally arrested, but released when law enforcement officials learned of the exemptions. Nevertheless it was a great inconvenience with lost work and family disruption. There were also challenges from non-Indian groups who also wanted the special exemption. In 1976, one such group, the Native American Church of New York, claimed federal restrictions on Peyote were unconstitutional. Members sought the right to use any psychedelic drug based on the First Amendment and the exemption given to the NAC. In 1979, the federal district court in New York rejected the group's claim, stating that they did not prove that they were a bona fide religion, yet concluded that they were eligible for the exception if they could prove their case. This was troubling commentary from this court's interpretation of federal regulations. Cases such as this posed a danger for the Peyote community. They feared for the future if non-Indian groups had legal access to their sacred herb, which was already in short supply.[25]

NAC leaders, such as Presidents Jackson and Long, used strong language to encourage church members to obey the law and follow the regulations concerning Peyote; failing to do so, might jeopardize the situation for all. They realized the potential threat from a small case working its way through the court system. They argued that Peyotism is an Indian religion and others should not be allowed to join or partake of the holy sacrament," especially as the lawsuit filed in Texas by the Peyote Way Church of God was still in the courts. Jackson is reported to have claimed that at the 1982 convention a resolution was passed supporting the one-fourth Indian-blood-quantum requirement for membership. (It is not in the convention minutes.) Two sources claim that Jackson informed the FBI about a white couple in North Dakota who were members of a local NAC chapter and had Peyote in their possession. They were arrested in 1984. A jury trial was held in federal court. Even though they were not American Indians, they were found innocent as they proved they were members of a Peyote congregation. This was troublesome to the NAC leadership, but it points to another contentious issue about the requirement for membership as not all Peyotists support a blood-quantum requirement.[26]

OREGON V. SMITH: A CHURCH CRISIS

The year 1990 was a watershed for religious freedom issues. While the U.S. Congress passed legislation protecting human remains, burial sites, and sacred objects, the U.S. Supreme Court narrowed the free exercise of religion clause of the First Amendment in regard to the sacramental use of Peyote by American Indians. After a considerable lobbying effort by American Indians over several decades, Congress passed the Native American Graves Protection and Repatriation Act. The law requires federal agencies and private museums and universities receiving federal funds to inventory their collection of human remains, associated funerary objects, sacred objects, and objects of cultural patrimony, notify the tribes of origin, and return the remains and objects if requested. Meanwhile the Supreme Court dealt a blow to the NAC by delivering a decision that some people consider one of the court's most infamous rulings: the narrowing of the free exercise of religion principle of the First Amendment.[27] This decision caused shock and dismay and led to a firestorm of protest culminating in new federal legislation in 1993 and 1994.

With the passage of AIRFA in 1978 the Peyote community was less concerned about federal interference than at any time in the past. There was still concern on the state level because some state laws differed from federal regulations. The fear that a minor incident could lead to a major crisis was realized in 1983–84, when two men, Alfred Smith (Klamath) and Galen Black (non-Indian), were fired as drug and alcohol abuse counselors for violating an agency policy against "abuse of substances." Both men had attended NAC services and had ingested Peyote. They were hired in 1982 by Douglas County (Portland, Oregon) Council on Alcohol and Drug Abuse Prevention and Treatment. When they applied for unemployment compensation from the Oregon Employment Division, they were turned down because they had been "terminated for misconduct" in using an illegal drug. In Oregon, the possession of Peyote was a felony, punishable by up to ten years in prison. Smith and Black filed a lawsuit against the Employment Division claiming that they were protected by the free exercise clause of the First Amendment; thus, they should receive unemployment compensation. The Court of Appeals reversed the decision of Employment Appeals Board and awarded both men unemployment compensation. The state of Oregon petitioned the Oregon Supreme Court to review the Appeals Court decision, which they affirmed in June 1986. The Oregon attorney general, David Frohnmayer, unhappy with this ruling, petitioned the Oregon Supreme Court to reconsider its decision. The petition was denied; however, the case did not end there as Frohnmayer appealed to the U.S. Supreme Court. At this point the NAC leadership became involved. Several amicus briefs were filed supporting Smith and Black. One was filed by attorneys Walter Echo-Hawk and Steven Moore of the Native American Rights Fund (NARF) on behalf of the NAC of North America and the NAC of Navajoland. Briefs were also filed by the American Jewish Congress and the ACLU in support of the religious liberty issues involved. In December 1987, the U.S. Supreme Court heard the case.[28]

As the decision was pending, one crucial case was settled and another was in litigation. In *Lyng v. Northwest Indian Cemetery Protective Association* (1988), a major religious freedom case was lost when the U.S. Supreme Court allowed the U.S. Forest Service to construct a highway through the Chimney Rock area in California's Six Rivers National Forest. A six-mile stretch of the area is considered a sacred site by three American Indian nations. They claimed the area was essential to their ceremonies and the road threatened their right to the free exercise of religion. In the other case, a suit filed by the Peyote Way Church of God challenging the special exemption for NAC members was pending in the Fifth Circuit Court of Appeals. The court would eventually support the DEA's exemption based on the federal government's responsibility to protect American Indian religions and cultures as required by AIRFA and as part of the federal government's "trust responsibility," but this outcome was not yet known. With the *Lyng* decision, Smith and the NAC feared the worst. If the court would not protect a sacred site, would it protect the sacramental use of a sacred herb and award unemployment compensation to Smith and Black? One week later, the court sent the case back to the Oregon Supreme Court asking them to determine if the sacramental ingestion of Peyote was a crime in Oregon.[29]

After hearing arguments from both sides, the Oregon Supreme Court decided not to rule on the legality of the issue as no one had been arrested and indicted. They concluded, however, that if a person were arrested for the good faith ingestion of a sacrament, his or her arrest would violate the First Amendment. The court cited AIRFA and pointed out that twenty-three states and the federal government had such exemptions. The judges ordered the Employment Appeals Board to award unemployment compensation. Frohnmayer saw some weaknesses in the ruling and refiled with the U.S. Supreme Court, which agreed to rehear the case. The stakes for the NAC could not have been higher. At its 1988 annual convention, the NAC of North America voted to use legal help from NARF and to try to prevent the case from reaching the Supreme Court. The attorneys discussed with Smith the possibility of withdrawing the case and not risking a negative decision by the court. There was tremendous pressure on Smith, but in the end he would not withdraw his case.[30]

Alfred Smith had had a difficult life with childhood trauma and alcohol problems, but in midlife he had a job, became a member of the NAC, and was living a sober life. Now he was in a legal quagmire for practicing his faith. He said:

> I was born on the Klamath reservation and by the age of eight was taken from my home and put in a parochial school. The remainder of my education was in boarding schools. . . . I was separated from my family and stripped of my language, my culture, and my identity. Eventually I became an alcoholic. At the age of thirty-six I stopped drinking and began a life of recovery. . . . That was the beginning of my introduction to the way my ancestors lived, and to this day I receive spiritual guidance through Native American ceremonies. . . . It was Native spirituality that brought my life into a totally new perspective. I learned how to live and how to understand the Creator in a natural way.[31]

In November 1989, when the U.S. Supreme Court began to hear arguments in the case, several hundred Peyotists traveled to Washington, D.C., to support Smith, to hold public prayer vigils and blessing ceremonies, and to sit in on the hearings. Viewpoints were mixed. Some Peyotists supported Smith; others had hoped he would withdraw. Aware of the lack of unity, Smith tried to rally his friends and supporters. Several days before the court's decision, he sent a letter to many acquaintances in the Peyote community outlining his reasons for not signing a withdrawal agreement. He said:

I was asked, by signing this document, to sacrifice my own religious freedom as well as the integrity and freedom of the Native American Church. . . . I believe that we have a right to our ceremonies and spiritual ways. I believe that it is wrong to deny any of us our chosen spiritual path. We have been pushed too long, too far and so, once faced with the threat to my religious freedom, I took a stand.[32]

On April 17, 1990, by a 6–3 vote, the Court ruled against Smith and Black, denying them unemployment compensation and upholding Oregon's statute prohibiting all use of Peyote. The decision meant that a state law may proscribe the use of a "drug" even if it prohibits a religious practice, provided that the law is neutral and applies to all citizens. It meant a state could now repeal its statutes that made an exemption for the sacramental use of Peyote without violating the First Amendment rights of NAC members. This narrowed the free exercise of religion clause and weakened the "compelling state interest" test that is usually applied in such cases. This meant a certain activity could be prohibited if it could be demonstrated that the activity does harm to the larger group. In *Smith* the Court did not argue that Peyote was harmful or demonstrate that the religious use of Peyote would harm the citizens of Oregon. The Court declared that Oregon had the right to control Peyote, even if it denied the free exercise of religion to two of its citizens. After the decision by the U.S. Supreme Court, a coalition of religious and civil liberties groups requested a rehearing. The request was denied.[33]

THE PEYOTE COMMUNITY FIGHTS BACK

The *Smith* case provoked outrage from many quarters. It was seen as a threat to religious freedom with the failure to apply the compelling interest doctrine and the narrowing of the free exercise clause of the First Amendment. As NARF attorney Walter Echo-Hawk pointed out, the ruling was a threat to all religions. Protest against *Smith* came from the left and the right. Both the *Washington Post* and the *National Review* criticized the decision. Two scholars wrote: "For United States citizens who are members of the Native American Church, the Bill of Rights is dead."[34] The only recourse to a Supreme Court decision was legislative relief in the form of a federal bill that would restore the compelling state interest test and guarantee the free exercise of religion to NAC members; otherwise states would have a patchwork of statutes, some exempting

Peyote and others prosecuting for possession of Peyote. This was an impossible situation, creating a legal quagmire for the Native American Church. The answer was to organize, publicize, create coalitions, and lobby Congress for legislative relief. A bipartisan effort was launched in Congress as some of its members had two concerns: the weakening of the compelling state interest test when applied to a First Amendment case, and the weakening of the right to the free exercise of religion. Outside of Congress, Reuben A. Snake, Jr., took the leadership role and created a coalition to overturn *Smith*. In addition to being a member of the NAC and a Roadman, he was a nationally known and highly respected American Indian leader. He had served as chairman of the Winnebago Tribe of Nebraska and as president of the National Congress of American Indians. He had served in the U.S. Army with the Green Berets. He became a political organizer in the late 1960s as he became committed to religious freedom and political self-determination for American Indian nations. He has been called "one of the greatest Native American leaders of this [twentieth] century."[35] In spite of his accomplishments, he remained modest and down to earth, with a sense of humor to carry him through difficult times. He sometimes signed his name "Reuben Snake, Your Humble Serpent." With full support from the NAC leadership he created a national coalition of more than a hundred organizations that included religious and environmental groups, American Indian organizations, and tribal governments. The coalition, called the American Indian Religious Freedom Project, became the lobbying arm of the Native American Church. They held academic conferences and media events to build support. A core team was put together to draft legislation that would specifically protect the sacramental use of Peyote. In 1992, Senator Daniel Inouye (D-Hawaii), chair of Native American Affairs subcommittee, called for Congressional hearings.[36] The previous year, in June, the Oregon legislature had passed a bill permitting a religious defense if one were arrested for using Peyote. Although this brought relief to Peyote groups in Oregon, it did not affect the Supreme Court's *Smith* decision.

As part of the effort to gain legislative relief from the *Smith* case, the American Indian Religious Freedom Project mailed out information packets to lawmakers, journalists, and scholars in late 1991. The packets contained documents on the history of the ceremonial use of Peyote, a summary of the draft legislation, and copies of newspaper articles and editorials. Included as well were statements by Reuben Snake and Senator Inouye and letters of support for new legislation by the chief administrator of the Drug Enforcement

Administration and the director of the Indian Health Service. Copies of articles from law journals and resolutions of support from various organizations, such as the National Council of Churches, the American Anthropological Association, and the Arizona and New Mexico legislatures, were included. There is also quite a powerful letter from Robert B. Whitehorse, president of the Native American Church of Navajoland, to Chief Justice William Rehnquist and the associate justices outlining the spiritual significance of Peyote and summarizing the Peyote origin narrative of the Diné. It is a lengthy information packet that proved quite helpful in building support for the new legislation. Although quite ill at the time, Reuben Snake worked tirelessly on this legislation.[37]

In an attempt to influence public opinion and to educate lawmakers, Reuben Snake and the coalition produced two documentary films. One was a short, fifteen-minute video, *The Traditional Use of Peyote*. After an introduction by Senator Inouye, Snake explained the reasons for holding Peyote services, and the famous religion scholar Huston Smith pointed out that "Peyote is not a mind-altering drug." The second film, *The Peyote Road: Ancient Religion in Contemporary Crisis*, is an appeal to the public and to Congress to pass the necessary legislation to protect the Peyote faith. The film analyses the crisis brought on by the *Smith* case. It includes an interview with Al Smith, and summarizes the history of Peyotism with a focus on Peyote as an ancient sacrament, comparable to bread and wine in Christianity. There are historic photographs, as well as interviews with male and female members of the Native American Church. There is a description of a Peyote religious service and an explanation of the ceremonial items that are used. The film ends with a dedication "to the ancestors who passed this way of worship through the generations, even through times of religious prosecution." The film is dedicated to the memory of anthropologist Omer Stewart, who died in 1991.

Peyote Road is an excellent film. It takes a historical approach by interspersing the development of the church with the attempts to prohibit Peyote and uses scholars, such as Vine Deloria, Jr., to describe the history. The historic view is balanced by an analysis of contemporary issues. The film gives one the sense of crisis and explores the actions needed to protect religious freedom. This award-winning film is significant as it was part of the struggle for religious freedom and the effort to promote new legislation. It demonstrates how activism, mobilization, and coalition building can affect public policy. The film is also important as an historic document. There are important interviews with Peyotists and analyses of Peyote ceremonies and symbolism, much of it illustrated by historic and contemporary film footage.[38] Sadly, Reuben Snake passed away before he could see the fruits of his labor. He not only left two important films but also brought together a coalition that lobbied successfully for new legislation. Senator Inouye delivered a speech on the floor of the Senate in his memory.[39]

The *Smith* decision led to two pieces of legislation, each one dealing with a different aspect of the case. The court's refusal to apply the compelling state interest doctrine to the Peyote case worried many legislators, legal scholars, and religious organizations. Without the application of this doctrine, it would be possible for state legislators to outlaw a specific religious practice without having to demonstrate it was contrary to state interests. Members of both houses of Congress introduced and passed the Religious Freedom Restoration Act of 1993, which required the application of the compelling state interest test to future First Amendment cases, at all government levels, that involved the free exercise of religion. As important as this legislation was in terms of religious freedom concerns, it did not specifically address the Peyote issue.[40]

By midyear, a new bill, the American Indian Religious Freedom Act Amendments of 1994, was submitted to Congress to address the free exercise of religion aspect of the *Smith* decision as it related to Peyote. The goal was a uniform national law "to provide for the traditional use of peyote by Indians for religious purposes." The new legislation had full support from the Department of Justice and the DEA, which stated in congressional hearings that they preferred a federal statutory exemption rather than the regulatory exemption that had been in place since 1965. It would eliminate the state-by-state patchwork of laws where twenty-eight states had an exemption and in twenty-two states any possession of Peyote was a felony. The bill ensures that "the use, possession, or transportation of peyote by an Indian for bona fide traditional ceremonial purposes in connection with the practice of a traditional Indian religion is lawful, and shall not be prohibited by the United States or any State." The bill reached the floor of Congress only after three years of hard work by the NAC, their attorneys, and their supporters. There were setbacks and uncertainty, but with the support of key congressional leaders the bill passed the House and the Senate by voice vote and was signed by President Bill Clinton on October 6, 1994. The bill overturned the Supreme Court's *Smith* decision by giving full legal protection for the sacramental use of Peyote.[41] This protection covered members of "Indian Tribes," which are recognized by the United States, and who are participating in an "Indian Religion," or in other words protection for members of federally recognized tribes. It does not say members of the Peyote faith; it does not mention the NAC of North American by name, or any blood-quantum requirement. The special exemption applies only to American Indians and has not opened the floodgates for the same exemption for non-Indian groups. The courts have supported this by ruling that the exemptions are based on the historic and special relationship between the United States and federally recognized tribes. The wording in the bill was designed to protect the exemption from legal challenges. In its testimony, the Department of Justice said the policy stands on solid constitutional ground. Subsequently, the Pentagon issued a ruling giving American Indians in the military who are members of the Native American Church the right to use Peyote as a sacrament without fear of court martial or denial of promotion. The Armed Forces Chaplain's Board drew up the policy to conform to the 1994 legislation. This ended another chapter in the long history of the struggle of the Native American Church for the constitutional right to the free exercise of religion.

NATIVE AMERICAN CHURCH ORGANIZATIONS

The several hundred thousand Peyotists belong to a number of international, state, county, local, and reservation-based organizations. The NAC of North America and the NAC of Navajoland, now Azee' Bee Nahaghá, are the largest, but there are other important groups, such as the NACs of Oklahoma and South Dakota. Most western states have chartered Peyote organizations comprising smaller affiliated groups or chapters. There are some Peyote communities not affiliated with the larger groups. This has been called a "loose confederation," sometimes contentious, but on legal issues such as constitutional protection and protecting the Peyote cactus there is cooperation and unity. One does not have to be an "official member" of a NAC group to obtain the exemption for the use of Peyote. One has to be a member of a federally recognized tribe and use Peyote as part of a religious ceremony. The larger organizations do not have theological or legal control over member groups or individuals. They do not train or sanction Roadmen, nor set ritual guidelines. They have the power of persuasion, or threats of invalidating affiliated status. The larger groups prefer that the local groups follow their bylaws and resolutions, but some groups insist on a degree of local autonomy. Following the *Smith* decision, a more coordinated effort was needed to support the effort for a congressional bill to guarantee the right to use Peyote as a sacrament.

Frank Dayish (Diné), then president of the NAC of North America, proposed a National Council of Native American Churches to provide leadership and to coordinate efforts with Reuben Snake's coalition. The council consists of the presidents of the NAC of North America, the Azee' Bee Nahaghá, and the NACs of Oklahoma and South Dakota. Past presidents are also invited as are members of the executive councils of the four organizations. Its purpose is to enhance communication to able to deal with issues that affect the entire Peyote community and to develop a common agenda to tackle those issues.

As the churches grew in membership and had to deal with myriad issues, they also grew bureaucratically. In addition to full participation in Peyote services, women have taken on additional responsibilities as these organizations have grown. Women are involved in the planning and organization of church events. They have been elected to administrative positions in most of the church organizations, as well as being elected locally to serve as voting delegates at state and national annual conferences, where they are active participants in policy discussions.

NATIVE AMERICAN CHURCH OF NORTH AMERICA, INC.

The NAC of North America is a coalition of church organizations that encompasses the United States, Canada, and Mexico; however a number of Peyote communities do not belong to this group, and some do not use the name Native American Church. As a corporate entity, the NAC of North America traces its origin to 1918 in Oklahoma and is presently incorporated in Oklahoma. As a corporation with tax exempt status it operates under a set of bylaws established by the membership over the years. The preamble establishes the purpose of the church: "the free exercise of their religious beliefs and in the unmolested practice of the rituals." The mission is the same as it was in 1918: "the protection of the sacramental use of Peyote." The church's affiliated chapter members are incorporated in their home states. The annual membership fee is $250.00 per chapter. Individual members must be one-quarter or more "Native American Indian blood" and either belong to a federally recognized Indian nation, be a member of the First Nations of Canada, or be a member of a traditional Indian people of Mexico. The blood-quantum requirement is not in federal law, but it is a NAC requirement. The legislative body is made up of delegates-at-large chosen by their constituents. Delegates elect the president, vice president, secretary, and treasurer to three-year terms with no compensation. The delegates, two from each district, represent approximately twenty to twenty-five districts from the United States and Canada. The number varies by who pays their dues and attends the annual conventions. The bylaws are very specific prohibiting non-Indians from using the holy sacrament and encouraging the membership to inform law enforcement officials if laws are broken.[42] The NAC of North America has been in the forefront of the struggle for religious freedom. The leadership has been involved in virtually every legal issue involving Peyote. They arrange for attorneys, provide expert testimony, and submit briefs to the courts. For example, they arranged for anthropologist Omer Stewart to be an expert witness at various trials. They played a role in helping convince the Navajo Tribal Council to rescind its restrictions on the use of Peyote. When Texas criminalized the possession of Peyote in 1967, the NAC sent representatives to meet with legislators and state officials to make the case for a special exemption for the religious use of Peyote. They did the same in the mid-1970s with Congress as it was considering an American Indian freedom of religion bill. After the *Smith* decision, they worked tirelessly with Reuben Snake's coalition. They maintain attorneys and keep in close liaison with other Peyote groups, with federal officials, and with the Department of Public Safety in Texas, which regulates the sale of Peyote. The NAC of North America has taken the lead in the struggle to maintain the right of all Peyotists to the free exercise of their beliefs.

The NAC annual conferences are the lifeblood of the organization (the leadership also meets semiannually). Peyotists from North America gather to hold official business meetings, to share information, to see old friends, to make new ones, and to enjoy companionship and prayer in nightly Peyote services. A local group sponsors the conference. In 2007, the Shoshone-Bannock of the NAC of Fort Hall, Idaho, sponsored the fifty-eighth annual conference. They provided entertainment, food, and youth activities and set up tepees to hold Peyote services. The 2008 conference was held on the Rocky Boy Reservation in Montana.

One issue that has not been addressed by the NAC is the 25 percent blood quantum in their bylaws as previously mentioned. The leadership believes this requirement for membership is essential for the long-term protection of the church. Outside the church, however, there is some opposition to using a blood-quantum requirement for any purpose. The critics, however, are not aiming their attacks at the NAC; they do not even mention the NAC. The focus is on those tribal governments that require a particular blood quantum for tribal citizenship. Susan Shown Harjo (Cheyenne/Muskogee), a prominent author and spokeswoman on American Indian issues, is one of the outspoken critics of the blood-quantum requirement. Her words are aimed at tribal governments as there are no federal regulations requiring blood-quantum information. Since the 1970s, tribal governments have determined their own criteria for citizenship. Harjo and others argue that the use of blood-quantum data can lead to a reduction in the number of federally recognized individuals as the children and grandchildren of present members may marry outside their group with subsequent offspring not being eligible for tribal citizenship since they could be below the required blood-quantum level. Even though tribal governments are the target of this criticism, it is also pointed out that it was the U.S. government that originally imposed the blood-quantum requirement on American Indians. In the American Indian Religious Freedom Act Amendments of 1994, there is no mention of blood quantum as a requirement for the sacramental use of Peyote. At present this is not on the agenda of the NAC but could become an issue in the future.[43]

NATIVE AMERICAN CHURCH, STATE OF OKLAHOMA

Oklahoma is the cradle of Peyotism in the United States. From the Comanches and Kiowas, with legendary leaders such as Quanah Parker, the modern Peyote ceremony, with its variants, developed in what was then known as Indian Territory. Building on ancient religious traditions from Mexico, Peyotism spread throughout the West. Facing attempts by Congress to criminalize the possession of Peyote, leaders in Oklahoma sought protection by incorporating in 1918 under the name Native American Church. For several decades, it was the "mother church," providing leadership and serving as a role model as other Peyote communities incorporated using the Oklahoma charter as a model. The Oklahoma Peyotists set the standard by proclaiming the principle that their faith and holy sacrament was protected by the First Amendment. As Peyotism expanded, a movement emerged to establish a national organization. In 1944, the Oklahoma charter was amended and a new name, the Native American Church of the United States, was adopted. As the national leadership was involved in a broad range of legal activities, many of the Oklahoma Peyotists wanted to return to their state organization and focus on state and local issues. In 1949, the original 1918 charter was amended using the former name, Native American Church, eventually adopting the name Native American Church,

State of Oklahoma. They did not oppose a national body; they wanted a state organization to maintain and protect their autonomy. This did not affect the status of the NAC of the United States as each group had its own charter and corporate status. As a state organization, the NAC of Oklahoma is affiliated with the larger body and is involved in the broad legal issues involving Peyote. They worked with the Oklahoma State Bureau of Narcotics and Dangerous Drug Control to develop a Special Exempt Persons regulation that protected NAC members using Peyote in "bona fide religious ceremonies of the Native American Church." In 1968, they proudly celebrated the golden anniversary of their original charter.

The state organization consists of more than twenty affiliated groups or chapters, most ethnically based, such as Cheyenne NAC Chapter #1. The state group holds annual conferences that are part business and part prayer service. The chapters run their own affairs but coordinate their broader concerns such as legal protections with the state and national organization. For example, the *Smith* case unified Peyotists from around the country, including Oklahoma Peyotists, who were part of the struggle for constitutional protection. They wanted their views to be heard and submitted a position paper to Congress asking for legislative protection. More recently they were involved in discussions with the DEA on the issue of wording and the federal exemption as various statutes and regulations do not use consistent language (more on this below). At the 2001 annual conference, the membership voted to support a letter by Rollin Haag, Sr. (Cheyenne), state chairperson of the NAC of Oklahoma, to the DEA, urging them to keep the name Native American Church in their regulations. A more recent example is Archie Hoffman's (Cheyenne) ten-page position paper "Peyote and the Native American Church." He outlines a series of recommendations on how to make the language of the exemptions consistent yet still maintain a historic tie to the NAC name.[44] In these discussions, however, Oklahoma Peyotists made it clear that no other group speaks for them. They are affiliated in spirit and share concerns with other groups but want their own voice.

AZEE' BEE NAHAGHÁ OF DINÉ NATION
(FORMER NATIVE AMERICAN CHURCH OF NAVAJOLAND)

From the Navajo (Diné) Tribal Council's prohibition of Peyote in 1940, to its overwhelming support for the post-*Smith* legislation protecting Peyotists, the

Diné Nation leadership has come a long way concerning the Peyote faith. The Peyote Road has been difficult for Diné Peyotists. They had opposition from missionaries, traditionalists, tribal officials, three state governments, and the federal government. Today close to half of the 225,000 Diné are Peyotists and are accepted by a large majority of non-Peyotists. Peyotism is no longer controversial. Harry Walters, a Diné traditional scholar, has suggested that the NAC is a "fifth Blessingway for the people."[45] As Peyotism expanded in the 1940s and 1950s, Peyote communities joined together, mostly on a regional basis, to establish organizations and file for incorporation. Individuals were involved with the national NAC and attended the annual conferences. In the mid-1940s, Diné Peyote communities incorporated in Utah, New Mexico, and Arizona. In the next decade, the NAC of Navajoland emerged as an important organization. Its membership was primarily from the southern part of the reservation, although there are members from all regions. In the 1950s they unsuccessfully challenged the Navajo Tribal Council to rescind the prohibition of Peyote. In 1966, NAC of Navajoland became an official chartered organization, though remaining independent of the NAC of North America. The Navajo Peyotists became chartered in Arizona, New Mexico, Utah, and Texas. Members continued to lobby the tribal council and, with support from other Peyote communities and President Raymond Nakai, they were able to convince the council to decriminalize the religious use of Peyote and to be recognized by the government of the Navajo Nation. Meanwhile in the northern part of the reservation, Peyotists established and chartered the Native American Church of the Four Corners. They became affiliated with the NAC of North America. There are other groups, such as the Northern Navajoland Native American Church Association, and other smaller groups, sometimes affiliated with larger groups, sometimes independent.

From the 1970s through the 1990s, Diné Peyotists continued to increase in numbers. Their organizations worked in coordination with other groups in the struggle for federal protection of Peyote. They were part of the massive effort to reverse the impact of the *Smith* decision. They also affected Diné politics. Then president Peterson Zah, not a Peyotist, gave full support to Reuben Snake's coalition and testified before Congress. Other Diné Peyotists also testified while some sent letters to U.S. senators and representatives. The Diné Nation Council authorized funds for a hundred NAC members to travel to Washington to lobby for the legislation. Later in the 1990s, the NAC of Navajoland turned to other concerns such as the illegal sale and nonceremonial use of Peyote, particularly among the youth. This posed a dilemma for the NAC: how to eliminate unauthorized use without restricting its use for ceremonial purposes. The problem was that Peyote was listed as a controlled substance in the Navajo Criminal Code of 1978, with an exemption for its use in "connection with recognized religious practices, sacrament or service of the Native American Church." The Peyote community wanted it removed from the controlled substances list out of respect for a holy sacrament; however, they did not call for complete decriminalization as this would have compounded the problem of abuse. Their recommendation was to remove Peyote from the controlled substances list but still restrict its use through new legislation. Jesse Thompson, then president of the NAC of Navajoland, advocated this approach by adding a new section to the criminal code, making the "unlawful possession or sale of Peyote" punishable except when used for religious purposes. Then it would not be labeled a "narcotic," but its use would still be restricted.

Meanwhile a new executive council was elected in 2000. The new president, David Clark, proclaimed "A New Beginning" to signify a "new millennium—a hoped-for period of happiness, peace, prosperity, and justice." The board of directors also called for a name change from the NAC of Navajoland to "Azee' Bee Nahaghá of Diné Nation" (ABNDN), meaning the "Peyote Ceremony of the Diné."

With the new name came a redesigned logo featuring the iconic tepee above a large Peyote button, surrounded by the Diné four sacred mountains. There are two cornstalks below and two eagle feathers above, all surrounded by two concentric circles. This is quite significant as it incorporates traditional Diné symbolism and Peyote symbolism within the logo. The new name is consistent with the trend to use the Diné language when referring to cultural and spiritual institutions and practices. The elimination of the name Native American Church would not present any legal problems since the AIRFA Amendments of 1994 do not mention the Native American Church by name; that legislation states that the exemption for ceremonial use of Peyote applies only to members of federally recognized tribes. Part of the problem is that the name Native American Church has become a generic term for anyone who practices the Peyote faith and not just members of a specific organization. This created a problem of how to define a member of the NAC. For example, the new music award for the Best Native American Church Music is not a reference to an organization; it is a generic reference to music that is part of the Peyote faith.

The ABNDN also recommended that the criminal code be revised so that it "reflects that the use of the peyote herb is part of a traditional bona fide Diné ceremony." This was based on the view that the use of Peyote should not be seen as part of a specific "church-religion organization," but as a "traditional ceremony" in compliance with AIRFA. This would avoid the appearance of giving special protection to one religious organization. It was hoped that the new legislation could better withstand constitutional scrutiny if non–federally recognized groups sought the exemption. The ABNDN proposed new legislation: the Peyote Ceremonial Act of 2003, which the Diné Nation Council tabled, seeking more information.

The bill was then reintroduced in October 2004 in two parts. The first part revised the Navajo Nation Criminal Code, Section 394:

> The listing of peyote (more commonly known as azee' in Subsection A) does not apply to the use of azee' by an enrolled member of an Indian tribe for bona fide ceremonial purposes in connection with nahagha. Individuals who use, possess or transport azee' for use in nahagha are exempt from this prohibition. Azee' is lawful on the Navajo Nation.

The second part of the legislation outlines the Peyote Ceremony and defines it as a "Diné-traditional ceremony" and states that the purpose is "to recognize, honor, and respect the Azee' Bee Nahaghá (Peyote Ceremony) as a Diné (Navajo) Traditional ceremony and the Azee' (Peyote) as one of the Diné sacred herbs as designated by the Holy People." In addition all references to the name Native American Church were deleted and replaced with Azee' Bee Nahaghá. Not all Diné Peyotists agreed with the name change; nevertheless in 2005 the Diné Nation Council passed the bill 63 to 1.[46] This is quite a significant development as Peyotism is now recognized by the Diné as a "traditional ceremony."

Like the NAC of North America, Azee' Bee Nahaghá is a coalition of local groups or chapters. In 1966 a constitution and bylaws were certified, stating the purpose of the organization and describing its administrative structure. The purpose is "to foster, promote, and preserve the use of peyote sacrament through bona-fide religious ceremonies." The executive officers—president, vice president, treasurer, and secretary—serve four-year terms as do the board of directors, who are elected by the local chapters. All serve without compensation. They hold annual conventions for the members and quarterly meetings for the officers and the board. Subcommittees are appointed and submit reports and resolutions to be voted upon. Each chapter has its own officers, pays an annual fee, and submits reports to the main body. This is coordinated from the administration headquarters in Chinle, Arizona. They are in the process of developing a records management system with a database and archives to house documents since the preservation of past records has not been systematic.[47]

The annual conventions, held at the Chinle Spiritual Grounds, are the highlight of the year. The forty-second annual convention in 2008 was very special as David Clark stepped down after eight years of a successful presidency and David Tsosie was inaugurated as the new president. Conventions are a mixture of business and worship and a place to debate the most pressing issues about the state of the Peyote faith, the Diné Nation, and other American Indian issues. The mornings begin with veterans raising the Diné Nation flag alongside the U.S. Stars and Stripes and singing the flag song. There are special activities ranging from Youth Appreciation Day, with workshops on how to "tie drum," to warnings on the dangers of illegal drugs. On the business side, elections are held, subcommittee reports are given, and resolutions are debated and voted upon. Peyote services are held on Saturday night followed by a feast on Sunday. There is an energizing atmosphere to the conventions. Along with debate and differences of opinion, there is camaraderie among people who have struggled to defend their faith. Through the course of the day, between meetings, you can hear Peyote music on someone's tape/CD player, or hear others practicing with drum and rattle. One can hear older people speaking Diné, sometimes complaining about the youth, who speak primarily English. The conventions play an essential role: they strengthen one's identity as a Diné and a Peyotist.

NATIVE AMERICAN CHURCH OF SOUTH DAKOTA

The various Sioux groups in North and South Dakota were introduced to Peyotism in the first decade of the twentieth century. Peyote communities emerged on the Pine Ridge, Rosebud, and Yankton Sioux Reservations. All faced harassment by federal and state officials and missionaries. Arrests were common and ritual paraphernalia was confiscated on all three reservations. In 1920, the superintendent of the Rosebud Reservation was ordered by the BIA "to prohibit the use, sale, or gift, etc. of peyote." The superintendent threatened to withhold funds and rations from those found participating in Peyote meetings.[48] Under these circumstances the Peyotists on Pine Ridge, using the Oklahoma model, formally incorporated in October 1922, as the

Native American Church of Allen [County]. The next month, the Yankton incorporated as the NAC of Charles Mix County. In 1923, the South Dakota legislature criminalized the possession of Peyote. The reaction was more incorporation. In July 1924, the NAC of Rosebud incorporated. The Peyotists at Pine Ridge, taking a leadership position in the state, amended their charter in November 1924 to become the statewide NAC of South Dakota, Inc. By the end of the 1930s there were eleven incorporated Peyote communities in South Dakota.

To avoid possible legal entanglements, Peyote is not mentioned in any of the early incorporation papers. There was a conscious attempt to make these charters sound as if they were Christian church organizations. The Yanktons are a case in point. In their original handwritten version of the charter, they referred to themselves as "the peyote church of christ [sic]" with the sacramental use of Peyote. In the final typed version of the charter submitted to the state, the wording had been changed. The Yanktons changed their organization's name to the Native American Church of Charles Mix County and deleted all references to Peyote; instead the charter said, "The purpose of the corporation is to foster and promote the Christian religious beliefs among the Sioux Indians." In charters written or amended in the 1930s, Peyote was described as a sacrament, as it is today.[49]

The NAC of South Dakota is organized like other state churches with a central administration and an executive council. The state organization remained independent of the national NAC organization for several decades; however, in 1959 the NAC of South Dakota formally affiliated with the NAC of North American and began taking an active role in national Peyote issues. The 2007 bylaws have a clearly articulated mission statement. The stated purpose is the

> promotion of morality, sobriety, industry, charity, right living and the cultivation of a Spirit of self-respect, brotherly love and union among its membership . . . and belief in an Almighty GOD and declare full, complete and everlasting faith in our church, through which we worship for religion and the protection of the sacramental use of Peyote.

The bylaws are divided into two parts: administrative duties and powers, and church officials' duties and powers. The latter come from the "Church Canons for Native American Church of 1948," a very detailed description of the responsibilities of the church officials not found in many other bylaws. The bylaws outline the duties of the members of the executive council, who serve three-year terms without compensation. There is also a board of directors as required by South Dakota law. Membership rules follow the AIRFA Amendments of 1994, requiring members to belong to a federally recognized tribe. In addition, following the requirements of the NAC of North America, a member must be "one-quarter Native American Indian blood." The affiliated chapters, which have their own elected executive councils, elect delegates who vote for the president, vice president, secretary, and treasurer. Recently, Sandor Iron Rope (Oglala Lakota) and Leonard Crow Dog, Jr. (Siçangu Lakota), have been elected president and vice president, respectively. In 2008, the NAC of South Dakota held its eighty-sixth annual convention.

The 1948 Church Canons are almost verbatim in the 2006 bylaws. They outline basic church rules and the duties and powers of church officials from high priest to local church leaders (Roadmen). There have only been four high priests since 1922. The first three are from the same Pine Ridge family: William Black Bear, Paul Oliver Spider, and Emerson Spider, Sr., who served from 1964 to 2004. The present high priest is Burnett Iron Shell. The high priest is the spiritual leader of the South Dakota Peyote community. Duties include running Peyote services, conducting marriages, baptisms, and funerals, caring for the sick, and generally being responsible for the spiritual health of the church. The bylaws also describe the duties of the chief drummer, cedarman, and fireman. The use of Peyote is prescribed: it must be blessed before partaking; it can be used only as a sacrament. The final section of the bylaws lists the ceremonial order of a Peyote service from opening announcements to a closing Lord's Prayer. Outlines are provided for a Peyote service in a tepee or a Peyote service in a house.[50]

One of the affiliated groups of the statewide organization is the Native American Church of Jesus Christ, whose members are mostly from the town of Porcupine on the Pine Ridge Reservation. It has received notoriety from its leader, Emerson Spider, Sr. (Oglala Lakota), who was also the high priest of the NAC of South Dakota for forty years (see figure 16). His group, which practices the Cross Fire Way, is very direct in proclaiming itself a Christian church, yet maintaining the primacy of Peyote. Spider believed that Peyote was put on earth to lead people to Jesus Christ and to prepare for the "second coming." He argued that no one should be excluded from Peyote services. The majority of South Dakota Peyotists disagreed with him, but he argued this from a theological perspective. In a 1999 interview he said, "God is love, if you exclude, how do you call yourself a church; let anyone in, enjoy Herb

Figure 16. The opening of a Native American Church of South Dakota business meeting, 1999. Emerson Spider, Sr., chief priest, is second from left, with drum. Photo taken by author with permission.

[Peyote]." At one time, he rejected Sioux traditional ceremonies by saying it was time to put away the Pipe and pick up the Bible. In his later years he modified his views, for example, by blessing the Sun Dance. As a Roadman, he conducted Cross Fire services with "Grandfather Peyote" placed on the Bible. The majority of the Sioux follow the Cross Fire Way, but many do not support Spider's view on inclusivity. Today the bylaws of the NAC of South Dakota prohibit non-Indians from the sacramental use of Peyote.[51]

TWENTY-FIRST CENTURY:
PROTECTION OF PEYOTE AND PEYOTISM

The Peyote faith has come a long way since its emergence in the United States. It has gone from pariah to widespread acceptance, from governmental attempts to criminalize the possession of Peyote to federal protection for its religious usage. As the church enters a new century, there are still problems and concerns, not the least being a fear of a changing legal or political environment that could threaten the church's present status. There is also a concern that non-Indian groups could acquire the exemption through a state or federal court ruling. With additional groups using Peyote the future supply of it would be a concern. To this end, efforts are under way to coordinate the language of federal laws and regulations with the bylaws of incorporated Peyote groups. The one issue that seems settled from a health point of view is the safety of Peyote.

In the first reports by reservation employees in the 1880s, Peyote was declared a dangerous substance. The basic strategy used by those who opposed Peyotism was to label it a "drug" or an "intoxicant" and describe the supposed harmful effects. There were always individuals such as James Mooney who said it was not harmful as well as a large number of American Indians who said it was beneficial and called it "medicine." In the second half of the twentieth century, negative opinions were modified as scientific evidence demonstrated that Peyote was not an addictive narcotic, it did not produce withdrawal symptoms, and one did not develop a tolerance to it. However, since Peyote contains a small amount of mescaline, it was added to the federal controlled-substances list in 1965. The Department of Justice added an exemption to the *Federal Register* for Peyote's religious use by NAC members. There was still misinformation among the public, some seeing it as a hallucinogen in a category with LSD. In actuality, the amount of mescaline in a Peyote button is minimal. Only 1 to 3 percent of its dry weight is mescaline. In terms of potency it has 1/2000 the potency of LSD. One of the problems in testing Peyote is that it is administered outside the context of a religious ceremony. One laboratory study of Peyote, unassociated with the NAC, reported that "some subjects go into fits of laughter."[52] With tens of thousands of examples of the sacramental use of Peyote, no one has reported fits of laughter.

The much-debated safety issue has recently been settled by a five-year study, completed in 2004, under the auspices of McLean Hospital, a psychiatric facility affiliated with the Harvard Medical School. The study was partially funded by the National Institute on Drug Abuse, a federal agency. The study was conducted on the Diné Reservation with the support of tribal officials and church leaders led by Dr. John H. Halpern, a psychiatrist, and Dr. Harrison G. Pope, Jr., director of the Biological Psychiatry Laboratory at McLean. They spent considerable time on the reservation, presenting their plan, convincing church leaders, and finding willing participants for the study. The researchers divided the participants, ages eighteen to forty-five, into three groups. The first was composed of lifelong Peyotists who had ingested Peyote over a long period of time and did not use alcohol or illicit drugs. The second group was composed of former alcoholics with at least a five-year history of excessive drinking, now sober for at least the last two months; and, a third comparison group of non-Peyotists with minimal use of alcohol or illegal substances during their lifetimes. The three groups were administered a battery of neuropsychological tests. The findings "yielded no significant differences between the peyote and comparison group on any measure, whereas the former alcoholic group showed poorer performance." The researchers concluded the long-term use of Peyote when ingested as a sacrament "is not associated with adverse residual psychological or cognitive effects"; in other words, there was no brain damage. The Halpern study received wide coverage in the mainstream media.[53] This study is also important for the future protection of church members as politicians or judges may want to revisit the safety question and the exemptions for the sacramental use of Peyote.

To further protect the Peyote exemption from future constitutional challenges, an effort is under way to coordinate the language of the exemption in various laws and regulations. The purpose is to close possible loopholes by which a court could rescind the exemption, which is not likely, or to open the exemption to non-Indian groups. In 2001, the DEA wrote to various American Indian leaders outlining a plan to reword the language of the exemption in the *Federal Register*. The following year. DEA officials held a series of regional meetings with tribal and church leaders to solicit input on the proposed changes. The DEA claims its purpose is to strengthen the protection given by Congress in 1994. The DEA regulation, now almost forty years old, gives the exemption to "members of the Native American Church." The DEA explains in its letter that the original intent was to protect all members of federally recognized tribes, not just NAC members. The new proposal will coordinate the exemption of the DEA guidelines in the *Federal Register* with the language of the AIRFA Amendments of 1994. This would also close the door on non-Indian groups who use the name NAC, such as happened in the Mooney case in Utah (see below). It means deleting all references to the "Native American Church" and substituting "federally recognized tribes." The change would eliminate or at least decrease questions regarding the constitutionality of the DEA regulations since the revised regulation is not based on special treatment for one group, such as the NAC, but meant to protect and preserve American Indian culture based on, as the DEA letter states, "the special relationship between the United States and the Indian tribes." The difference in the language of the exemptions has caused confusion. The changes would protect the exemption from a First Amendment challenge that "Congress shall make no law respecting an established religion," and a Fourteenth Amendment challenge based on equal protection under the law.[54] A regulation that seems to favor one church group could be challenged, a regulation protecting American Indian cultures and practices would be less so. Not all Peyote groups agree with the proposed changes. Both the NACs of Oklahoma and South Dakota prefer to keep the name Native American Church in the regulation. The name has historic meaning to many individuals who struggled to keep their faith. One argument is that using the criteria of federally recognized tribes is too narrow. For example, it excludes Canadian and Mexican Peyotists and American Indians who for one reason or another are not enrolled in a federally recognized tribe. It also excludes the non-Indian spouses of NAC members, and possibly their children.[55] As of 2009 the issue has not been settled.

There are a number of court cases that strengthen the argument in favor of the changes in the wording. An older case relevant to the present debate is *U.S. v. Boyll.* In 1990 a grand jury in New Mexico indicted Robert Boyll, a non-Indian member of the NAC, for the illegal possession of Peyote. A federal judge dismissed the charges on the grounds that Peyote as a controlled substance was exempted when used by NAC members and Boyll, though not an American Indian, was a member of the church. The dismissal of the charges was not seen as favorable to the NAC as it could have opened the door for other non-Indian individuals or groups to use Peyote.

A more vexing case is that of James and Linda Mooney of Utah, who were arrested by state authorities in 2000 and charged with twelve first-degree felonies for possession of 12,000 Peyote buttons. They are the founders of the Oklevueha EarthWalks Native American Church of Utah. Mr. Mooney claims membership in the Oklevueha Band of Yamasee Seminoles, which is not federally recognized. The government claims the membership was obtained fraudulently and the group has since revoked his membership. The Mooneys filed a countersuit claiming their home was entered illegally. The NAC of North America opposed the Mooneys and disavowed any connection to them. In 2004 the case reached the Utah Supreme Court, which ruled in the Mooneys' favor, much to the surprise of the Peyote community and federal officials. The court ruled that Utah law had incorporated the DEA's exemption for the religious use of Peyote by members of the Native American Church and the

Mooneys were using the name Native American Church. This had serious implications since it meant that non-Indian members could not be prosecuted. The NAC of North America and its attorneys began an active campaign to have the Utah legislature close this loophole. Church officials went to Utah to meet with state legislators. At this point, the Department of Justice became involved and after the state charges were voided, federal officials arrested the Mooneys and charged them with breaking federal law in the distribution of Peyote as they were not members of a federally recognized tribe. Department of Justice officials negotiated with the Mooneys in 2006 and offered to drop all charges if they agreed to never acquire, use, or distribute Peyote. On February 22, 2006, an agreement was signed. This case was a great concern to the NAC as it threatened their special exemption. In addition, if the Mooneys were ultimately successful in a federal court, this could open up widespread use of Peyote and further threaten the supply.[56] Later in the year, with the help of NAC president Milton Miller, the Utah legislature amended its controlled substance regulation to bring it into line with federal law, making membership in a federally recognized tribe the sole criteria for an exemption. An argument was made by some Utah officials that this was not a First Amendment issue, but the responsibility of the state to protect the rights of American Indians. This is the same argument used by the DEA in its 2001 letter to NAC officials. This represents a moving away from a First Amendment defense of Peyote use to the argument that the exemption comes from the unique trust relationship between American Indian nations and the federal government.

Ironically, just the day before the Mooney settlement, the U.S. Supreme Court issued a ruling concerning a group that was indicted for importing a hallucinogenic tea for use in religious services. The court voted 8–0 in *Gonzales v. O Centre Espirita Beneficente União do Vegetal*, upholding the group's right to import the tea, called *hoasca*. U.S. Customs had seized the tea as a controlled substance that was to be used for communion by about 130 members a Brazilian-based faith. The plaintiffs argued that an exemption had been made for the religious use of Peyote and that the exemption had been in place for forty years. The court referred to the 1993 Religious Freedom Restoration Act to support its decision. That bill prohibits the federal government from restricting religious freedom unless it can demonstrate a compelling interest to do so. Chief Justice Roberts wrote that the government failed to demonstrate a compelling interest in banning the tea. The plaintiffs won the case based on the 1993 legislation, but their argument for the application of the equal protection clause failed. For the equal protection clause to be applied, the two groups must be similarly situated. The court ruled that they were not similarly situated as American Indians have a unique legal and political relationship to the U.S. government, which has a trust responsibility to protect and preserve American Indian cultures. Roberts added that the government assertion that the law allowed no exceptions for controlled substances was weakened by the long-standing exemption for the religious use of Peyote. The NAC had mixed emotions with this outcome. The right to an exemption for a controlled substance was upheld, but this case could be a dangerous precedent. This makes it crucial that the NAC fight to maintain an exemption based on membership in a federally recognized tribe. It is unclear if this poses a long-range threat to the exemption, although a U.S. attorney was quoted as saying it would have no impact on Peyote, but it could affect the discussions on rewording the DEA's regulations. In the midst of these two threatening cases, the NAC received strong editorial support from *Indian County Today* supporting the right of the NAC to its sacrament but realizing the danger of the plethora of cases going through the courts.[57]

These two cases point to the concerns of the Peyote community. Compounding the supply issue is the continuing rise in the price of Peyote buttons as church membership increases and supply decreases. Prices have skyrocketed, putting pressure on Peyote communities to raise money for Peyote and funds to travel to Texas.

A sample of prices for the past fifty years illustrates the increase.

- 1955—$9.50–15.00 per 1,000 Peyote buttons
- 1966—$15.00 per 1,000
- 1981, 1983 (two reports)—$80.00 per 1,000
- 1988—$100 per 1,000
- 1995—$150–170 per 1,000
- 1999—$130 per 1,000
- 2005—$250 per 1,000
- 2007—$290–300 per 1,000
- 2008—$350 per 1,000
- 2007–2008—$35 per 100[58]

Prices have increased mostly because of less available land from which to harvest Peyote as well as the ecological deterioration of the Peyote fields. With fewer plants, some get harvested before maturity, which has a negative effect on their ability to regenerate. The supply of Peyote is a topic of debate at virtually all NAC conventions. In some places, it has led to buying smaller amounts because of the high price. It has also exacerbated the concern about non-Indians having access to Peyote in prayer meetings or trying to establish separate churches. At this point the legal issue in not debatable; it is more theological, as mentioned in discussing Emerson Spider, Sr. He and others believe that Peyote is a gift of God to be shared with all humanity so no one should be excluded. According to federal law, there is no problem with anyone's attending a Peyote service; it is the ingestion of Peyote that is the issue. If a person is not a member of a federally recognized tribe, he or she can be arrested for the use of Peyote. The leadership of the NAC of North America makes this clear. It is in their bylaws as well as the bylaws of state NAC organizations. For example, the Utah NAC bylaws are very specific. One must be a member of a federally recognized tribe. Not following the law could jeopardize the church. The NAC is unequivocal about this as it continually reminds the membership about the law. However, given the non-hierarchical structure of the NAC of North America, it is difficult to impose this on local groups, much less to know what is going on in the hundreds of local Peyote communities. At the 2007 national convention, President Milton Miller stressed the need to follow federal law and to educate local chapters on this issue. He said, "Take care of the medicine for the sake of the future."[59] The only exception in the NAC bylaws is for Canadian and Mexican Peyotists. In 2001, the NAC passed a resolution proposing that Canadian and Mexican Peyotists be treated the same as members of federally recognized tribes as they hold an equivalent status in their countries. At present, the sacramental use of Peyote in Canada for First Nations people is legal; however Canadian and Mexican Peyotists in the United States cannot buy, transport, or use Peyote as they are not members of federally recognized tribes. American Indian members of the NAC can take Peyote into Canada. For the NAC leadership, the protection of the right to use Peyote is of the highest order. There are no easy answers to the supply question. Other options include importation from Mexico, cultivation, and purchasing land in the Peyote-growth region.

The Peyote cactus is abundant in northern Mexico, but Peyote use is illegal there, and Peyote cannot be exported to the United States. There have been discussions about the possibility of importation, but it is difficult to see this changing with the Mexican government's public support for a "war on drugs." The Huicholes, however, are accommodated in their traditional use of Peyote.

In 1994, their sacred sites in the Peyote fields were declared a protected ecological and cultural sanctuary by the Mexican government. According to the DEA and the Texas Department of Public Safety (TDPS), smuggling is not a problem. The profit is too low, the risk great, and those willing to take the risk could smuggle much more lucrative items into the United States. Cultivation might be a possibility, but at present it is illegal even for horticulturists or cactus collectors. If cultivation were legal it would be costly. It is the same with purchasing land in Texas. It is expensive and not feasible at this time.

One effective way to protect the Peyote supply is the regulation of its harvesting and sale, especially since it is listed as a controlled substance and only available to eligible American Indians. Peyoteros are required to register with the Department of Justice's Drug Enforcement Agency and the Texas Department of Public Safety. Others who harvest Peyote are subject to arrest. In 1969, when Texas established an exemption for the religious use of Peyote, the state legislature developed regulations for the plants' harvesting and sale. In 2002, the regulations were revised to be consistent with the language of federal regulations. To legally ingest Peyote in Texas, one must be a member of a federally recognized tribe ingesting the Peyote in a bona fide religious ceremony, the same as under federal law. The requirements for purchasing Peyote in Texas from peyoteros are more stringent. One must be "an individual with not less than 25% Indian blood who is an enrolled member of a federally recognized tribe under federal law and a certified member of the Native American Church." The requirements to be a distributor are also stringent. Distributors must register and be licensed each year by the TDPS and obtain a certificate of registration and an identification card. Their employees must also carry identification cards. In addition, the distributors need to have an agreement with a land owner, usually in the form of a six- or twelve-month lease, to have legal access to private property. A record of each transaction, including the number of Peyote buttons sold, the price, and information on the purchaser must be kept and submitted quarterly to the TDPS. In addition the distributors are not authorized to cultivate Peyote or to ingest any themselves, and they must dry the buttons in locked wire mesh cages.[60] Peyotists who travel to Texas must have the proper identification, showing they meet the requirements to purchase Peyote. These strict policies control Peyote distribution as it is a controlled substance under Texas law. According to the TDPS, the program is effective as illicit Peyote is not a problem. For example, in 2005 they confiscated only nineteen pounds of Peyote compared to 538,828 pounds of marijuana.[61]

The number of peyoteros has varied since the system was implemented. According to various sources, there were eight in 1970, and twenty-seven in 1974, eleven in 1994, six in 2002, four in 2004, and only three from 2005 to 2009. Each distributor today has three to fifteen employees. Salvador Johnson, one of today's peyoteros, has been selling Peyote for more than forty years. In a recent interview, he said he harvests 300,000 to 500,000 Peyote buttons per year. He claims that with four workers he could harvest 30,000 buttons on twenty-five acres in five hours if the plants were abundant.[62] According to the TDPS, based on data from 1986 to 2007, an average of 1,840,000 buttons has been harvested annually for the last twenty-two years. The lowest year for sales was 1988, with 1,570,000 sold; the highest was 1997, with 2,317,000 sold. The higher sales years show the growth of NAC membership. From 1994 to 2001, an average of more than 2 million per year were sold. Since 2002 there has been a steady decline in the sale of Peyote to a low of 1,605,000 in 2007, or approximately a 25 percent decline. It indicates problems with the Peyote habitat. However, the gross income of the peyoteros has increased to its highest level. In 2007, the gross amount was $474,321.[63] Considering expenses and salaries for the employees, this is not a lucrative business. The number of Peyote buttons being harvested is insufficient for the needs of the nation's Peyote communities. As supply declines and prices increase, a degree of tension has emerged between landowners and peyoteros, with visiting NAC members unhappy with the situation, not only prices but being unable to harvest any Peyote themselves. The NAC leadership is supportive of these regulations as the supply is protected. What happens in Texas is crucial; it is the only natural growth region for Peyote in the United States.

The NAC of North America and the state organizations want consistent laws, regulations, and enforcement. They insist the membership follow the law or risk losing the right to the "medicine." Misuse can create concern in Congress or create negative public opinion. There are twenty-eight states with various regulations exempting Peyote; however the federal AIRFA Amendments of 1994 supersede state laws, except for Texas's blood-quantum requirement for purchasing Peyote. The remaining dilemma in federal regulations is that the DEA regulations exempt NAC members, while federal law in the AIRFA Amendments of 1994 exempts members of federally recognized tribes. The latter is the prime criteria, however, as the DEA has stated that was its intention all along. Today being a member of a federally recognized tribe is the sole criteria. This may seem clear cut, except when a court is adjudicating a case and having to work with inconsistent language in the regulations.

Peyotists are cognizant of the century-long struggle to reach the present situation. They are aware of the sacrifices their ancestors made to protect their faith. Since 1994, the federal courts have protected the First Amendment right to the religious use of Peyote, but continued vigilance is necessary as there will be court challenges. The ultimate legal protection, however, comes from U.S. Congress. Vigilance is required on the legal front, especially at the state level, where a local situation could develop into a major problem such as what happened in the *Smith* case, which began as an unemployment compensation dispute. Vigilance is needed in Texas to protect the natural habitat of the Peyote cactus. It is also necessary to bring the youth into the church and to encourage them to follow the Peyote Road. This is not an easy task with all the distractions for today's youth. The NAC community follows the general precept that it has a responsibility to the ancestors to preserve the faith for future generations, or to the "seventh generation," a metaphor that reflects one's commitment to preserve the past for the future. The only way to do this is to follow the Peyote Road. All the NAC organizations have special youth days, youth programs and activities to teach the young people how to drum and sing, to understand the Peyote ceremonies, and to appreciate the heritage of their ancestors. The 2007 annual convention of the NAC of North America was dedicated to "Empowering Our Youth through Knowledge," as they are the only guarantee of a future for the Peyote faith.

Conclusion

The emergence and growth of the Peyote faith has had a significant impact on American Indians. At the same time, this epic struggle for religious freedom has affected all Americans. Recognizing this has brought support from Christian and Jewish organizations and other groups intent on protecting the First Amendment. Senator Daniel Inouye of Hawaii observed that "the right to freely exercise our religion is the right that millions have sacrificed their lives for." There is no doubt that the Peyote faith deserves constitutional protection.

In the early years, the Peyote faith became a source of community when American Indian communities were under assault. In the pre-reservation era, the extended family, band, clan, or village provided community, but by the twentieth century they were rarely functioning as corporate groups. Peyotism helped reestablish community during difficult times by fostering economic self-sufficiency, family unity, respect for parents, and care for the elderly. In many cases, the Peyote community evolved into an extended family. As a result of a century of opposition, people forged communal bonds in the heat of struggle. Cooperation was essential to survival. Working together meant facing the opposition with one voice. This does not mean that Peyotists have always gotten along with each other or not had significant differences of opinion or personality clashes, but on one issue the sense of community prevailed: the survival of the Peyote religion and the right to the sacramental use of Peyote.

Of great importance also is the impact of Peyotism on the family as the members participate in a "way of life." In a 2005 editorial in *Indian Country Today,* the Native American Church was praised for taking "a rich and highly humanistic approach to family life and culture," which the writer said has stabilized families and communities. There are countless stories of those who have overcome alcoholism, and there is a relative absence of alcohol abuse in Native American Church families.

Peyotism has also been described by a number of scholars, particularly anthropologists, as having an additional impact. Since the 1950s, and continuing today in a number of scholarly works, Peyotism has been labeled a Pan-Indian movement. Because the NAC is intertribal in nature, some scholars have assumed that it is helping to create a "generic American Indian." Part of the issue hinges on how one defines Pan-Indianism. One of the earliest formulations of Pan-Indianism was developed in the mid-1950s by anthropologist James Howard. He defined it as a process by which American Indian groups were losing their tribal distinctiveness, developing a generalized nontribal Indian identity, and evolving into the so-called generic Indian. He said the Native American Church and the powwows offered two examples of this trend. I would argue emphatically that Peyotism has not weakened tribal identity. To make a case for the development of a "generic Indian," one has to look elsewhere. Being a Peyotist affects one's identity, but not at the expense of one's ethnicity. I originally arrived at this conclusion after spending much time with Yankton Sioux Peyotists. They are no less Yankton, and they are certainly not generic Indians. They are proudly the Ihanktonwan Dakota Oyate, the Yankton Sioux Nation. It can be further argued that Peyotism has actually reinforced ethnic identities, especially since indigenous languages are valued in Peyote communities and used in song and prayer. One could make the case that a higher percentage of Peyotists speak the languages of their ancestors than do a similar group of non-Peyotists, although this point needs more research. The NAC is certainly a pan-Indian institution, and belonging to a Peyote community reinforces a member's identity as a Peyotist, but not at the expense of a person's tribal heritage. One could not possibly argue that Diné Peyotists are less Diné than those that are not Peyotists. This is true for many groups, such as the Kiowas, Cheyennes, Comanches, Winnebagos/Ho-Chucks, Crows, Omahas, the Lakotas of Pine Ridge and Rosebud, as well as many others. They maintain a strong tribal identity in spite of other influences. Nelson and Harding Big Bow, two Kiowa Peyotists, said in an interview that they associate Peyotism with maintaining Kiowa culture and keeping the old ways alive.

One could also argue that Peyotism with its roots in indigenous cultural values may be a factor in resisting the homogenizing forces of the twenty-first century. Part of the explanation for the survival of strong tribal identities may be related to the many American Indians who maintain multiple religious affiliations, as discussed in chapter 2. A Diné may be a Peyotist, attend traditional curing ceremonies, and be a Catholic. In South Dakota, many Peyotists are also Sun Dancers, and they may also be Episcopalians. Peyotists do not see themselves as part of a Pan-Indian movement that is creating a generic Indian. The viewpoint that Peyotism is partially responsible for Pan-Indianism is not coming from American Indian scholars. I believe the scholars who identify Peyotism as part of "Pan-Indian movement" are misled by its intertribal nature and an assumption that the faith is weakening other identities. It is understandable that Howard perceived this in the 1950s with termination and relocation, but there has been a strong shift in the intervening half century.

The future of the Native American Church is not in question now, but the Peyote supply is a concern. There are human and ecological factors that pose threats to the Peyote cactus. Regulation by the Texas Department of Public Safety has helped protect the cactus. The federal standard for the sacramental use of Peyote, still classified as a Schedule I controlled substance, is membership in a federally recognized tribe. This has been referred to as the "triumph of the Native American Church." To some this requirement is unsatisfactory, but it has provided a workable standard in a complex situation. It offers a middle ground between no restrictions and total prohibition. Few members advocate either extreme. It is the location of the middle ground that engenders the debate. Church leaders fear that widening the exemption would threaten the supply, but narrowing the exemption from its present form would threaten the church.

The Native American Church has come a long way. No one calls it the "peyote cult" any more or makes accusations about the evils of Peyote. The past fifty years have been marked by a strong shift, not only in federal government policy, but in a powerful American Indian cultural renaissance, economic self-sufficiency, strong governments, and a commitment to a future that includes respect for the past. All this has aided the Native American Church in becoming a significant force in American Indian life. The church is now taking its place alongside other U.S. and world religious organizations. As Pawnee attorney Walter Echo-Hawk said recently at a world religions conference, it is time for all American Indians "to get a seat at the table." Nevertheless, the Native American Church must remain vigilant; religious persecution of American Indians has a long history, and the struggle for religious freedom is never ending.

Epilogue

As the Native American Church moves into the second decade of the twenty-first century, its members are filled with hopes and aspirations as well as lingering concerns for the Peyote faith. The leaders of the various Peyote groups have been making special efforts to reach out to young people, a difficult task given everything out there competing for their attention. The leadership knows that integrating young people into the church is critical to the future of Peyotism.

The courts are also a central concern to members of the Peyote faith. At this time, the purchase of Peyote and the use of Peyote as a sacrament by members of federally recognized tribes appear to be well established in federal policy. There is also a positive working relationship among the U.S. Drug Enforcement Agency, the Texas Department of Public Safety, which regulates the harvesting and sale of Peyote, and the NAC. Yet in the past, courts have rendered decisions unfavorable to the NAC, and the church worries that future decisions will prove to be unfavorable as well or have negative effects.

Peyotists fear that the church's exemption for the sacramental use of a controlled substance could be weakened by a court giving other religious groups a similar exemption even though their members do not belong to federally recognized tribes. As discussed in chapter 6, the U.S. Supreme Court issued a ruling in 2006 allowing a religious group, União do Vegetal, to import a tea, called *hoasca*, that contains controlled substances. The group had argued that because an exemption had been granted to the NAC, it should also be granted to them as well. Ultimately, however, the court based its decision on the 1993 Religious Freedom Restoration Act, not on the NAC exemption.

Three years later, in 2009, a similar case entered the courts. A group of the followers of Santo Daime, a Brazilian-based religion, that consumes a hallucinogenic tea as a sacrament, filed for an exemption in federal court. The tea, called *ayahoasca,* is made from a variety of plants in Brazil and imported into the United States. On March 18, 2009, the U.S. district court in Oregon ruled in favor of the Santo Daime group, allowing it to use ayahoasca in their religious ceremonies. Again, the court referred to the Religious Freedom Restoration Act in its decision. The NAC was not involved in the Santo Daime case; NAC members believed that the decision would not have any impact on the sacramental use of Peyote since the Peyote exemption only covers members of federally recognized tribes. The judge noted that ayahoasca, like Peyote, is not harmful or habit-forming when used in a ceremonial manner. He quoted psychiatrist John H. Halpern, who has studied the effects of Peyote and ayahoasca and has found no negative medical effects when these substances are used in a ceremonial setting.

The two groups involved in the cases described above were granted exemptions allowing them to use controlled substances. The long-range fear for Peyotists is that if courts award too many exemptions, a state legislature or the U.S. Congress could intervene with prohibitive legislation, or as with the *Smith* case in 1990, a court might uphold the right of a state to prohibit all controlled substances without making an exemption for religious use. Members of the Peyote community have not forgotten the *Smith* case.

One of the reasons for NAC's concern over these cases, besides restrictive legislation that could ensue, is the dwindling supply of Peyote. This problem is compounded by recent weather trends, as extended droughts have reduced the size of the Peyote cacti and thus the overall supply. The dwindling supply has become a significant concern for both the NAC of North America (NACNA) and Azee' Bee Nahaghá of Diné Nation (ABNDN).

In 2009 NACNA held its sixtieth annual conference in Window Rock, Arizona. Window Rock is in the northern part of the Diné Reservation where the NACNA has always had members. The regional group, NACNA, State of Arizona, Inc., was the sponsor. This sponsorship was special to all NAC members because the president of the Arizona chapter of the NACNA is Emerson Jackson, a former president of NACNA as a whole. Jackson has spent the last fifty years fighting for and defending the Peyote faith.

At this conference, NACNA members elected a new administration. Earl Arkinson (Chippewa/Cree), from Montana, who previously had served two terms as president, was elected as the new president, and Sandor Iron Rope, president of the NAC of South Dakota, was elected vice president. Iron Rope stepped down as president of the South Dakota group to focus on his new position. The NAC of South Dakota elected Dwayne Shields (Yankton Sioux), from a famous family of Peyote singers, as its president, and Leonard Crow Dog, Jr. (Siçangu Lakota), as vice president. The major issues at the 2009 conference involved the use of eagle feathers, the rights of prisoners to the free exercise of religion, the integration of youth into the church, and the dwindling supply of Peyote buttons. By unanimous vote the attendees passed a resolution calling for the implementation of traditional spiritual activities for American Indian inmates in prison, in particular to allow inmates access to pipes, rattles, drums, cedar, sage, eagle feathers, and other items necessary for spiritual growth and renewal. The resolution did not call for prisoners to have access to Peyote. A second resolution was passed concerning the possession and use of eagle feathers. This issue emerged as some members believed that Peyotists were being unfairly targeted by the U.S. Fish and Wildlife Service. Federal agents were investigating poachers and sellers of eagle parts and may have cast their net too widely.

Members of federally recognized tribes, which include NAC members, are exempt from restrictions on the possession and use of endangered birds for spiritual activities. In order to clarify the issue, the U.S. Fish and Wildlife Service was invited to send a representative to the 2009 conference. The agent that spoke told the conferees that his agency was not targeting Peyotists, but rather individuals who were poaching and selling eagle feathers. The agent went on to explain the regulatory issues and the exemptions for possession of eagle feathers. He explained that members of federally recognized tribes were permitted to own, use, give as gifts, or trade eagle parts, but were not allowed to sell them for a profit. Nevertheless, the membership passed a resolution reaffirming the rights of Peyotists to use eagle feathers for spiritual purposes.

As important as these two resolutions are, the leadership of the NACNA believes that the supply issue is paramount. As the supply of Peyote buttons decreases, the price correspondingly increases. There is no easy solution to this dilemma.

In a recent interview with the author, President Arkinson addressed this concern. He pointed out that the membership of the NAC is continuing to grow, while Peyote cacti are being overharvested and harvested too early, resulting in fewer and smaller plants. One possible solution is the much larger supply of Peyote in Mexico. The problem is that the Mexican government does not allow the export of Peyote. The federal Drug Enforcement Administration is not opposed to the importation of Peyote for use by the NAC. President Arkinson is trying to make arrangements to meet with President Obama, with the hope of obtaining his help in working with the Mexican government. Attorneys that work with the NAC are also investigating the possibility of working with the Mexican government.

Vice President Iron Rope expressed similar concerns in a recent interview, particularly regarding the continuing rise in the cost of Peyote for people who cannot afford such high prices. While recognizing the importance of ceremonial issues to the church, Iron Rope wants to focus more on young people, and on the business aspect in running an international organization as well as running the many affiliated chapters. He sees the involvement of youth in a broad manner. He believes that the NAC's holistic approach to well-being can be used to help solve the wider problems on today's reservations. There is also a problem of what Iron Rope calls "spiritual exploitation," which involves non-Indians using American Indian spirituality for personal gain and profit.

The ABNDN held its forty-third annual conference in Chinle, Arizona, in 2009. A special day was set aside that year as part of the effort to rebuild "spiritual bridges" between elders and youth. Some of today's Diné elders have concerns about the youth. It is not so much that young people are not participating in ABNDN; they are, in great numbers. Instead, it is that the youth do not always follow traditional ceremonial etiquette, for instance in their excessive talking, in not showing enough respect for the details of the Peyote ceremony, or in going outside too often for social smoking. In order to close what some call a "Peyote cultural gap," a special youth day was scheduled as part of the annual conference. In addition, members made a proposal "to develop educational plans/programs aimed at teaching the proper use of Azee' [Peyote] under Tribe, State, and Federal Laws and to re-instill the old traditional teachings of our elders." They also proposed that each church chapter throughout the reservation establish a youth council and institute a local youth day. Older members are similarly concerned about Diné youth away at college. One way to reinforce the Peyote faith among college students is for church members to organize campus groups, such as the ABNDN organization at Northern Arizona University.

At the ABNDN conference business meeting, members discussed a variety of important issues, including a warning to the membership not to allow people who are not members of a federally recognized tribe to participate in the sacramental use of Peyote, as this could jeopardize the future of the church. Another issue on the agenda was the possibility of unifying all the Peyote organizations across Navajoland, as such unity would be good for the future of the church.

With so many critical issues to discuss, some ABNDN members seek a better means of communication. The organization has had a website for some time and some members have established an ABNDN blog allowing individuals to communicate directly with one another (as well as with the larger community) and share ideas and information. There is also a growing concern about the cost of running a large organization with tens of thousands of members spread across a vast land. Suggestions for strengthening the organization's funds include the development of an endowment, individual membership fees, and initiating fundraising campaigns.

A major issue discussed at all levels of the ABNDN is the supply of Peyote. At the 2009 conference there was some debate over recent attempts to purchase Peyote by weight rather than by the number of Peyote buttons, as is the present practice. As Peyote buttons have become smaller in size, the buyer is receiving less and less Peyote for the same price. One long-range answer to the shortage is to raise money and purchase land in the "Peyote gardens" of Texas. This would be costly but it would lessen the problem of relying on farmers to give permission for access to their land. If the ABNDN purchases such land, it could request the Texas Department of Public Safety to license additional peyoteros to harvest the Peyote buttons. Raising money for such a purchase would be very difficult, but the possibility is a recurrent topic of discussion.

For the hundreds of thousands of members of the Peyote faith, there will always be problems to solve and concerns about new or worsening problems. Yet after more than a century of struggle they maintain a strong belief in the spiritual destiny of the Peyote faith. Church members have put their faith in Peyote to protect their way of life and guarantee that future generations will continue to follow the Peyote Road.

Notes

CHAPTER 1

1. Schultes and Hofmann, *Botany and Chemistry of Hallucinogens*, 194; C. Boyd, "Pictographic Evidence."

2. C. Boyd, "Pictographic Evidence."

3. Quoted in Schultes and Hofmann, *Plants of the Gods*, 132; Stewart, *Peyote Religion: A History*, 19; Slotkin, "Peyotism, 1521–1891," 204–207.

4. Furst, *Flesh of the Gods*, 142–43; Stewart, *Peyote Religion: A History*, 20–21; Leonard, "A Decree against Peyote."

5. Quoted in Stewart, *Peyote Religion: A History*, 20.

6. Ibid., 17–26; Slotkin, *Peyote Religion: A Study*, 205, 208; La Barre, *Peyote Cult*, 29–40; Schultes and Hofmann, *Plants of the Gods*, 132–35.

7. Meyerhoff, *Peyote Hunt*, 73–77, 112; Furst, *Flesh of the Gods*, 141–46.

8. Meyerhoff, *Peyote Hunt*, 126–37; Furst, *Flesh of the Gods*, 156.

9. Meyerhoff, *Peyote Hunt*, 155–71, 175. This version is from Meyerhoff's pilgrimage in the 1960s; other accounts have variations. Furst, *Flesh of the Gods*, 175–80.

10. Meyerhoff, *Peyote Hunt*, 218–20.

11. Quotes from ibid., 121, 189, 227–28.

12. Ibid., 190.

13. Stewart, *Peyote Religion: A History*, 30.

14. Ibid., 34, 46; La Barre, *Peyote Cult*, 122; Slotkin, *Peyote Religion: A Study*, 210–12; Slotkin, "Early Eighteenth Century Documents."

15. Stewart, *Peyote Religion: A History*, 49–50; Morris Opler, "Description"; Morris Opler, "Use of Peyote."

16. Morris Opler, "Use of Peyote"; Stewart, *Peyote Religion: A History*, 46–50; La Barre, *Peyote Cult*, 122.

17. Stewart, *Peyote Religion: A History*, 49–50, 57; Morris Opler, "Use of Peyote"; Morris Opler, "Description."

18. Stewart, *Peyote Religion: A History*, 58–60, includes photo of Chiwat.

19. Hagan, *Quanah Parker*, 36–61, includes photo of his mother, Cynthia Parker, 53; La Barre, *Peyote Cult*, 85; Stewart, *Peyote Religion: A History*, 71.

20. Stewart, *Peyote Religion: A History*, 71–72.

21. Ibid., 74, 79.

22. Stewart, *Peyote Religion: A History*, 79–83; Howard, "Half Moon Way."

23. Mooney, "Mescal Plant," 7.

24. H. Smith and Snake, *One Nation under God*, 24.

25. Hodge, *Handbook of American Indians*, 1:959, photograph. It is also in Stewart, *Peyote Religion: A History*, 85.

26. Stewart, *Peyote Religion: A History*, 48–50, 94–95; Mooney, "Wichita," 949; Morris Opler, "Description," 433; La Barre, *Peyote Cult*, 117.

27. Stewart, *Peyote Religion: A History*, 91; Swan, *Peyote Religious Art*, 31–32; Petrullo, *Diabolic Root*, 80–85.

28. Petrullo, *Diabolic Root*, 32–43; Stewart, *Peyote Religion: A History*, 95–96, 106.

29. La Barre, *Peyote Cult*, 52, 127–28; Hagan, *Quanah Parker*, 52–54, 62; Stewart, *Peyote Religion: A History*, 128–29.

30. Hagan, *Quanah Parker*, 115–20.

31. Quannah [*sic*] Parker to Commissioner Valentine, October 9, 1908, Central Classified File (CCF), 1907–39, Liquor Traffic, Box 4, Record Group (RG) 75, National Archives (NA), Washington, D.C. (hereafter cited as Liquor Traffic).

32. "Peyotists at Carlisle," Folder: Leaders and Indian Schools, Box 65, Omer Stewart Papers, University of Colorado Archives, Boulder (hereafter cited as Stewart Papers).

33. The best study of the Ghost Dance Movement is still Mooney, *Ghost Dance Religion and the Sioux Outbreak*.

34. Slotkin, "Peyotism, 1521–1891," 212.

35. Annual Report, Commissioner of Indian Affairs (ARCIA), 1905: 253; Radin, *Autobiography of a Winnebago Indian*, 389, 393; Stewart, *Peyote Religion: A History*, 144–45. In addition to the above *Autobiography*, see Sam Blowsnake's autobiography (his pseudonym is Crashing Thunder), which was reissued in an expanded version in 1926 as Radin, *Crashing Thunder*. See also autobiographical material on Blowsnake (Sam's brother), in Radin, "Personal Reminiscences of a Winnebago Indian," and on Sam and his sister, in Lurie, *Mountain Wolf Woman*. There is additional autobiographical material by John Rave, Albert Hensley, and Jesse Clay in Radin, *Winnebago Tribe*. Today the Wisconsin Winnebagos call themselves the Ho-Chunks; however, throughout the twentieth century they were called Winnebagos. For consistency with the sources, I use Winnebago, except when referring to the present-day group in Wisconsin.

36. Radin, *Winnebago Tribe*, 391; Radin, "Sketch of the Peyote Cult," 5–12; La Barre, *Peyote Cult*, 121.

37. Radin, *Autobiography of a Winnebago Indian*, 55n153.

38. Albert Hensley to Commissioner of Indian Affairs (CIA), October 9, 1908, Correspondence of Chief Special Officer, Law and Order, Box 1, RG 75, NA (hereafter cited as Law and Order).

39. Harry Keefe to BIA, March 19, 1912, CCF, 1907–39, Liquor Traffic, Box 4; Hearing before Assistant Commissioner of Indian Affairs on Use of Mescal, March 19, 1912; "A Petition to Cato Sells," CIA, February 20, 1915. Quoted in Stewart, *Peyote Religion: A History,* 163–64, 406.

40. Stewart, *Peyote Religion: A History,* 230; Slotkin, *Peyote Religion: A Study,* 60.

41. Stewart, *Peyote Religion: A History,* 149–51, 167; La Barre, *Peyote Cult,* 162–65.

42. Anderson, *Peyote: The Divine Cactus,* 44–45; La Barre, *Peyote Cult,* 73–74; Radin, *Winnebago Tribe,* 394–97, 400, 411–12; Radin, "Sketch of the Peyote Cult," 10–11.

43. Radin, *Winnebago Tribe,* 400.

44. Ibid., 420; Radin, "Sketch of the Peyote Cult," 11, 17–18.

45. Albert Hensley to CIA, October 9, 1908, Correspondence of Chief Special Officer, Law and Order.

46. William Johnson to Superintendent Walter Runke, April 17, 1911, CCF, 1907–39, Liquor Traffic, Box 3; ARCIA, 1909: 13–14.

47. Johnson to CIA, September 11, 1911, Correspondence of Chief Special Officer, Law and Order; Radin, *Winnebago Tribe,* 415.

48. Radin, *Winnebago Tribe,* 417; La Barre, *Peyote Cult,* 121; Stewart, *Peyote Religion: A History,* 158–59.

49. Slotkin, "Menomini Peyotism," 575–76; La Barre, *Peyote Cult,* 121; Hurt, "Factors in the Persistence of Peyote," 18. For an in-depth view of contemporary Winnebago Peyotism, see Noah White, interview by Herbert Hoover, June 25, 1970, American Indian Research Project (AIRP), Tape 507, Institute of American Indian Studies, University of South Dakota, Vermillion (hereafter cited as IAIS); Sterling Snake, interview by Herbert Hoover, July 29, 1970, AIRP, Tape 534, IAIS. Excerpts are published in Cash and Hoover, *To Be an Indian.*

50. Radin, *Winnebago Tribe,* 74.

51. Office of Indian Affairs to Harry Black Bear et al., October 6, 1911, CCF, 1907–37, Liquor Traffic, Box 3; Lurie, *Mountain Wolf Woman,* 44–45; Stewart, *Peyote Religion: A History,* 181.

52. Jim Blue Bird to Omer Stewart, January 13, 1949, Folder 1,946, Box 46, Stewart Papers.

53. Crow Dog and Erdoes, *Crow Dog,* 83, 94.

54. Walter Runke to William Johnson, March 30, 1911, CCF, 1907–39, Liquor Traffic, Box 3.

55. Superintendents' Annual Narrative and Statistical Reports, Yankton Agency, 1911, RG 75, NA (National Archives Microfilm Publication M 1011, roll 72) (hereafter cited as Supts' Annual Narrative).

56. A. W. Leech to Commissioner of Indian Affairs, February 10, 1912, CCF, Yankton, Box 7, RG 75, NA (hereafter cited as Yankton). For a detailed analysis of the introduction of Peyote to the Yanktons, see Maroukis, *Peyote and the Yankton Sioux,* 89–95.

57. Statement signed by Charles Jones, February 12, 1912, CCF, Yankton.

58. F. H. Abbott, Assistant Commissioner of Indian Affairs to Leech, March 8, 1912, CCF, Yankton; Supts' Annual Narrative, 1913, roll 72.

59. Report of S. A. M. Young, April 18, 1914, CCF, Yankton; E. B. Merritt, Assistant Commissioner of Indian Affairs to Young, May 6, 1914; Leech to Henry Larson, November 13, 1916, Correspondence of Chief Special Officer, Law and Order; David A. Richardson, M.D. to Leech, November 10, 1916, RG75.

60. ARCIA, 1906: 268, 321.

61. Quoted in La Barre, *Peyote Cult*, 217; Slotkin, *Peyote Religion: A Study*, 57–58.

62. Blair, *Indian Tribes of the Upper Mississippi Valley*, 282.

63. Stewart, *Peyote Religion: A History*, 223; Slotkin, *Peyote Religion: A Study*, 135n11.

64. Stewart, *Peyote Religion: A History*, 223; Slotkin, *Peyote Religion: A Study*, 58, 136nn15–16.

65. Slotkin, *Peyote Religion: A Study*, 53–54; Hertzberg, *Search*, 254.

66. Lake Mohonk Conference, Reports of the 32nd, 33rd, 34th, 35th *Lake Mohonk Conference*. Lake Mohonk, N.Y., 1914–17.

67. Seymour, "Peyote Worship," 181–84; H. Welsh, "Peyote: An Insidious Evil"; Stewart, *Peyote Religion: A History*, 217; Slotkin, *Peyote Religion: A Study*, 53–54.

68. Prucha, *Great Father*, 787; Hertzberg, *Search*, 259–72.

69. House Subcommittee on Indian Affairs, *Peyote: Hearings on H.R. 2614*, 65th Congress, 2nd sess., 1918 (hereafter cited as *H.R. 2614*), 58–59, 145; Moses, *Indian Man*, 200–201; D. Welch, "Zitkala-Ša," 137–44; Hertzberg, *Search*, 264–66.

70. D. Welch, "Zitkala-Ša," 133–34; Stewart, "Gertrude Simmons Bonnin."

71. *Peyote*, Hearings on HR 2614, 128; D. Welch, "Zitkala-Ša," 84–85, 133–43, 148; Stewart, *Peyote Religion: A History*, 198–200, 221; Slotkin, *Peyote Religion: A Study*, 58; La Barre, *Peyote Cult*, 169.

72. *H.R. 2614*, 139–42; Hertzberg, *Search*, 39–42, 263–64.

73. Hertzberg, *Search*, 48–53, 145–46.

74. Mooney, "Mescal Plant," 7–11; Mooney, "Peyote," 237; Moses, *Indian Man*, 57–60, 182–84, 200–203; Stewart, *Peyote Religion: A History*, 220.

75. *H.R. 2614*, 80, 113, 137, 147.

76. U.S. Congress, Documents and Reports, *Prohibition of the Use of Peyote*, 65th Congress, 2nd sess., May 13, 1918.

77. Whitewolf, *Life of a Kiowa-Apache Indian*, 130.

78. Moses, *Indian Man*, 203–207; Hertzberg, *Search*, 272; Stewart, *Peyote Religion: A History*, 222–25.

79. Moses, *Indian Man*, 205–10.

CHAPTER 2

1. Mooney, "Mescal Plant," 9; Radin, "Sketch of the Peyote Cult," 12; Schultes, "Appeal of Peyote," 698–715; Stewart, *Peyote Religion: A History*, 248; La Barre, *Peyote*

Cult, 58, 85; Hultkrantz, *Attraction of Peyote*, 105. In American Indian studies the words *religion* and *traditional* are contested. Native scholars criticize the use of the word *religion* as being too narrow, indicating a secular/sacred dichotomy that does not exist in American Indian cosmologies. Spiritual leaders and elders refer to a "Way of Life" in which all things are integrated in a spiritual universe that encompasses all of life. The parts cannot be separated from the whole. Nevertheless it is impossible when writing in English to find suitable alternatives when analyzing spiritual beliefs systems. *Traditional* has been used by western scholars to imply a static or unchanging past in nonwestern societies. Life in the past has always changed, giving the word *traditional* an unclear meaning. Does "traditional plains culture" mean before or after the introduction of the horse? I use *traditional* in a very precise way to refer to the spiritual, cultural, and social values and structures that existed on the eve of the reservation era to help explain how pre-reservation belief systems interfaced with the expansion of the Peyote faith.

2. Crow Dog and Erdoes, *Crow Dog*, 91–113; Catches, "Native American Church," 17–24; Spider, "Native American Church of Jesus Christ," 189–210; D. Long, "Religious Freedom and Native Sovereignty," 188–194. Address by Douglas Long at a twenty-fifth anniversary conference of American Indian Religious Freedom Act.

3. Vecsey, *Imagine Ourselves Richly*, 153–81, contains an analysis of many Peyote origin narratives.

4. Mooney, "Kiowa Peyote Rite," 329–30.

5. M. Boyd, *Kiowa Voices*, 103–104.

6. Brant, "Peyotism among the Kiowa-Apache," 213–14. The interview was conducted in 1949.

7. Roger Stops, interview by Stuart W. Conner, 1970, American Indian Research Project (AIRP), Tape 569, IAIS.

8. Alice Bulltail, interview by William Fraser, 1970, Pryor, Montana, AIRP, Tape 598, IAIS; D. Long, "Religious Freedom and Native Sovereignty."

9. Brant, "Peyotism among the Kiowa-Apache," 219.

10. Radin, *Autobiography of a Winnebago Indian*, 31–35, 52–57; Radin, "Sketch of the Peyote Cult," 4–9.

11. Aberle, *Peyote Religion among the Navaho*, 183; d'Azevedo, *Straight with the Medicine*, 45.

12. H. Smith and Snake, *One Nation under God*, 18; *Traditional Use of Peyote*, filmed interview with Reuben Snake.

13. Aberle, *Peyote Religion among the Navaho*, 181–82.

14. Hultkrantz, *Attraction of Peyote*, 103.

15. Ibid., 103–104; Wiedman, "Big and Little Moon Peyotism" 377–84; Davies, *Healing Ways*, 47, 181; Malouf, "Gosiute Peyotism," 100–101; Dick Fool Bull, interview by George Nielsen, 1971, Rosebud Reservation, AIRP, Tape 710, IAIS (hereafter cited as Fool Bull interview).

16. Davies, *Healing Ways*, 49, 181.

17. Ibid., quoted on 183.

18. La Barre, *Peyote Cult*, 166; Radin, "Sketch of the Peyote Cult," 9; Deloria, "Politics and Religion," 7301.

19. Brant, "Peyotism among the Kiowa-Apache," 218.

20. d'Azevedo, *Straight with the Medicine*, 7.

21. Medicine, "Indian Women," 161.

22. Deloria, *Singing for a Spirit*, 33.

23. Crow Dog and Erdoes, *Crow Dog*, 137.

24. H. Smith and Snake, *One Nation under God*, 20.

25. d'Azevedo, *Straight with the Medicine*, 20–21.

26. Howard, *Ponca Tribe*, 73.

27. Stewart, *Peyote Religion: A History*, 354.

28. Ibid., 372–73, reproduces a Gosiute "Meeting Program" from 1940. It lists the activities done in sequences of four.

29. La Barre, *Peyote Cult*, 78–79; Cousineau, *A Seat at the Table*, 90.

30. Speck, "Notes on the Life of John Wilson," 547.

31. Spider, "Native American Church of Jesus Christ," 200–201.

32. Ibid.

33. Shonle, "Peyote, the Giver of Visions," 53–75; La Barre, *Peyote Cult*, 58; Hultkrantz, *Attraction of Peyote*, 117; Anderson, *Peyote: The Divine Cactus*, 62; Young, "Intertribal Religious Movements," 1005–1007.

34. Petrullo, *Diabolic Root*, 22, 55; Slotkin, *Peyote Religion: A Study*, 41–45; Stewart, *Peyote Religion: A History*, 91; Stewart, "Anthropological Theory," 279–80; Schultes, "Appeal of Peyote," 704; Cash and Wolff, *Ponca People*, 78.

35. Maroukis, *Peyote and the Yankton Sioux*, 157–58.

36. H. Smith and Snake, *One Nation under God*, 39.

37. Fikes, "Brief History," 173; Swan, *Peyote Religious Art*, 92.

38. Crow Dog and Erdoes, *Crow Dog*, 100.

39. Stewart, *Peyote Religion: A History*, 344.

40. Brown, *The Sacred Pipe*, 69.

41. Crow Dog and Erdoes, *Crow Dog*, 98–99; Catches, "Native American Church," 20; Gerald Primeaux, interviews by the author, Marty, S.D., March 1, 2003, and June 3, 2007.

42. Hultkrantz, *Attraction of Peyote*, 84. For a discussion of these paradigms see the "classification of social movements" in Aberle, *Peyote Religion among the Navaho*, 315–33. Hultkrantz also discusses many of the theories of diffusion.

43. Petrullo, *Diabolic Root*, 63, 84–85; Stewart, *Peyote Religion: A History*, 92 and 354. Item #281 in Stewart's "Peyote Element Distribution List" has all Peyote communities accepting Peyote as a teacher; Fool Bull interview.

44. H. Smith and Snake, *One Nation under God*, 40–41.

45. Maroukis, *Peyote and the Yankton Sioux*, appendix 1.

46. Aberle, *Peyote Religion among the Navaho*, 180–81.

47. Radin, "Sketch of the Peyote Cult," 5, 11; Brant, "Peyotism among the Kiowa-Apache," 219.

48. d'Azevedo, *Straight with the Medicine*, 47.

49. H. Smith and Snake, *One Nation Under God,* 53–55; Kracht, "Kiowa Religion in Historical Perspective," 249.

50. Howard, *Ponca Tribe,* 99; Charles Kills Enemy, interview by Herbert Hoover, July 2, 1971, AIRP, Tape 71, IAIA; Collins, " A Descriptive Introduction," 448; Stewart, "History of Peyotism in Nevada," 290; Iverson, *Diné,* 306.

51. Davies, *Healing Ways,* 46, 181–82; Aberle, *Peyote Religion among the Navaho,* 178, 181.

52. Begay and Maryboy, "Whole Universe Is My Cathedral"; *Navajo Times,* "Centenarians," February 22, 2007, C1–2.

53. Snake, *Reuben Snake,* 229.

54. Spider, "Native American Church," 190.

55. H. Smith and Snake, *One Nation under God,* 79; Stewart, *Peyote Religion: A History,* 339. This section on the Cross Fire and Half Moon services is a composite from many sources, particularly from the voices of NAC members. I also used two films, *The Peyote Road* and *The Traditional Use of Peyote,* both containing interviews with prominent church members.

56. Swan, *Peyote Religious Art,* 49–56.

57. Noah White, interview by Herbert Hoover, 1970, Prairie Island Indian Community, Minnesota, AIRP, Tape 507, IAIS.

CHAPTER 3

1. Chronological File, Folder 1916–21, Box 43, Stewart Papers.

2. E. B. Merritt to Superintendents, March 28, 1919, Circular 1522, "Peyote," CCF, 1907–39, Liquor Traffic, Box 2. Copies of the responses can be found in Box 43, Stewart Papers. The originals are in CCF, 1907–39, Liquor Traffic.

3. E. G. Merritt, *Concerning Peyote* (U.S. Bureau of Indian Affairs, 1919).

4. Prucha, *Great Father,* 789.

5. ARCIA, 1922: 20.

6. Ibid.

7. Stewart, *Peyote Religion: A History,* 226–27.

8. Newberne, *Peyote: An Abridged Compilation,* 1–2. Includes the 1919 questions sent to superintendents, 27.

9. Ibid., 6–8, 11, 13.

10. Ibid.

11. Ibid., 33–36.

12. Ibid.; ARCIA, 1923: 23.

13. Newberne, *Peyote: An Abridged Compilation,* 25–36.

14. *Peyote,* Bulletin 21 (Office of Indian Affairs, Department of the Interior, 1923), 4; Anderson, *Peyote: The Divine Cactus,* chapters 5 and 6 contain a thorough analysis of the pharmacology and chemistry of Peyote.

15. Klüver, "Mescal Visions," 502–15; Rouhier, *La Plante qui fait les yeux émerveilles,* 337, 340; Klüver, *Mescal,* 91, 101.

16. Work, *Indian Policies*, 8; Hertzberg, *Search*, 202–203, 275; Prucha, *Great Father*, 788–89.

17. Meriam, *Problem of Indian Administration*, 222, 629; Prucha, *Great Father*, 807–809, 836–39.

18. ARCIA, 1930: 1–2, 32.

19. Stewart, "Gertrude Simmons Bonnin"; Stewart, "Peyote and the Law,"47–48.

20. Stewart, "Gertrude Simmons Bonnin"; Stewart, "Friend to the Ute," 274–75; Stewart, *Peyote Religion: A History*, 199–200.

21. Zitkala-Ša [Gertrude Bonnin], *American Indian Stories*; D. Welsh, "Zitkala-Ša," 168–69.

22. *Proceedings of the Senate: State of South Dakota* (Pierre, S.D.: State Publishing, 1923), 103, 106, 109, 127; *Proceedings of the House of Representatives: State of South Dakota* (Pierre, S.D.: State Publishing, 1923), 110–11, 130, 143; Stewart, *Peyote Religion: A History*, 227–28; Maroukis, *Peyote and the Yankton Sioux*, 142.

23. Stewart, "Gertrude Simmons Bonnin"; D. Welsh, "Zitkala-Ša," 47.

24. Slotkin, *Peyote Religion: A Study*, 56; Stewart, *Peyote Religion: A History*, 226–27; Stewart, "Peyote and the Law," 47–48; Stewart, "Ute Peyotism," 5; Stewart, "Peyote Religion," in d'Azevedo, *Great Basin*, 680.

25. Charles Burke, foreword to Lindquist, *Red Man*, v–vii.

26. Work, *Indian Policies*, 6.

27. Lindquist, *Red Man*, xiv, 65, 69–76.

28. Maroukis, *Peyote and the Yankton Sioux*, 208–209.

29. D. Welsh, "Zitkala-Ša,"178–79.

30. Ibid., 209–21; Hertzberg, *Search*, 207–209.

31. Willard, "First Amendment," 39–40.

32. Stewart, *Peyote Religion: A History*, 223.

33. Ibid., 228–30; Hertzberg, *Search*, 277.

34. Slotkin, *Peyote Religion: A Study*, 62, 137n22, preamble to the 1934 charter; Hertzberg, *Search*, 284.

35. Jim Blue Bird to Harold Ickes, March 16, 1937, CCF, 1907–39, Liquor Traffic, Box 4.

36. Stewart, *Peyote Religion: A History*, 232–37; Collins, "A Descriptive Introduction," 427–49.

37. Ibid., 237–38; *Documents on Peyote*, no. 137817, pt. 1, Bureau Report on S. 1399, 75th Cong., 1st sess., February 8, 1937.

38. Petrullo, *Diabolic Root*; Petrullo, "Peyotism as an Emergent Indian Culture," 51–60; Maroukis, *Peyote and the Yankton Sioux*, 210–11.

39. Richard Schultes to Commission John Collier, March 31, 1937, Folder 1937, Box 45, Stewart Papers.

CHAPTER 4

1. Stewart, *Peyote Religion: A History*, chapters 9 and 10.

2. L. Villegas to F. M. Skillman, Broken Bough, NB., April 5, 1909, CCF, 1907–39, Liquor Traffic, Box 3.

3. Morgan, "Man, Plant," 84–95; Julius Wormser to Omer Stewart, September 20, 1938, Folder Peyote Persons, U–Z, Box 40, Stewart Papers; Stewart, *Peyote Religion: A History*, 229; Stewart, "Ute," 7; Slotkin, "Menomini Peyotism," 681.

4. Folder Blue Bird, Box 32, Stewart Papers. In a thirty-eight-page interview, Blue Bird listed the names of the major Peyotists of this era.

5. Stewart, *Peyote Religion: A History*, 172–73, 215; Slotkin, "Menomini Peyotism," 577, 676–77; Hurt, "Factors in the Persistence of Peyote," 16–27.

6. Lieber, "Opposition to Peyotism," 387–96; Slotkin, *Peyote Religion: A Study*, 47.

7. Stewart, *Peyote Religion: A History*, 184–89; La Barre, *Peyote Cult*, 214.

8. Marvin Opler, "Character and History," 465–68; Newberne, *Peyote: An Abridged Compilation*, 33–35.

9. Malouf, "Gosiute Peyotism," 93–94, 100–102; Stewart, *Peyote Religion: A History*, 266–67.

10. Stewart, "History of Peyotism," 279–91.

11. D'Azevedo, *Straight with the Medicine*, 93.

12. Ibid., xi–xiv; Stewart, *Peyote Religion: A History*, 279, 286, Stewart attended Peyote meetings with Lancaster in 1938; d'Azevedo, "Washoe," 496.

13. Iverson, *Diné*, 50–65, 134.

14. Aberle, *Peyote Religion among the Navaho*, 109; Stewart, *Peyote Religion: A History*, 294.

15. Quotes from Iverson, *Diné*, 153; Aberle, *Peyote Religion among the Navaho*, 164–66.

16. Aberle, *Peyote Religion among the Navaho*, 110–11, 124; Aberle, "Peyote Religion among the Navaho," 558, 564.

17. Aberle, *Peyote Religion among the Navaho*, 113–15, reprints the full resolution; Stewart, *Peyote Religion: A History*, 296–98.

18. Iverson, *Diné*, 197–204.

19. Wyman, "Navajo Ceremonial System," 531.

20. Iverson, *Diné*, 3; Aberle, *Peyote Religion among the Navaho*, 119.

21. Quintero, "Gender, Discord, and Illness," 84.

22. Davies, *Healing Ways*, 46–47; Aberle, "Peyote Religion among the Navaho," 563; Newton and Bydone, "Identity and Healing in Three Navajo Religious Traditions."

23. Slotkin, *Peyote Religion: A Study*, 62; copies of charters in Stewart Papers, Box 45.

24. Slotkin, *Peyote Religion: A Study*, 60–61; Stewart, *Peyote Religion: A History*, 240.

25. "Button, Button . . ."; Stewart, *Peyote Religion: A History*, 301; Aberle, *Peyote Religion among Navaho*, 403–405.

26. "Statement on Peyote."

27. Minutes, NAC National Convention, Macy, Nebraska, August 6–8, 1953, Folder NAC 1953, Box 46, Stewart Papers.

28. *Quarterly Newsletter of the Native American Church of the United States* 1, no. 1 (1955), Box 46, Stewart Papers (hereafter cited as *Quarterly Newsletter of the NAC*). With volume 1, issue 4, the title of the publication was changed to the *NAC of North America*.

29. Slotkin, *Peyote Religion: A Study*, 62.

CHAPTER 5

1. The Azee' Bee Nahaghá (Peyote Ceremonial Act) of 2005, Exh. A, section 4:3; NAC of South Dakota, Bylaws, 2007; NAC of North America, Bylaws, 2007.

2. Swan, *Peyote Religious Art*, x.

3. Ibid., 39 fig. 2:16, 18 fig. 4:19.

4. Gerald Primeaux, Sr., interview by author, Marty, S.D., June 15, 2000.

5. Swan, *Peyote Religious Art*, 56–59.

6. Ibid., 37–38.

7. Ibid., 45–47, 67–69; La Barre, *Peyote Cult*, 67n59.

8. La Barre, *Peyote Cult*, 68.

9. Azee' Bee Nahaghá, Exh. A.

10. Lohrmann and Ah Be Hill, "'As Long As I Can Thread a Needle,'" 16; Swan, *Peyote Religious Art*, 41–46, photographs of Peyote fans.

11. Lessard, "Instruments of Prayer," 24–27; Swan, *Peyote Religious Art*, 46, 94–97; Wiedman, "Staff, Fan, Rattle & Drum," 38–45; Merriam and d'Azevedo, "Washo Peyote Songs," 619.

12. Jewelry from Douglas and Marriott, "Metal Jewelry of the Peyote Cult," 81; Swan, *Peyote Religious Art*, 62–65. Swan, "Contemporary Navajo Peyote Arts," 49–50.

13. Greene, *Silver Horn:* 120–21; Donnelley, *Transforming Images*, 60–84.

14. Donnelley, *Transforming Images*, illus., 156–57; Wiedman and Greene, "Early Kiowa Peyote Ritual and Symbolism: The 1890 Drawing Books"; Greene, *Silver Horn*, 64–67, 120–24. The four sketchbooks are in the Field Museum of Natural History, Chicago.

15. Greene, *Silver Horn*, 126, plate 22; Swan, *Peyote Religious Art*, 70–71.

16. Swan, *Peyote Religious Art*, 72–75, illus. 4:12–13.

17. M. Boyd, *Kiowa Voices*, 126–27, photo of the Kiowa Five in dance regalia.

18. Donnelley, *Art of Silver Horn*, plate #41.

19. Denman, *Peyote Ritual*, 3.

20. Ibid., 7.

21. *Peyote Design* is the title of both paintings. See SIRIS (Smithsonian Institution Research Information System, NAAINV 0874300, NAAINV 8799100).

22. Swan, *Peyote Religious Art*, 70–79, illus. 4:8–10; Prucha, *Great Father*, 947, 973–76, illus. #65.

23. Denman, *Peyote Ritual*, 13–14.

24. Wiedman and Greene, "Early Kiowa Peyote Ritual and Symbolism: The 1891 Drawing Books," 32–41; Douglas and d'Harnoncourt, *Indian Art*, 210. This painting

is known by several different names: *The Cormorant, Messenger Bird, Between Earth and the Greats.*

25. Lessard, "Instruments of Prayer," 24; Swan, *Peyote Religious Art*, xi; Swan, "Contemporary Navajo Peyote Arts," 47. This has also been my experience. Swan's observation refers to the 1990s. He adds that this has since changed.

26. M. Boyd, *Kiowa Voices*, frontispiece.

27. Swan, *Peyote Religious Art*, 99.

28. Primeaux, June 3, 2007, interview.

29. McAllester, *Peyote Music*, 36, and song index, 18.

30. Snake, *Humble Serpent*, 226.

31. For example, the Rockboy family of the late Clarence Rockboy (Yankton Sioux) donated his lifelong collection of Peyote music to the Institute of American Indian Studies, University of South Dakota.

32. Merriam and d'Azevedo, "Washo Peyote Songs," 621.

33. Primeaux, June 3, 2007, interview.

34. McAllester, *Peyote Music*, 65–80.

35. Merriam and d'Azevedo, "Washo Peyote Songs," 627; Maroukis, *Peyote and the Yankton Sioux*, 220–22.

CHAPTER 6

1. "Button, Button . . . ," 6, 8.

2. Folder Blue Bird, Box 32, Stewart Papers; Stewart, *Peyote Religion: A History*, 243.

3. Frank Takes Gun to Members, October 31, 1957, Folder 1957, Box 47, Stewart Papers; Stewart, *Peyote Religion: A History*, 244.

4. *Quarterly Newsletter of the NAC*, vols. 1–3 (1955); Stewart, "Peyote and the Law," 57–58; Stewart, *Peyote Religion: A History*, 244.

5. *Arizona v. Mary Attakai*, no. 4098, 178 (Ariz. Sup. Ct., Coconino Cty., 1960); C. Long, *Religious Freedom and Indian Rights*, 17–18; Stewart, *Peyote Religion: A History*, 305–308; Stewart, "Peyote and the Law," 49.

6. *Native American Church v. Navajo Tribal Council*, 272 F.2d 131 (10th Cir. 1959); Stewart, *Peyote Religion: A History*, 302–305; Stewart, "Peyote and the Law," 56–57; Aberle, *Peyote Religion among the Navaho*, 121; Iverson, *Diné*, 204.

7. *Navajo Times* (21 November 1968), quoted in Stewart, *Peyote Religion: A History*, 310.

8. *People v. Woody*, 394 P.2d 813, (Cal. 1964), 815; C. Long, *Religious Freedom and Indian Rights*, 17–18; Stewart, "Peyote and the Law," 50–52.

9. Stewart, *Peyote Religion: A History*, 245–46.

10. Ibid., 304–305; Aberle, *Peyote Religion among the Navaho*, xlii; *Navajo Times*, November 21, 1968.

11. Constitution and Bylaws, 1966, Folder Oklahoma, Box 62, Stewart Papers.

12. Ginsberg, *Howl and Other Poems*, 10.

13. Food and Drugs, 31 *Federal Register* 4679 (1966); Stewart, "Peyote and the Law," 52; Stewart, *Peyote Religion: A History*, 246–47, 333–34.

14. Food and Drugs, Title 21 Sec.1307.31, *Federal Register* (1970).

15. NAC of North America, Minutes, September 10–12, 1971, Folder 1964–75, Box 48, Stewart Papers.

16. *Whitehorn v. Oklahoma*, 561 P.2d 539 (Okla. 1977).

17. *State of Oregon v. Soto*, 537 P.2d 142 (Ore. 1975).

18. Harjo, "American Indian Religious Freedom Act," also contains the transcripts from a conference on the Twenty-fifth Anniversary of AIRFA; C. Long, *Religious Freedom and Indian Rights*, 20–21.

19. d'Azevedo, *Straight with the Medicine*, 52.

20. Morgan, "Biogeography of Peyote," 50–57; Morgan and Stewart, "Peyote Trade," 282.

21. Morgan, "Man, Plant," 85; Anderson, "'Peyote Gardens,'" 67.

22. Interview with Cárdenas in Morgan, "Man, Plant," 125; "Peyote Pioneer Dies at 100," *Laredo Morning Times*, September 8, 2005; "Honoring a Pioneer: Ceremony Celebrates Life of a Mirando Woman," *Laredo Times*, September 11, 2005.

23. Morgan, "Man, Plant," 102–104.

24. Ibid., 105–10; Anderson, "'Peyote Gardens,'" 70–72; Morgan and Stewart, "Peyote Trade," 280, 293; Stewart, *Peyote Religion: A History*, 334–35.

25. *Native American Church of New York v. U.S.*, 468 F.Supp. 1247 (S.D. N.Y. 1979).

26. Archie D. Hoffman, Sr., Vice-Chair, *Cheyenne Native American Church*, chapter 2, "Peyote and the Native American Church," unpublished paper, 2004; Stewart, *Peyote Religion: A History*, 333–34.

27. Botsford and Echo-Hawk, "Legal Tango," 134.

28. C. Long, *Religious Freedom and Indian Rights*, 30.

29. Ibid., 144–47; *Lyng v. Northwest Indian Cemetery Protective Assn.*, 485 U.S. 439 (1988); *Peyote Way Church of God v. Thornburgh*, 922 F.2d 1210 (5th Cir. 1991).

30. C. Long, *Religious Freedom and Indian Rights*, 151–52, 171–78, details the pressures on Smith.

31. H. Smith and Snake, *One Nation under God*, 51–52. For a more personal view on the trials and tribulations of Smith's life, see Epps, *To an Unknown God*, 8–19.

32. Al Smith to Asa Primeaux, Sr., April 13, 1990. A copy of this letter is in possession of the author.

33. *Employment Division, Dept. of Human Resources of Oregon v. Smith* 494 U.S. 872 (1990); Fisher, *Religious Liberty in America*, 186–88; C. Long, *Religious Freedom and Indian Rights*, 185–97.

34. Lawson and Morris, "Native American Church and the New Court." More than one hundred scholarly articles have been published on the *Smith* case. See bibliographic essay in C. Long, *Religious Freedom and Indian Rights*.

35. Botsford and Echo-Hawk, "Legal Tango," 139.

36. Peregoy, Echo-Hawk, and Botsford, "Congress Overturns Supreme Court's Peyote Ruling," 19–20.

37. A copy of the information packet is in the author's possession.

38. *Peyote Road* (film, exec. prod. Reuben A. Snake); *Traditional Use of Peyote* (film).

39. Reprinted in *Native American Rights Fund Legal Review* 20, no. 1 (1995): 3–5.

40. Fisher, *Religious Liberty in America*, 189–93; C. Long, *Religious Freedom and Indian Rights*, 273; Percgoy, Echo-Hawk, and Botsford, "Congress Overturns Supreme Court's Peyote Ruling," 16–17. The Supreme Court, in *City of Boerne v. Flores*, 521 U.S. 507 (1997), ruled that parts of the Religious Freedom Restoration Act, 1993, that applied to state and municipal law were unconstitutional on the basis that it violated the principles of federalism and the separation of powers. The *Boerne* decision has not affected the 1994 American Indian Religious Freedom Act Amendments protecting the sacramental use of Peyote.

41. Botsford and Echo-Hawk, "Legal Tango," 140–41.

42. "Native American Church of North America, Bylaws," revised June 15, 2007.

43. Harjo, "Vampire Policy Is Bleeding Us Dry," 42–44. For an in-depth look at the DNA issue, see Tallbear, "DNA, Blood, and Racializing."

44. Rollin Haag, Sr., to Linden Barber, Office of Chief Counsel, DEA, n.d. [January 2002], copies in possession of the author; Archie D. Hoffman, "Peyote and the Native American Church," unpublished paper, 2004.

45. 1999 interview with Peter Iverson, *Diné*, 319.

46. *ABNDN Newsletter*, June 2004; "Resolution of the Navajo Nation Council, 2005."

47. *ABNDN Newsletter*, June 2004 .

48. Assistant Commissioner Merritt to Supt. Covey, March 3, 1920, Rosebud, Folder 7, Box 3, RG 75, NA.

49. Maroukis, *Peyote and the Yankton*, 134–42. The South Dakota secretary of state was under pressure not to issue these charters, but he said there was no legal way to reject them.

50. "Native American Church of South Dakota, Inc. BYLAWS," 2007; "Church Canons for Native American Church of South Dakota, 1948." The Church Canons are reprinted in Stewart, *Peyote Religion: A History*, appendix C.

51. Emerson Spider interview with author, Marty, S.D., June 25, 1999; Spider, "Native American Church of Jesus Christ."

52. Kimber and McDonald, "Sacred and Profane Uses of the Cactus *Lophophora Williamsii*," 188. The authors are quoting a 1979 study. This article begins with a misleading sentence: "Peyote is one of the best-known plant sources for a psychedelic experience," 182. The data on Peyote is from Olive, *Peyote and Mescaline*, 43, 69, and Anderson, *Peyote: The Divine Cactus*, 125.

53. Halpern et al., "Psychological and Cognitive Effects," 625–28; Gardner, "Peyote Use by Native Americans."

54. Laura M. Nagel, Deputy Assistant, Office of Diversion Control, DEA, Department of Justice to "Tribal Leader," December 18, 2001. A copy of this letter is in the possession of the author.

55. Hoffman, "Peyote and the Native American Church"; Sandor Iron Rope, President, NAC of South Dakota, personal communication with author, June 26, 2008.

56. "Charges Dropped vs. Couple."

57. "Native American Church Deserves Its Sacrament."

58. These prices come from a variety of published sources and by personal communication.

59. "NACNA Conference Addresses Legal Issues Involving Peyote Medicine."

60. Anderson, "'Peyote Gardens,'" 67; Hampton, "Peyote and the Law," 180.

61. Minutes, Public Safety Commission, Department of Public Safety, Pey 9602.SalesXLS, February 25, 2002; "Crimes in Texas," Department of Public Safety, Drug Seizures, 2005.

62. Morgan, "Man, Plant," 99; Anderson, "'Peyote Gardens,'" 70–72; "Mirando City Journal: A Forbidding Landscape"; "Down in Texas Scrub"; Moreno, "A Rare and Unusual Harvest."

63. "Peyote Totals," Controlled Substances Registration, TDPS, July 2008.

Bibliography

BOOKS

Aberle, David F. *The Peyote Religion among the Navaho.* Chicago, Ill.: Aldine, 1966; 2nd ed., Chicago: University of Chicago Press, 1982. Reprint, Norman: University of Oklahoma Press, 1991. Page references are to first edition.

———. "Peyote Religion among the Navaho." In Ortiz, *Southwest,* vol. 10 of *Handbook of North American Indians,* 558–69.

———, and Omer C. Stewart. *Navajo and Ute Peyotism: A Chronological and Distributional Study.* Boulder: University of Colorado Press, 1957.

———, and Omer C. Stewart, "Navaho and Ute Peyotism: A Chronological and Distributional Study." In *Peyotism in the West,* edited by Omer C. Stewart and David Aberle, 129–265. Boulder: University of Colorado Press, 1984.

Anderson, Edward F. *Peyote: The Divine Cactus.* 1980; 2nd ed., Tucson: University of Arizona Press, 1996. Page references are to second edition.

Bailey, Garrick, and Daniel C. Swan. *Art of the Osage.* Seattle: University of Washington Press, 2004.

Benitz, Fernando. *In the Magic Land of Peyote.* Austin: University of Texas Press, 1975.

Berlo, Janet C. *Plains Indian Drawings 1865–1935.* New York: Harry N. Abrams, 1996.

Blair, Emma Helen. *The Indian Tribes of the Upper Mississippi Valley and Region of the Great Lakes.* Cleveland: Arthur H. Clark, 1912.

Bodine, John J. "Taos Pueblo." In Ortiz, *Southwest,* vol. 9 of *Handbook of North American Indians,* 255–67.

Botsford, James, and Walter Echo-Hawk. "The Legal Tango: The Native American Church v. The United States of America." In H. Smith and Snake, *One Nation under God,* 123–42.

Boyd, Carolyn E. "Pictographic Evidence of Peyotism in the Lower Pecos, Texas Archaic." In *The Archeology of Rock-Art*, edited by Christopher Chippendale and Paul Tacon, 227–46. Cambridge: Cambridge University Press, 1998.

Boyd, Maurice. *Kiowa Voices: Ceremonial Dance, Ritual, and Song*. Kiowa Voices Series, vol. 1. Fort Worth: Texas Christian University Press, 1981.

Brito, Silvester J. *The Way of the Peyote Roadman*. New York: Peter Lang, 1989.

Brown, Joseph Epes. *The Sacred Pipe: Black Elk's Account of the Seven Rites of the Oglala Sioux*. Norman: University of Oklahoma Press, 1953.

Cash, Joseph H., and Herbert T. Hoover, eds. *To Be an Indian: An Oral History*. New York: Holt, Rinehart and Winston, 1971. Reprint, St. Paul: Minnesota Historical Society, 1995. Page references are to reprint.

———, and Gerald Wolff. *The Ponca People*. Phoenix: Indian Tribal Series, 1975.

Chamberlain, Alexander. "Music and Musical Instruments." In Hodge, *Handbook of American Indians North of Mexico*, 1:958–61.

Collier, John. *From Every Zenith: A Memoir*. Denver: Sage Books, 1963.

Cousineau, Phil, ed. *A Seat at the Table: Huston Smith in Conversation with Native Americans on Religious Freedom*. Los Angeles: University of California Press, 2006.

———, and Gary Rhine. "The Peyote Ceremony." In H. Smith and Snake, *One Nation under God*, 75–102.

Crow Dog, Leonard, and Richard Erdoes. *Crow Dog: Four Generations of Sioux Medicine Men*. New York: Harper Collins, 1995.

Daily, David W. *Battle for the B. I. A.: G. E. E. Lindquist and the Missionary Crusade against John Collier*. Tucson: University of Arizona Press, 2004.

Davies, Wade. *Healing Ways: Navajo Healing in the Twentieth Century*. Albuquerque: University of New Mexico Press, 2001.

———. "Western Medicine and Navajo Healing: Conflict and Compromise." In *The Politics of Healing: Histories of Alternative Medicine in Twentieth-Century North America*, edited by Robert D. Johnston, 83–94. New York: Routledge, 2004.

Davis, Leslie B. *Peyotism and the Blackfeet Indians of Montana: An Historical Assessment*. Museum of the Plains Indian Studies, no. 1. Browning, Mont.: U.S. Office of Indian Affairs, 1961.

D'Azevedo, Warren L., ed. *Great Basin*, vol. 11 of *Handbook of North American Indians*. Washington, D.C.: Smithsonian, 1986.

———. *Straight with the Medicine: Narratives of the Washoe Followers of the Tipi Way as Told to Warren L. d'Azevedo*. Reno: University of Nevada Press, 1978. Reprint, Berkeley: Heyday Books, 1985. Page references are to reprint.

———. "Washoe." In d'Azevedo, *Great Basin*, 466–98.

Deloria, Vine, Jr. "Politics and Religion: Politics and Native American Religious Traditions." In *Encyclopedia of Religion*, edited by Lindsay Jones, 11:7299–7304. Detroit: Macmillan, 2005.

———. *Singing for a Spirit: A Portrait of the Dakota Sioux*. Santa Fe: Clear Light, 1999.

DeMallie, Raymond J., ed. *Plains*, vol. 13 of *Handbook of North American Indians*. Washington, D.C.: Smithsonian, 2001.

———, and Clifford M. Lytle. *The Nations Within: The Past and Future of American Indian Sovereignty*, 2nd ed. Austin: University of Texas Press, 1998.

DeMallie, Raymond J., and Douglas R. Parks, eds. *Sioux Indian Religion: Tradition and Innovation*. Norman: University of Oklahoma Press, 1987.

Denman, Leslie Van Ness. *The Peyote Ritual: Visions and Descriptions of Monroe Tsa Toke*. San Francisco: Grabhorn Press, 1957.

Donnelley, Robert G. *Transforming Images: The Art of Silver Horn and His Successors*. Chicago: University of Chicago Press, 2000.

Douglas, Fredrick H., and R. d'Harnoncourt. *Indian Art of the United States*. New York: Museum of Modern Art, 1941.

Duthu, N. Bruce. *American Indians and the Law*. New York: Viking, 2008.

Eisgruber, Christopher L., and Lawrence G. Sager. *Religious Freedom and the Constitution*. Cambridge, Mass.: Harvard University Press, 2007.

Epps, Garrett. *To an Unknown God: Religious Freedom on Trial*. New York: St. Martin's, 2001. Reprint, *Peyote vs. The State: Religious Freedom on Trial*. Norman: University of Oklahoma Press, 2008.

Fikes, Jay C. "A Brief History of the Native American Church." In H. Smith and Snake, *One Nation under God*, 165–74.

Fisher, Louis. *Religious Liberty in America: Political Safeguards*. Lawrence: University of Kansas Press, 2002.

Furst, Peter T., ed. *The Flesh of the Gods: The Ritual Use of Hallucinogens*. New York: Praeger, 1972.

———. "To Find Our Life: Peyote among the Huichol Indians of Mexico." In Furst, *Flesh of the Gods*, 136–84.

Gilmore, Melvin R., *Uses of Plants by the Indians of the Missouri River Region*. Washington, D.C.: Bureau of American Ethnology, 1919.

Ginsberg, Allen. *Howl and Other Poems*. San Francisco: City Lights, 1956.

Greene, Candace. *Silver Horn: Master Illustrator of the Kiowas*. Norman: University of Oklahoma Press, 2001.

Hafen, P. Jane. "Gertrude Simmons Bonnin: For the Indian Cause." In *Sifters: Native American Women's Lives*, edited by Theta Perdue, 127–40. New York: Oxford University Press, 2001.

Hagan, William T. *Quanah Parker, Comanche Chief*. Norman: University of Oklahoma Press, 1993.

Hampton, Carol. "Peyote and the Law." In *Between Two Worlds: The Survival of the Twentieth-Century Indian*, edited by Arrel Gibson, 166–83. Oklahoma City: Oklahoma Historical Society, 1986.

Harjo, Susan Shown. "Vampire Policy Is Bleeding Us Dry—Blood Quantums be Gone!" In *America Is Indian Country*, edited by José Barreiro and Tim Johnson, 42–44. Golden, Colo.: Fulcrum, 2005.

Hertzberg, Hazel W. *The Search for an American Indian Identity: Modern Pan-Indian Movements*. Syracuse: Syracuse University Press, 1971.

Hirschfelder, Arlene, and Paulette Molin. *The Encyclopedia of the Native American Religions: An Introduction*, 2nd ed. New York: Facts on File, 2001.

Hodge, Frederick W., ed. *Handbook of American Indians North of Mexico*. 2 vols. Washington, D.C.: GPO, 1907–10.

Hoover, Herbert T. *The Yankton Sioux*. New York: Chelsea House, 1988.

Howard, James H. *The Ponca Tribe*. Washington, D.C.: Smithsonian Institution, 1965. Reprint, Lincoln: University of Nebraska Press, 1995. Page references are to reprint.

Howell, Carol L., comp. and ed. *Cannibalism Is an Acquired Taste, and Other Notes, from Conversations with Anthropologist Omer C. Stewart*. Niwot: University Press of Colorado, 1998.

Hultkrantz, Ake. *The Attraction of Peyote: An Inquiry into the Basic Conditions for the Diffusion of the Peyote Religion in North America*. Stockholm: Almqvist and Wiksell, 1997.

Irwin, Lee, ed. *Native American Spirituality: A Critical Reader*. Lincoln: University of Nebraska Press, 2000.

Iverson, Peter. *Diné: A History of the Navajos*. Albuquerque: University of New Mexico Press, 2003.

———, ed. *"For Our Navajo People:" Diné Letters, Speeches & Petitions, 1900–1960*. Albuquerque: University of New Mexico Press, 2003.

———. *"We Are Still Here": American Indians in the Twentieth Century*. Wheeling, Ill.: Harlan Davidson, 1998.

Jocks, Christopher Ronwanièhte. "Spirituality for Sale: Sacred Knowledge in the Age." In Irwin, *Native American Spirituality*, 61–77.

Kimber, Clarissa T., and Darrel McDonald. "Sacred and Profane Uses of the Cactus *Lophophora Williamsii* from the South Texas Peyote Gardens." In *Dangerous Harvest: Drug Plants and the Transformation of Indigenous Landscapes*, edited by Michael K. Steinberg, 182–208. New York: Oxford, 2004.

Klüver, Heinrich. *Mescal: The "Divine" Plant and Its Psychological Effects*. London: K. Paul, Trench, Trubner, 1928. Reprint, *Mescal and Mechanisms of Hallucinations*. Chicago: University of Chicago Press, 1966. Page references are to reprint.

Kracht, Benjamin R. "Kiowa Religion in Historical Perspective." In Irwin, *Native American Spirituality*, 236–55.

La Barre, Weston. *The Peyote Cult*. New Haven: Yale University Press, 1938. 5th ed., Norman: University of Oklahoma Press, 1989. Page references are to 5th edition.

Lindquist, G. E. E. *The Red Man in the United States*: New York: George H. Dorian, 1923.

Long, Carolyn. *Religious Freedom and Indian Rights: The Case of Oregon v. Smith*. Lawrence: University Press of Kansas, 2000.

Lurie, Nancy O., ed. *Mountain Wolf Woman, Sister of Crashing Thunder: Autobiography of a Winnebago Indian*. Ann Arbor: University of Michigan Press, 1961.

Maroukis, Thomas C. *Peyote and the Yankton Sioux: The Life and Times of Sam Necklace*. Norman: University of Oklahoma Press, 2004.

Marriott, Alice, and Carol K. Rachlin. *Peyote*. New York: Thomas Y. Crowell, 1971.

McAllester, David P. *Peyote Music*. New York: Viking Fund, 1949. Reprint, New York: Johnson Reprint, 1971. Page references are to first edition.

McDonnell, Janet. *The Dispossession of the American Indian, 1887–1934*. Bloomington: University of Indiana Press, 1991.

Medicine, Beatrice. "Indian Women and the Renaissance of Traditional Religion." In DeMallie and Parks, *Sioux Indian Religion*, 159–71.

Meriam, Lewis. *The Problem of Indian Administration*. Baltimore: Johns Hopkins, 1928.

Meyerhoff, Barbara G. *Peyote Hunt: The Sacred Journey of the Huichol Indians*. Ithaca: Cornell University Press, 1974.

Mooney, James. *Ghost Dance Religion and the Sioux Outbreak*. Washington, D.C.: GPO, 1896. Reprint, Lincoln: University of Nebraska Press, 1991. Page references are to reprint.

———. "Peyote." In Hodge, *Handbook of American Indians North of Mexico*, 2:237.

Morgan, George R. "Recollections of the Peyote Road." In *Psychedelic Reflections*, edited by Lester Grinspoon and James Bakalar, 91–95. New York: Human Sciences, 1983.

Moses, L. G. *The Indian Man: A Biography of James Mooney*. Chicago: University of Illinois Press, 1984.

Mount, Guy. *The Peyote Book: A Study of Native Medicine*. 1987; 3rd ed., Arcata, Calif.: Sweetlight, 1987. Page references are to 3rd edition.

"Native American Religious Freedom Project: Materials, Traditional Use of Peyote" (American Indian Religious Freedom Coalition, 1991). [Loose-leaf collection of Peyote documents distributed by the Coalition.]

Neeley, Bill. *The Last Comanche Chief: The Life and Times of Quanah Parker*. Hoboken, N.J.: John Wiley, 1995. Reprint, Edison, N.J.: Castle Books, 2007. Page references are to reprint.

Newberne, Robert E. L. *Peyote: An Abridged Compilation from the Files of the Bureau of Indian Affairs*. Washington, D.C.: GPO, 1922.

Olive, M. Foster. *Peyote and Mescaline*. New York: Chelsea House, 2007.

Ortiz, Alfonso, ed. *Southwest*, vols. 9 and 10 of *Handbook of North American Indians*. Washington, D.C.: Smithsonian, 1979–83.

Petrullo, Vincenzo. *The Diabolic Root: A Study of Peyotism, the New Indian Religion among the Delawares*. Philadelphia: University of Pennsylvania Press, 1934. Reprint, New York: Octagon Books, 1975. Page references are to reprint.

Prucha, Francis Paul. *The Great Father: The United States Government and the American Indian*. 2 vols. Lincoln: University of Nebraska Press, 1984. Unabridged ed., 1 vol., 1995. Page references are to 1995 edition.

Radin, Paul, ed. *The Autobiography of a Winnebago Indian: Life Ways, Acculturation, and the Peyote Cult*. Berkeley: University of California Publications in Archeology and Ethnology, 1920. Reprint, New York: Dover, 1963. Page references are to reprint.

———, ed. *Crashing Thunder: The Autobiography of a Winnebago Indian*. New York: Appleton, 1926. Reprint, Lincoln: University of Nebraska Press, 1983. Page references are to reprint.

———. *The Winnebago Tribe*. Washington, D.C.: Bureau of American Ethnology, 1923. Reprint, Lincoln: University of Nebraska Press, 1970. Page references are to reprint.

Rouhier, Alexandre. *La Plante qui fait les yeux émerveilles—Le Peyotl*. Paris: Doin, 1927. Reprint, 1975.

Schaefer, Stacy B., and Peter T. Furst, eds. *People of the Peyote: Huichol Indian History, Religion, and Survival*. Albuquerque: University of New Mexico Press, 1996.

Schultes, Richard E., and Albert Hofmann. *The Botany and Chemistry of Hallucinogens*. Springfield, Ill.: Charles C. Thomas, 1973.

———. *Plants of the Gods: Their Sacred, Healing and Hallucinogenic Powers*. Rochester, Vt.: Healing Arts Press, 1992.

Siskin, Edgar E. *Washo Shamans and Peyotists*. Salt Lake City: University of Utah Press, 1983.

Slotkin, J. S. *The Peyote Religion: A Study in Indian-White Relations*. Glencoe, Ill.: Free Press, 1956. Reprint, New York: Octagon Books, 1975. Page references are to first edition.

Smith, Huston, and Reuben Snake, eds. *One Nation under God: The Triumph of the Native American Church*. Santa Fe: Clear Light, 1996.

Snake, Reuben. *Reuben Snake, Your Humble Serpent: Indian Visionary and Activist*. Santa Fe: Clear Light, 1995.

Spider, Emerson, Sr. "The Native American Church of Jesus Christ." In DeMallie and Parks, *Sioux Indian Religion*, 189–210.

Steinmetz, Paul B. *Pipe, Bible, and Peyote among the Oglala Lakota*. Knoxville: University of Tennessee Press, 1990.

Stewart, Omer C. "Friend to the Ute" [1982]. In Stewart and Aberle, *Peyotism in the West*, 269–75.

———. "The History of Peyotism in Nevada" [1982]. In Stewart and Aberle, *Peyotism in the West*, 279–91.

———. "The Native American Church." In *Anthropology on the Great Plains*, edited by W. Raymond Wood and Margot Liberty, 188–96. Lincoln: University of Nebraska Press, 1980.

———. "Peyote and the Law." In Vecsey, *Handbook of American Indian Religious Freedom*, 44–62.

———. "The Peyote Religion." In d'Azevedo, *Great Basin*, 673–81. Washington, 1986.

———. "Peyote Religion." In *Native America in the Twentieth Century: An Encyclopedia*, edited by Mary B. Davis, 446–49. New York: Garland, 1996.

———. *Peyote Religion: A History*. Norman: University of Oklahoma Press, 1987.

———. *Ute Peyotism*. Boulder: University of Colorado Press, 1948.

———. "Ute Peyotism: A Study of a Cultural Complex" [1948]. In Stewart and Aberle, *Peyotism in the West*, 3–46.

———. "Washo-Northern Paiute Peyotism: A Study in Acculturation" [1944]. In Stewart and Aberle, *Peyotism in the West*, 47–127.

———, and David F. Aberle. *Peyotism in the West*. Salt Lake City: University of Utah Press, 1984.

Swan, Daniel C. "The Osage Peyote Religion." In Bailey and Swan, *Art of the Osage*, 109–35.

———. *Peyote Religious Art: Symbols of Faith and Belief.* Jackson: University of Mississippi Press, 1999.

Tsa Toke, Monroe. *The Messenger Bird.* San Francisco: Grabhorn, 1948.

Vecsey, Christopher, ed. *Handbook of American Indian Religious Freedom.* New York: Crossroad, 1991.

———. *Imagine Ourselves Richly: Mythic Narratives of North American Indians.* New York: Crossroad, 1988. Reprint, New York: Harper Collins, 1991. Page references are to reprint.

Vennum, Thomas, Jr. "Music." In d'Azevedo, *Great Basin*, 682–704.

Vestal, Paul, and Richard E. Schultes. *The Economic Botany of the Kiowa Indians as It Relates to the History of the Tribe.* Cambridge, Mass.: Harvard Botanical Museum, 1939.

Vogel, Virgil J. *American Indian Medicine.* Norman: University of Oklahoma Press, 1970.

Wagner, Roland M. "Peyotism, Traditional Religion, and Modern Medicine: Changing Healing Traditions in the Border Area." In *Modern Medicine and Medical Anthropology in the United States-Mexico Border Population*, edited by Boris Velimirovic, 139–146. Washington, D.C.: Pan-American Health Organization, 1978.

Walker, Deward E., Jr., ed. *Plateau*, vol. 12 of *Handbook of North American Indians*, Washington, D.C.: Smithsonian, 1998.

———, and Helen H. Schuster. "Religious Movements." In Walker, *Plateau*, 499–514.

White, Phillip M. *Peyotism and the Native American Church: An Annotated Bibliography.* Westport, Conn.: Greenwood, 2000.

Whitewolf, Jim. *The Life of a Kiowa-Apache Indian*, edited by Charles S. Brant. New York: Dover, 1969.

Work, Hubert. *Indian Policies: Comments on the Resolutions of the Advisory Council on Indian Affairs.* Washington, D.C.: GPO, 1924.

Wyman, Leland C. "Navajo Ceremonial System." In Ortiz, *Southwest*, vol. 10 of *Handbook of North American Indians*, 536–57.

Young, Gloria. "Intertribal Religious Movements." In DeMaillie, *Plains*, 996–1010.

Zitkala-Ša [Gertrude Bonnin]. *American Indian Stories.* Washington, D.C.: Hayworth, 1921. Reprint Lincoln: University of Nebraska Press, 1985.

JOURNALS AND MAGAZINES

Anderson, Edward F. "The 'Peyote Gardens' of Southern Texas: A Conservation Crisis?" *Cactus and Succulent Journal* 67 (1995): 67–73.

Arth, Malcolm J. "A Functional View of Peyotism in Omaha Culture." *Plains Anthropologist* 7 (1956): 25–29.

Bannon, John Thomas, Jr. "The Legality of the Religious Use of Peyote by the Native American Church: A Commentary on the Free Exercise, Equal Protection, and Establishment Issues Raised by the Peyote Way Church of God Case." *American Indian Law Review* 22, no. 2 (1998): 475–505.

Barber, Bernard. "A Socio-Cultural Interpretation of the Peyote Cult." *American Anthropologist* [*AA*] 43 (1944): 376–75.

Barber, Carroll. "Peyote and the Definition of Narcotic." *AA* 61 (1959): 641–46.

Bass, Althea. "James Mooney in Oklahoma." *Chronicles of Oklahoma* 22, no. 3 (1954): 246–62.

Begay, David, and Nancy C. Maryboy. "The Whole Universe Is My Cathedral: A Contemporary Navajo Spiritual Synthesis." *Medical Anthropology Quarterly* 14, no. 4 (2000): 498–520.

Bergman, Robert L. "Navajo Peyote Use: Its Apparent Safety." *American Journal of Psychiatry* 128, no. 6 (1971): 695–99.

Bergquist, Laura. "Peyote: The Strange Church of Cactus Eaters." *Look*, December 10, 1957, 36–41.

Brant, Charles S. "Joe Blackbear's Story of the Origin of the Peyote Religion." *Plains Anthropologist* 8 (1963): 180–81.

———. "Peyotism among the Kiowa-Apache and Neighboring Tribes." *Southwest Journal of Anthropology* 6, no. 2 (1950): 212–22.

Brosius, S. M. "The Ravages of Peyote." *Annual Report of the Indian Rights Association* 34 (1916): 37–41.

"Button, Button . . . " *Time*, June 18, 1951, 82–83.

Campbell, Thomas. "Origin of the Mescal Bean Cult." *AA* 60 (1958): 156–60.

"The Case against Peyote." *The Outlook*, May 24, 1916, 162–63.

Catches, Vincent. "Native American Church: The Half-Moon Way." *Wicazo Sa Review* 7, no. 1 (1991): 17–24.

"Charges Dropped vs. Couple in Peyote Case." *New York Times*, February 22, 2006.

Collier, John. "The Peyote Cult." *Science* 115 (1952): 503–504.

Collins, John J. "A Descriptive Introduction to the Taos Peyote Ceremony." *Ethnology* 7, no. 4 (1968): 427–49.

Cook-Lynn, Elizabeth. "A Monograph of a Peyote Singer: Asa Primeaux, Sr." *Wicazo Sa Review* 7, no. 1 (1991): 1–15.

———. "Profile: Asa Primeaux." *Wicazo Sa Review* 1, no. 1 (1985): 2–4.

Deloria, Vine. "Secularism, Civil Religion, and the Religious Freedom of American Indians." *American Indian Culture and Research Journal* 16, no. 2 (1992): 9–20.

Densmore, Frances. "Native Songs of Two Hybrid Ceremonies among the American Indians." *AA* 43, no. 1 (1941): 77–82.

Douglas, Frederic H., and Alice Marriott. "Metal Jewelry of the Peyote Cult." *Material Culture Notes* [Denver Art Museum] 17 (1942): 98–109.

"Down in Texas Scrub, 'Peyoteros' Stalk Their Elusive Prey." *Wall Street Journal*, May 12, 2004.

Echo-Hawk, Walter R. "Native American Religious Liberty: Five Hundred Years after Columbus." *American Indian Culture and Research Journal* 17, no. 3 (1993): 33–52.

Ellis, Havelock. "Mescal: A Study of a Divine Plant." *Popular Science Monthly* 41 (1902): 52–71.

Gardner, Amanda. "Peyote Use by Native Americans Doesn't Damage Brain." *New York Times*, November 4, 2005.

Garrity, John F. "Jesus, Peyote, and the Holy People: Alcohol Abuse and the Ethos of Power in Navajo Healing." *Medical Anthropology Quarterly* 14, no. 4 (2000): 521–42.

Gilmore, Melvin R. "The Mescal Society among the Omaha Indians," *Nebraska State Historical Society* 19 (1919): 163–67.

Gray, Autumn. "Effects of the American Indian Religious Freedom Act Amendments on Criminal Law: Will Peyotism Eat Away at the Controlled Substance Act?" *American Journal of Criminal Law* 22, no. 3 (1995): 769–95.

Halpern, John H., et al. "Psychological and Cognitive Effects of Long-Term Peyote Use among Native Americans." *Biological Psychiatry* 58 (2005): 624–31.

Harjo, Susan Shown. "American Indian Religious Freedom Act after Twenty-Five Years." *Wicazo Sa Review* 19, no. 2 (2004): 129–36

Hinojosa, Servando Z. "Human-Peyote Interaction in South Texas." *Culture & Agriculture* 22, no. 1 (2000): 29–36.

Hoover, Herbert T. "Interview: Noah White." *South Dakota Review* 8, no. 3 (1970): 171–77.

Howard, James H. "Half Moon Way: The Peyote Ritual of Chief White Bear." *Museum News: South Dakota Museum* 25, nos. 1–2 (1967): 1–39.

———. "The Mescal Bean Cult of the Central and Southern Plains: An Ancestor of the Peyote Cult?" *AA* 59 (1957): 75–85.

———. "Mescalism and Peyotism Once Again." *Plains Anthropologist* 5 (1960): 84–85.

———. "The Pan-Indian Culture of Oklahoma." *Scientific Monthly* 18, no. 5 (1955): 215–20.

———. "Pan-Indianism in Native American Music and Dance." *Ethnomusicology* 27, no. 1 (1983): 71–82.

Hurt, Wesley R. "Factors in the Persistence of Peyote in the Northern Plains." *Plains Anthropologist* 5, no. 9 (1960): 16–27.

Johnson, David L., and Raymond Wilson. "Gertrude Simmons Bonnin, 1876–1938: Americanize the First American." *American Indian Quarterly* 12 (1988): 28–40.

Jopling, Carol F. "Art and Ethnicity: Peyote Painting, a Case Study." *Ethnos: Journal of Anthropology* 49, nos. 1–2 (1984): 98–118.

Kelsey, F. E. "The Pharmacology of Peyote." *South Dakota Journal of Medicine and Pharmacy* 12, no. 6 (1959): 231–33.

Klüver, Heinrich. "Mescal Visions and Eidetic Visions." *American Journal of Psychology* 37 (1926): 502–15.

Kroeber, Alfred. "The Arapaho: Peyote Worship." *Bulletin of the American Museum of Natural History* 18, no. 4 (1902): 398–410.

La Barre, Weston. "Mescalism and Peyotism." *AA* 59 (1957): 708–11.

———. "Statement on Peyote." *Science* 114, November 30, 1951, 582–83.

———. "Twenty Years of Peyote Studies." *Current Anthropology* 1, no. 1 (1960): 45–60.

Lawson, Paul E., and C. Patrick Morris. "The Native American Church and the New Court: The Smith Case and Indian Religious Freedoms." *American Indian Culture and Research Journal* 15, no. 1 (1991): 79–91.

———, and Jennifer Scholes. "Jurisprudence, Peyote, and the Native American Church." *American Indian Culture and Research Journal* 10, no. 1 (1986): 13–27.

Leonard, Irving A. "A Decree against Peyote, Mexican Inquisition, 1620." *AA* 44 (1942): 324–26.

Lessard, Dennis. "Instruments of Prayer: The Peyote Art of the Sioux." *American Indian Art Magazine* 9, no. 2 (1984): 24–27.

Lewis, David Rich. "Reservation Leadership and the Progressive-Traditional Dichotomy: William Wash and the Northern Utes, 1865–1928."*Ethnohistory* 38, no. 2 (1991): 124–48.

Lieber, Michael D. "Opposition to Peyotism among the Western Shoshone: The Message of Traditional Belief." *Man* 7, no. 3 (1972): 387–96.

Lohrmann, Charles J., and Jeri Ah Be Hill. "'As Long As I Can Thread a Needle,' Southern Plains Beadworkers and Their Art." *Native Peoples Magazine* 6, no. 4 (1993): 10–18.

Long, Douglas. "Religious Freedom and Native Sovereignty: Protecting Native Religion through Tribal, Federal, and State Law." *Wicazo Sa Review* 19, no. 2 (2004): 188–94.

Malouf, Carling. "Gosiute Peyotism." *AA* 44, no. 1 (1942): 93–103.

McAllester, David P. "Menomini Peyote Music." *Transactions of the American Philosophical Society* 42, no. 4 (1952): 681–700.

McNickle, D'Arcy. "Peyote and the Indian." *Scientific Monthly* 57 (1943): 220–29.

Merriam, Alan, and Warren L. d'Azevedo. "Washo Peyote Songs." *AA* 59, no. 4 (1957): 615–41.

"Mirando City Journal: A Forbidding Landscape That's Eden for Peyote." *New York Times*, May 7, 2007.

Mooney, James. "A Kiowa Mescal Rattle." *AA* 5 (1892): 64–65.

———. "The Kiowa Peyote Rite," *Der Urquell* 1 (1897): 329–33.

———. "Mescal Plant and Ceremony." *Therapeutic Gazette*, 3rd ser., 12, no. 1 (1896): 7–11.

Moore, Steven C. "Reflections on the Elusive Promise of Religious Freedom for the Native American Church." *Wicazo Sa Review* 7, no. 1 (1991): 42–50.

Moreno, Sylvia. "A Rare and Unusual Harvest: Man Collects Peyote Buttons from Cactus for American Indian Rites." *Washington Post,* September 18, 2005.

Morgan, George R. "The Biogeography of Peyote in South Texas." *Harvard University Botanical Museum Leaflets* 29, no. 2 (1983): 73–86.

———. "Hispano-Indian Trade of an Indian Ceremonial Plant, Peyote (*Lophophora Williamsii*), on the Mustang Plains of Texas." *Journal of Ethnopharmacology* 9 (1983): 319–21.

———, and Omer C. Stewart. "Peyote Trade in South Texas." *Southwestern Historical Quarterly* 87, no. 3 (1984): 269–96.

"NACNA Conference Addresses Legal Issues Involving Peyote Medicine." *Sho-Ban News*, June 18, 2007.

"Native American Church Deserves Its Sacrament." *Indian Country Today*, September 22, 2005.

Newton, Elizabeth L., and Victoria Bydone. "Identity and Healing in Three Navajo Religious Traditions: *Sà ah Naaghái Bik' eh Hózhó.*" *Medical Anthropology Quarterly* 14, no. 4 (2000): 476–97.

Opler, Marvin K. "The Character and History of the Southern Ute Peyote Rite." *AA* 42, no. 3 (1940): 463–78.

———. "Fact and Fancy in Ute Peyotism." *AA* 44 (1942): 151–59.

Opler, Morris E. "A Description of a Tonkawa Peyote Meeting Held in 1902." *AA* 41, no. 3 (1939): 433–39.

———. "The Influence of Aboriginal Pattern and White Contact on a Recently Introduced Ceremony, the Mescalero Peyote Rite." *Journal of American Folklore* 49 (1936): 143–66.

———. "The Use of Peyote by the Carrizo and Lipan Apache Tribes." *AA* 40, no. 2 (1938): 271–85.

Parker, Christopher. "A Constitutional Examination of the Federal Exemptions for Native American Religious Peyote Use." *B.Y.U. Journal of Public Law* 16 (2001): 89–112.

Pavlik, Steve. "The U. S. Supreme Court Decision on Peyote in Employment Division v. Smith: A Case Study in the Suppression of Native American Religious Freedom," *Wicazo Sa Review* 8, no. 2 (1992): 30–39.

Peregoy, Robert, Walter R. Echo-Hawk, and James Botsford. "Congress Overturns Supreme Court's Peyote Ruling." *Native American Rights Fund Legal Review* 20, no. 1 (1995): 1, 6–25.

Petrullo, Vincenzo. "Peyotism as an Emergent Indian Culture." *Indians at Work* 8, no. 8 (1940): 51–60.

Philp, Kenneth R. "John Collier and the Crusade to Protect Indian Religious Freedom, 1920–1926." *Journal of Ethnic Studies* 1, no. 1 (1973): 22–38.

Quintero, Gilbert A. "Gender, Discord, and Illness: Navajo Philosophy and Healing in the Native American Church." *Journal of Anthropological Research* 51, no. 1 (1995): 69–89.

Rachlin, Carol K. "The Native American Church in Oklahoma." *Chronicles of Oklahoma* 42, no. 3 (1964): 262–72.

Radin, Paul. "Personal Reminiscences of a Winnebago Indian [Crashing Thunder]." *Journal of American Folklore* 26 (1913): 293–318.

———. "A Sketch of the Peyote Cult of the Winnebago: A Study in Borrowing." *Journal of Religious Psychology* 7, no. 1 (1914): 1–22.

Rhodes, Willard. "Study of Musical Diffusion Based on the Wandering of the Opening Peyote Song." *Journal of the International Folk Music Council* 10 (1958): 42–49.

Schultes, Richard Evans. "The Aboriginal Therapeutic Uses of *Lophophora Williamsii.*" *Cactus and Succulent Society of America Journal* 12 (1940): 177–81.

———. "The Appeal of Peyote (*Lophophora Williamsii*) as a Medicine." *AA* 40, no. 4 (1938): 698–715.

———. "Peyote and Plants Confused with It." *Botanical Museum Leaflets, Harvard University* 5, no. 5 (1937): 61–89.

———. "Peyote and the American Indian." *Nature Magazine* 30, no. 3 (1937): 155–57.

———. "Peyote Cult." *Literary Digest*, November 13, 1937, 24–26.

Seymour, Gertrude. "Peyote Worship: An Indian Cult and a Powerful Drug." *Survey* 34, May 13, 1916, 181–84.

Shonle, Ruth. "Peyote, the Giver of Visions." *AA* 27 (1925): 53–75.

Slotkin, J. S. "Early Eighteenth Century Documents on Peyotism North of the Rio Grande." *AA* 53, no. 1 (1951): 420–27.

———. "Menomini Peyotism: A Study of Individual Variation in a Primary Group with a Homogeneous Culture." *American Philosophical Society* 42, no. 4 (1952): 565–700.

———. "The Peyote Way." *Tomorrow: Quarterly Review of Psychical Research* 4, no. 3 (1956): 64–70.

———. "Peyotism, 1521–1891." *AA* 57 (1955): 202–30.

Smith, Maurice G. "A Negro Peyote Cult." *Journal of the Washington Academy of Sciences* 24, no. 10 (1934): 448–53.

Speck, Frank G. "Notes on the Life of John Wilson, the Revealer of Peyote, as Recalled by His Nephew, G. Anderson." *General Magazine Historical Chronicle* 35 (1933): 539–56.

Stewart, Omer C. "American Indian Religion: Past, Present, Future." *Wassaja: The Indian Historian* 13, no. 1 (1980): 15–18.

———. "Anthropological Theory and History of Peyotism." *Ethnohistory* 26, no. 3 (1979): 277–81.

———. "Gertrude Simmons Bonnin." *Bulletin of the Institute of American Indian Studies: University of South Dakota* 87 (May 1981).

———. "Origins of the Peyote Religion in the United States." *Plains Anthropologist* 19 (1974): 211–23.

———. "Peyote and Colorado's Inquisition Law." *Colorado Quarterly* 5, no. 1 (1956): 77–90.

———. "Peyote and the Arizona Court Decision." *AA* 63, no. 6 (1961): 1134–37.

———. "The Peyote Religion and the Ghost Dance." *Indian Historian* 3, no. 4 (1972): 27–30.

———. "Peyotism in Idaho," *Northwest Anthropological Research Notes* 22, no. 1 (1988): 1–11.

———. "The Southern Ute Peyote Cult." *AA* 43 (1941): 303–308.

———, and Bernard Gorton. "Peyote and the Arizona Court Decision." *AA* 63, no. 6 (1961): 1334–37.

Swan, Daniel C. "Contemporary Navajo Peyote Arts." *American Indian Art Magazine* 34, no. 1 (2008): 44–55, 94.

———. "Early Osage Peyotism." *Plains Anthropologist* 43, no. 163 (1998): 51–71.

———. "Peyote Arts in the Collections of the Gilcrease Museum." *American Indian Art Magazine* 24, no. 2 (1999): 37–45.

Talbot, Steve. "Spiritual Genocide: The Denial of American Indian Religious Freedom, from Conquest to 1934." *Wicazo Sa Review* 21, no. 2 (2006): 7–39.

Tallbear, Kimberly. "DNA, Blood, and Racializing the Tribe." *Wicazo Sa Review* 18, no. 1 (2003): 81–107.

Tepker, Harry F., Jr. "Hallucinations of Neutrality in the Oregon Peyote Case." *American Indian Law Review* 16, no. 1 (1991): 1–56.

Thurman, Melburn D. "Supplementary Material on the Life of John Wilson, 'The Revealer of Peyote.'" *Ethnohistory* 20, no. 3 (1973): 279–87.

Troike, Rudolph. "Origins of Plains Mescalism." *AA* 64, no. 5 (1962): 946–63.

Wagner, Roland M. "Pattern and Process in Ritual Syncretism: The Case of Peyotism among the Navajo." *Journal of Anthropological Research* 31, no. 2 (1975): 162–81.

———. "Some Pragmatic Aspects of Navajo Peyotism." *Plains Anthropologist* 20, no. 69 (1975): 197–206.

Welsh, Herbert. "Peyote: An Insidious Evil." *Indian Rights Association,* 114 (1915): 1–6.

Wiedman, Dennis. "Big and Little Moon Peyotism as Health Care Delivery Systems." *Medical Anthropology* 12, no. 4 (1990): 371–87.

———. "Staff, Fan, Rattle & Drum: Spiritual and Artistic Expressions of Oklahoma Peyotists." *American Indian Art Magazine* 10, no. 3 (1985): 38–45.

———, and Candace Greene. "Early Kiowa Peyote Ritual and Symbolism: The 1890 Drawing Books of Silverhorn (*Haungooah*)." *American Indian Art Magazine* 10, no. 3 (1985): 38–45.

———. "Early Kiowa Peyote Ritual and Symbolism: The 1891 Drawing Books of Silverhorn (*Haungooah*)." *American Indian Art Magazine* 13, no. 4 (1988): 32–41.

Willard, William. "The First Amendment, Anglo-Conformity and American Indian Religious Freedom." *Wicazo Sa Review* 7, no. 1 (1991): 25–41.

PEYOTE MUSIC: SELECTED DISCOGRAPHY

(Recordings marked with * were nominated for "Best Native American Church Recording" by the Native American Music Awards, 2007; recordings marked with ** were winners of the 2007 or 2008 award.)

Abdo, Joe Sr., et al. *Yankton Sioux Peyote Songs.* Vols. 1–4, IH 4371C-IH 4374C, Indian House, 1976–1978.

*Becenti, Denise. *Morning Blessing.* CRM 11605, Cool Runnings Music, 2006.

Comanche Peyote Songs. Vol. 1–2, IH 2401-02, Indian House, 1969.

Kiowa. Recorded by Willard Rhodes. AAFS L35, Library of Congress, 1954.

*Meewasin Oma. *In Loving Memory.* 30095, Turtle Island Music, 2006.

Music of the Sioux and Navajo. Recorded by Willard Rhodes. P 401, Folkways Records, 1953.

Navajo. Recorded by Willard Rhodes. AFS L41, Library of Congress, 1954.

*Patterson, Shane. *Native American Church Songs of Prayer and Praise.* SSCD 4522, Sunshine Records, 2006.

Peyote Songs: Music of the Native American Church. ARP 6054, Canyon Records, 1967.

Ponca Peyote Songs. Vol. 1–3, IH 2005-07, Indian House, 1971.

Primeaux, Sr., Asa, and Sons. *Yankton Sioux Peyote Harmonizing Songs.* Vol. 1–6, 1171A-1171F, Indian Records, [1970s].

Primeaux, Gerald, Sr. *Into the Future.* CR-6441, Canyon Records, 2008.

———. *Songs of Prayer for Life.* CRM050402, Cool Runnings Music, 2002.

**———. *Voice of a Dakota: Harmonized Healing Songs.* CR-6408, Canyon Records, 2006.

———. *Yankton Sioux Peyote Songs.* CRM 081100, Cool Runnings Music, 2000.

Primeaux, Verdell, and Terry Hanks. *Stories Told: Harmonized Peyote Songs.* CR 6432, Canyon Records, 2008.

———, and Johnny Mike. *Bless the People: Harmonized Peyote Songs.* CRM, Canyon Records, 2001.

———. *Primeaux & Mike: Peyote Songs in Sioux & Navajo.* CR-16301, Canyon Records, 1993.

Red Bear, Rachel (Siçangu Lakota). *Peyote Songs: Flying High Woman.* CRM010400, Cool Runnings Music, 2000.

Shields, Joe Sr., et al. *Yankton Sioux Peyote Songs.* Vol. 5–8, IH 4375C–IH 4378C, Indian House, 1980–81.

Sioux. Recorded by Willard Rhodes. AFS L40, Library of Congress, 1954.

*Stoner, Brian. *With Love and Faith We Pray.* Drumgroups, 2006.

Toppah, Cheevers, and Kevin Zazzie. *First Light: Harmonized Peyote Songs in Diné and Kiowa.* CR 6436, Canyon Records, 2008.

**Turtle, Janette. *New Beginning.* CRM 122006, Cool Runnings Music, 2008.

Washo-Peyote Songs. Recorded by Warren L. d'Azevedo. FE 4384, Folkways, 1972.

*White Hawk and Crowe. *Wikiwam Ahsin.* Drumgroups, 2006.

Yazzie, William. *Navajo Peyote Songs.* CRM091003, Cool Running Music, 2002.

FILMS

To Find Our Life: The Peyote Hunt of the Huichols of Mexico. Los Angeles: UCLA, 1969.

The Peyote Road: Ancient Religion in Contemporary Crisis. Exec. prod. Reuben A. Snake. San Francisco: Kifaru Productions, 1993.

The Traditional Use of Peyote by Members of the Native American Church of North America. San Francisco: Kifaru, 1993.

THESES, DISSERTATIONS

Brito, Silvester John. "The Development and Change of the Peyote Ceremony through Time and Space." PhD diss., Indiana University, Bloomington, 1975.

Hampton, Carol McDonald. "American Indian Religion under Assault: Opposition to the Peyote Faith." PhD diss., University of Oklahoma, 1984.

McAllester, David P. "Peyote Music." PhD diss., Columbia University, 1950.

Morgan, George R. "Man, Plant, and Religion: Peyote Trade on the Mustang Plains of Texas." PhD diss., University of Colorado, 1976.

Schultes, Richard Evans. "Peyote in American Indian Life: A Practical Consideration of the Plant and the Part It Is Playing in the Daily Life of the American Indian Today." Master's thesis, Harvard University, 1937.

Swan, Daniel C. "West Moon East Moon: An Ethnohistory of the Peyote Religion among the Osage Indians, 1890–1930." PhD diss., University of Oklahoma, 1990.

Wagner, Roland M. "Western Navajo Peyotism: A Case Analysis." PhD diss., University of Oregon, 1974.

Welsh, Deborah S. "Zitkala-Ša: An American Indian Leader, 1876–1938." PhD diss., University of Wyoming, 1985.

Index

Aberle, David, 65, 140, 149
ACLU. *See* American Civil Liberties Union
Advisory Council on Indian Affairs, 112, 113
Agave angustifolia, 6, 7
Agency (defined), 109
Agriculture, U.S. Department of, 49, 104, 128
AIRFA. *See* American Indian Religious Freedom Act
Alcoholism: Peyote as cure for, 10, 33, 45, 48, 55, 57, 64–65, 67, 68, 137, 143, 222, 231; prohibition of alcohol, on reservations, 39, 113
Allotment system, 50, 115
American Anthropological Association, 207
American Civil Liberties Union (ACLU), 186–89, 203
American Ethnology, Bureau of, 51, 55
American Horse, Joe, 88
American Indian Association, 122
American Indian Defense Association, 114, 122
American Indian Federation, 141
American Indian Magazine, 116–17, 121
American Indian Movement, 196
American Indian Religious Freedom Act (AIRFA) (1978), 12, 196–97, 202–204
American Indian Religious Freedom Act Amendments (1994), 208, 212, 215, 222, 228
American Indian Religious Freedom Coalition, 12
American Indian Religious Freedom Project, 206–207
American Indians: art exhibitions, 168–71; Christian Indians, 120, 123; cultural renaissance of 1960s, 170, 191; custom marriage and divorce, 107; eagle, significance

of, 83; fires and fireplaces in religion of, 85; music, 173–74, 177; opposition to Peyote among, 46, 135; sacred circle, 72–74; sacred numbers, 74–77; sacred plants, 77; sickness and disease among, 64; spiritual revival, 1960s, 171; traditional culture and ceremonies, federal opposition to, 4, 113; traditional religions of, 69–71; traditional spiritualities, Peyote faith and, 83; traditional spiritual leaders, 71–72; vision experience in religions of, 80
American Indians, Society of, 49, 51–55, 116, 121
American Indian Sound Chiefs, 176
American Indian Stories (Gertrude Bonnin), 116
American Indian Studies, Institute of, 7
American Jewish Congress, 203
American Journal of Psychology, The, 111
Anadarko, Oklahoma, 31
Anderson, George, 79, 80–81, 133
Anderson, John, 133
Anderson, Leon B., 189
Anti-Peyote crusade, 9–10, 33, 45, 48–58, 103, 107–108; by missionaries, 119–20; by nongovernmental groups, 118–21; by nonsectarian groups, 121–22; by state governments, 115–18
Anti-Peyote literature, 49, 50, 52, 104, 107–11, 116, 119, 120, 149
Anti-Saloon League of America, 40, 51, 52
Apache John, 29
Apaches: and Peyote music, 179; sacred numbers, 76
Apiatan, 29

Arapahos, 31, 36, 40, 110, 136, 158; music, 176
Architah, 29
Arikaras, 134
Arizona, 116, 131, 140, 186, 187, 195, 214. *See also* Public Safety, Arizona Department of
Arkinson, Earl, 236, 237
Armed Forces Chaplain's Board, 209
Asah, Stephen, 167
Assimilation policies, U.S., 4, 9, 46, 49, 50, 107, 113, 114, 183; and cultural pluralism, 126; missionaries and, 119–20
Assiniboines, 131
Atcitty, James, 190
Atlantic Monthly, 116
Attakai, Mary, 187
Auchiah, James, 167
Aunguoe, James, 177
Ayahoasca, 235
Azee', 66
Azee' Bee Nahagha of Diné Nation, 209, 215, 237–38; and criminal code, 216; logo, 215; and National Council of Native American Churches, 210; and young people, 237–38. *See also* Native American Church of Navajoland
Aztecs, 15, 16

Bannocks, 11, 131, 211
Beadwork, 153, 154, 161, *162,* 163, 172
Bearskin, John, 42
Beat generation, Peyote use among, 191–92
Becenti, Denise, 177
Bergman, Robert L., 193
Best Native American Church Music awards, 11, 215
Best Native American Church Recording awards, 177–78
Best Native American Music Album, 177
Best Native American Music awards, 11
Best Traditional Music award, 177
BIA. *See* Bureau of Indian Affairs
Bible, use of, in Peyotism, 38–39, 42, 46, 79, 89, 94, 96, 100, 122, 123, 156, 220
Big Bow, Harding, 171, 177, 231
Big Bow, Nelson, 177, 231
Big Looking Glass, 29
Big Moon Way (Wilson Moon Way; Moonhead Way), 30, 31, 38, 79, 88; altar, 93–94, *95;* tobacco in, 98. *See also* Cross Fire Way
Big Tree, 27
Bird in Flight (Tsatoke), 170
Bird of Dawn, The (Tsatoke), 167
Birds, symbolism of, 84
Black, Galen, 202–203, 205
Black Bear, Harry, 42, 43
Black Bear, William, 34, 42, 43, 219
Black Elk, 85, 86
Blackfeet, 131
Black Owl, Archie, 169
Bless the People: Harmonized Peyote Songs (Mike and Primeaux), 11, 177

Blood-quantum requirement: for Native American Church membership, 219; for Peyote use, 193, 194, 200–202; for purchasing Peyote in Texas, 227; for tribal citizenship, 210–12
Blowsnake, Sam (Crashing Thunder), 34, 65
Blue Bird, Jim, 34, 42, 43, 65, 127, 133, 185
Boarding schools. *See* Indian boarding schools
Boley, Ray, 177
Bolton, Frances, 145
Bonnicastle, Arthur, 55
Bonnin, Gertrude Simmons (Zitkala-Ša; Red Bird), 51–54, 56, 57, 115–17, 121, 122
Bonnin, Raymond, 52, 116, 121
Boyd, Carolyn, 15
Boyll, Robert, 223
Boynton, Paul, 34, 55
Brace, Ned, 146
Brant, Charles S., 64
Brookings Institution (Institute for Government Research), 114
Brosius, Samuel M., 53, 116
Bryan, William Jennings, 112
Bull Bear, Jack, 31
Bull Bear, Jock (Arapaho Bull), 40
Bulltail, Alice, 63
Bureau of Indian Affairs (BIA), 4, 9, 10, 32, 33, 37, 148; boarding schools, 34; campaign to abolish Peyote use, 39–40, 42, 48–51, 58, 103–10, 112–14; Chavez bill opposed by, 128; and Diné livestock reduction program, 139–40; legality of Peyote, 45; missionary groups and, 118, 119, 120; questionnaire, 105–106, 108, 109; revised assimilation policies of, 120; and state anti-Peyote movement, 115
Burke, Charles H., 106, 107, 113, 118, 119
Burroughs, William, 191
"Button, Button . . ." (*Time* magazine article), 149

Caddos, 17, 22, 23, 27, 29, 30, 36, 56, 60
California, 10, 11, 117, 131, 136, 184, 186, 189
Canada, 130, 131, 134, 151, 210, 223, 226; NAC music, 177; Peyote imported into, 185
Canyon Records, 177
Cárdenas, Amanda and Carlos, 198–99
Cardenas, Juan de, 16
Carlisle Indian Boarding School, Pennsylvania, 34, 37, 43, 52, 54, 132
Carrizos, 17, 22, 23, 24, 29
Carson, Kit, 139
Carving, 153
Catches, Vincent, 61, 86
Catholic Church, 21, 91, 92, 127, 199; anti-Peyote campaign by, 15, 16
Catholic Indian Herald, The, 120
Catholic Indian Missions, Bureau of, 51, 53
Catholic Sioux Herald, The, 120
Cavalry, U.S.: Seventh, 35
Cedar, 77–79, 98, 99, 101, 155

Peyotism (*continued*)
curing in, 68, 81, 100, 143, 145, 159, 174; history of, 7–9; livestock reduction program and growth of, 140; Meriam Report's assessment of, 114; moral code and ethical system, 87–89; and multiple religious affiliations, 90–92, 136, 145, 232; non-Peyotists' support of, 188; in Northwest and Great Basin, 130–38; number of, 109, 110; opposition and the growth of, 142–43; origin of, 86–87; as pan-Indian movement, 231, 232; Quanah Parker's importance to, 24–25, 27; pilgrimages to Peyote Gardens, 197–98; poverty and, 142; proselytizers, 43; protection of, in twenty-first century, 220–29; railroads and spread of, 33–34; and reservation system, 24; sacred circle in, 72–74; sacred foods in, 69–70, 101–102; sacred numbers in, 74–77; sacred plants in, 77–80; sense of sacredness in, 70; spiritual beliefs and practices, 9, 11, 15–18; symbolism in, 41, 153, 154, 163; traditional beliefs and, 67, 69, 71, 83; and tribal identity, 133, 231; uniformity of, 151; vision experience in, 80–83. *See also* Native American Church
Philanthropic organizations, opposition to Peyote by, 118–21
Piawo, Wilbur, 55
Piercing, sacrifice of, 78
Pine Ridge Reservation, South Dakota, 42, 43, 53, 81, 124, 131, 217, 218, 219; number of Peyotists on, 109–10, 185
Pinero, 24
Pipe Carrier, 91
Plains Apaches: and Peyote music, 179
Plains Indians, 82; pictorial tradition of, 165; sacred foods of, 70
Ponca Agency, 110
Ponca Reservation, Oklahoma, 48, 131
Poncas, 27, 29, 36, 55, 76, 81, 91, 110
Pope, Harrison G., Jr., 221
Porcupine, South Dakota, 219
Postal Service, U.S., 49, 110, 128, 145, 185
Potawatomi, 110
Prairie sage. *See* Sage
Pratt, Richard, 34, 50, 51, 57
Prayer: as function of Peyote artworks, 173; music as, 174, 182; in Peyote Gardens, 198
Primeaux, Adrian, *175*
Primeaux, Asa, 91, 178
Primeaux, Gerald, Sr., 86, 174, *175*, 177, 178, 180
Primeaux, Harry, 174, 178
Primeaux, Verdell, 11, 177
Prisoners, religious rights of, 196, 236
Prohibition movement, 39, 105, 121
Prohibition of the Use of Peyote (U.S. Congress), 56
Propagation of the Gospel, Society for the, 119
Protestant churches, 119
Psychotropic plants, 15–16
Public Safety, Arizona Department of, 195

Public Safety, Texas Department of, 201, 211, 227, 234, 238
Pueblo Indians, 127

Quanah Parker. *See* Parker, Quanah
Quanah Parker Way (Comanche Way). *See* Half Moon Way
Quapaws, 30, 36, 95
Quarterly Bulletin of the Native American Church, 145, 185
Quitting (Closing) Song, 101, 180

Radin, Paul, 36–37, 40, 41, 60, 69
Railroad system, 33–34
Rattles, 45, 155
"Ravages of Peyote" (Brosius), 116
Rave, John, 36–39, 41, 42, 60, 65, 79, 88
Red Bear, Charles, 42
Red Bird. *See* Bonnin, Gertrude Simmons
Redbird, Robert, 171, 172
Red Man in the United States, The (Lindquist), 119
Red Nest, Willie, 42
Rehnquist, William, 207
Relative depravation theory, 140
Religion (term), Native American use of, 243n1
Religious freedom, 3, 11–12, 33, 46, 57, 58, 146, 184, 230; American Indian Religious Freedom Act, 196–97; Attakai case, Arizona, 187; narrowing of principle of, 202, 205
Religious Freedom Restoration Act (1993), 208, 224, 235
Relocation, U.S. policy of, 183, 184
Reservation system, U.S., 9, 23–24, 25, 113, 184; BIA questionnaire, 105–106; Collier's Circular #2970, 126; and Ghost Dance, 35; and internal opposition to Peyote, 135; living conditions on, study of, 113–14; missionaries and, 118; Peyotists in, 82, 103, 104, 132; state governments and, 117
Rhoads, Charles J., 114
Rhodes, Willard, 176
Rice, Joseph V., 161
Richardson, David A., 45
Roadmen, in Peyote meeting, 10, 14, 25, 29, 31, 35, 43, 55, 60, 64, 66, 76, 79, 91, 94, 98–102, 127, 135; attire of, 97; and expansion of Peyotism, 65, 133; language used by, 69; music and, 174, 175, 177; paraphernalia of, 84, 156–59; ritual modifications and, 96; songs of, 180–81; staff of, 74, 98, 99, 155, 157–58, 181; and traditional spiritual leaders, 71–72
Roberts, John G., Jr., 224–25
Rock art, Peyote use depicted in, 14–15
Rockboy, Joe, 34
Rocky Boy Reservation, Montana, 134, 211
Roman Nose, 34
Roosevelt, President Franklin D., 121, 126
Roosevelt, President Theodore, 33, 39
Root plowing, and Peyote supply, 200

and medicinal properties of Peyote, 60; music, 176; number of Peyotists, 110
Wirikuta, 18
Wisconsin, 36, 42, 48, 131, 134, 146; percentage of Peyotists in, 111
Women: and Diné livestock reduction program, 140; in Lakota/Dakota/Nakota belief system, 67–68; and Native American Church organizations, 210; in Peyote ceremonies, 23, 60, 69, 72, 79, 101, 138, 144–45, 166; and Peyote music, 178; in Peyote origin narratives, 61–63
Women's Christian Temperance Union (WCTU), 52, 116
Women's National Indian Association, 121
Woody, Jack, 189
Woody et al, 195
Wool yarn paintings, 20
Work, Herbert W., 112, 119
World War II, 90, 142, 148
Wormser Brothers, Laredo, Texas, 131
Wounded Knee, Massacre of (1890), 35, 53
Wovoka (Jack Wilson), 35
Wyoming, 111, 117, 131, 136

Yale University, 53
Yamasee Seminoles, 223
Yankton Agency, 110
Yankton Sioux, 82, 86, 88, 94, 95–96, 109, 110, 120; Primeaux family, 178; songs, 177, 181; tribal identity, 231
Yankton Sioux Peyote Songs: In Loving Memory (Primeaux and Dion), 177
Yankton Sioux Reservation, South Dakota, 40, 42–45, 91, 105–106, 116, 131, *175,* 217, 218
Yazz, Beatien, 169
Yellow Hammers, The (Tsatoke), 167
YMCA (Young Men's Christian Association), 51, 53, 121
Young, Gloria, 80, 81
Young, S. A. M., 45
Young Men's Christian Association (YMCA), 51, 53, 121

Zacatecos, 17
Zah, Peterson, 214
Zango Music, 177

CPSIA information can be obtained at www.ICGtesting.com
Printed in the USA
LVOW072241170112

264343LV00002B/2/P